WORKS

OF

ORVILLE DEWEY, D.D

VOL. II.

DISCOURSES

ON THE

NATURE OF RELIGION;

AND ON

COMMERCE AND BUSINESS;

WITH SOME

OCCASIONAL DISCOURSES

BY

ORVILLE DEWEY, D.D..

NEW YORK:
CHARLES S. FRANCIS.
1868.

CONTENTS.

Discourses on the Nature of Religion.

Discourses on Commerce and Business.

Miscellaneous and Occasional Discourses.

DISCOURSES.

ON THE NATURE OF RELIGION.

I.

SPIRITUAL INTERESTS REAL AND SUPREME.

LABOUR NOT FOR THE MEAT THAT PERISHETH, BUT FOR THAT MEAT WHICH ENDURETH UNTO EVERLASTING LIFE. John vi. 27.

THE interests of the mind and heart, spiritual interests, in other words—the interests involved in religion, are real and supreme. Neglected, disregarded, ridiculed, ruined as they may be; ruined as they may be in mere folly, in mere scorn; they are still real and supreme. Notwithstanding all appearances, delusions, fashions and opinions to the contrary, this is true, and will be true forever. All essential interests centre ultimately in the soul; all that do not centre there, are circumstantial, transitory, evanescent; they belong to things that perish.

This is what I have endeavoured to show in a previous discourse, and for this purpose I have appealed in the first place, to Society.

My second appeal is to Providence; Society, indeed, is a part of the system of Providence; but let me invite you to consider under this head, that the interest of the soul urged in the Gospel, is in every respect, the great object of heaven's care and providence.

The world, which is appointed for our temporary dwelling place, was made for this end. The whole creation around us, is to the soul, a subject and a ministering creation. The mighty globe itself, with all its glorious apparatus and furniture, is but a theatre for the care of the soul, the theatre of its redemption. This vast universe is but a means. But look at the earth alone. Why was it made such as it is? Its fruitful soils, its rich valleys, its mountain-tops, and its rolling oceans; its humbler scenes, clothed with beauty and light, good even in the sight of their Maker, fair —fair to mortal eyes—why were they given? They were not given for mere sustenance and supply; for much less would have sufficed for that end. They need not have been so beautiful to have answered that end. They could have spared their verdure and flowers and fragrance, and still have yielded sustenance. The groves might never have waved in the breeze, but have stood in the rigidity of an iron forest; the hills might not have been moulded into forms of beauty, the streams might not have sparkled in their course, nor the ocean have reflected the blue depths of heaven, and yet they might have furnished all needful sustenance. No, they were not given for this alone: but they were given to nourish and kindle in the human soul, a glory and a beauty, of which all outward grandeur and loveliness are but the image. They were given to show forth the majesty and love of God, and to form in man a resemblance to that majesty and love. Think then, of a being in such a position and with such a ministry, made to be the intelligent companion of God's glorious works, the interpreter of nature, the Lord of the creation-made to be the servant of God alone. And yet this being—Oh! miserable disappointment and failure!—makes himself the slave of circumstances, the slave of outward goods and advantages, the slave of everything that he ought to command.

I know that he must toil and care for these things. But wherefore? Why must he toil and care? For a reason, I answer, which still urges upon him the very point we are considering. It had been as easy for the Almighty to have caused nature spontaneously to bring forth all that man needs, to have built as a part of the frame of the earth, enduring houses for us to dwell in, to have filled them with all requisite comforts, and to have relieved us, in short, from the necessity of labour and business. Why has he not done this? Still, I answer, for the same cause, with the same moral design, as that with which the world was made. Activity is designed for mental improvement; industry for moral discipline; business for the cultivation of manly and high and noble virtues. When, therefore, a man enters into the active pursuits of life, though he pleads the cares of business as an excuse for his neglect, yet it is then especially, and that by the very teaching of Providence, that he should be reminded of his spiritual welfare. He could not with safety, to his moral being, be turned full and free into the domain of nature. He goes forth, therefore, bearing burdens of care, and wearing the shackles of necessity. The arm that he stretches out to his toil, wears a chain; for he *must* work. And on the tablet where immortal thoughts are to be written, he writes words of worldly care and foresight; for he *must* provide. And yet, how strange and passing strange is it!—the occupations and objects that were given for discipline, and the trial of the spirit, and the training of it to virtue, are made the ultimate end and the chief good; yes, these which were designed for humble means of good to the soul, are made the engrossing pursuits, the absorbing pleasures and possessions, in which the soul itself is forgotten and lost!

Thus spiritual, in its design, is nature. Thus spiritual, in its just aspects, is the scene of life; no dull scene when rightly regarded; no merely wearisome, uncompensated toil, or perplexing business; but a ministration to purposes of infinite greatness and sublimity.

We are speaking of human interests. God also looks upon the interest of his creatures. But he seeth not as man seeth. Man looketh on the outward appearance; but God looketh on the heart. He sees that all human interests centre there. He sees there, the gathering, the embosoming, the garnering up, of all that is precious to an immortal creature. Therefore, it is, that as the strongest proof of his love to the world, he gave his Son to live for our teaching and guidance, and to die for our redemption from sin and death and hell. Every bright example, every pure doctrine, every encouraging promise, every bitter pang endured, points to the soul, for its great design and end. And let me say that if I have seemed to any one to speak in language over refined or spiritual, I can no otherwise understand the teachings of the great Master. His words would often be mystery and extravagance to me, if I did not feel, that the soul is everything, and that the world is nothing but what it is to the soul. With this perception of the true value of things, I require no transcendental piety, I require nothing but clear seeing, to understand what he says, when he pronounces men to be deaf, and blind, and diseased and dead in sins. For to give up the joys of the soul for the joys of sense; to neglect the heart, for the outward condition; to forego inward good in the eagerness for visible good; to forget and to forsake God amidst his very works and mercies—this is, indeed, a mournful blindness, a sad disorder of the rational nature, and when the evil is consummated, it is a moral death! True, there may be no tears for it, save in here and there one, who retires from the crowd to think of the strange delusion, and the grievous mis fortune, and the degrading unworthiness. There are no tokens of public mourning for the calamity of the soul. Men weep when the body dies; and when it is borne to its last rest, they follow it with sad and mournful procession. But for the dying *soul* there is no open lamentation; for the lost soul there are no obsequies. And yet, when the great account of life is made up, though the words we now speak, can but approach to the truth, and may leave but slight impression, the things we may then remember—life's misdirected toil, the world's delusions, the thoughts unguarded, the conscience every day violated, the soul for ever neglected—these, Oh! these will weigh upon the spirit, like those mountains, which men are represented in prophetic vision as vainly calling upon to cover them.

III. But I am now verging upon the third and final argument which I proposed to use for the care of our spiritual interests, and that is to be found in their value.

I have shown that society in all its pursuits, objects and scenes, urges this care; that nature, and providence and revelation minister to it; and I now say, that the soul is intrinsically and independently worth this care. Put all consequences to social man out of sight, if it be possible; draw a veil over all the bright and glorious ministry of nature; let the teachings of Providence all be silent; let the Gospel be a fable; and still the mind of man has a value which nothing else has; it is worth a care which nothing else is worth; and to the single, solitary individual, it ought to possess an interest which nothing else possesses.

Indeed, at every step by which we advance in this subject, the contrast between what is, and what ought to be, presses upon us. Men very well understand the word, value. They know very well what interests are. Offices, stocks, monopolies, mercantile privileges, are interests. Nay, and even the chances of profit, are interests so dear, that men contend for them and about them, almost as if they were striving for life. And value—how carefully and accurately and distinctly is that quality stamped upon every object in this world! Currency has value, and bonds have value, and broad lands and freighted ships and rich mines are all marked down in the table of this strict account. Go to the exchange, and you shall know what they are worth; and you shall know what men will give for them. But the stored treasures of the heart, the unfathomable mines that are to be wrought in the soul, the broad and boundless realms of thought, the freighted ocean of man's affections and hopes—who will regard them? Who will seek for them, as if they were brighter than gold, dearer than treasure?

The mind, I repeat—how little is it known or considered! That all which man permanently is, the inward being, the divine energy, the immortal thought, the boundless capacity, the infinite aspiration; how few value this, this wonderful mind, for what it is worth! How few see it, that brother mind, in others; see it, through the rags with which poverty has clothed it, beneath the crushing burthens of life, amidst the close pressure of worldly troubles, wants and sorrows, and acknowledge and cheer it in that humble lot, and feel that the nobility of earth, that the commencing glory of heaven is *there*! Nor is this the worst, nor the strongest view of the case. Men do not feel the worth of their own minds. They are very proud perhaps; they are proud of their possessions; they are proud of their *minds*, it may be, as distinguishing them; but the intrinsic, the inward, the infinite *worth* of their own minds they do not perceive. How many a man is there who would feel, if he were introduced into some magnificent palace, and were led through a succession of splendid apartments, filled with rich and gorgeous furniture, as if he, lofty, immortal being as he is, were but an ordinary thing amidst the tinselled show around him; or would feel as if he were a more ordinary being, for the perishing glare of things, amidst which he walked! How many a man, who, as he passed along the way-side, saw the chariot of wealth rolling by him, would forget the intrinsic and eternal dignity of his own mind, in a poor, degrading envy of that vain pageant—would feel himto be an humbler creature, because, not in mind, but in mensuration, he was not quite so high! And so long as this is the case, do you believe that men understand their own minds, that they know what they possess within them? How many, in fact, feel as if that inward being, that mind, were respectable, chiefly, because their bodies lean on silken couches, and are fed with costly luxuries! How many respect themselves and look for respect from others, in proportion as they grow more rich and live more splendidly, not more wisely,—and fare more sumptuously every day! Surely it is not strange, while all this is true, that men should be more attracted by objects of sense and appetite, than by miracles of wisdom and love. And it is not strange that the spiritual riches which man is exhorted to seek, are represented in Scripture as "hid treasures;" for they are indeed hidden in the depths of the soul—hidden, covered up, with worldly gains and pomps and vanities. It is not strange that the kingdom of heaven, that kingdom which is within, is represented as a treasure buried in a field: the flowers bloom and the long grass waves there, and men pass by and say it is beautiful; but this very beauty, this very luxuriance conceals the treasure. And so it is in this life, that luxury and show, fashion and outward beauty, worldly pursuits and possessions, attract the eyes of men, and they know not the treasure that is hidden in every human soul.

Yes, the treasure; and the treasure that is in every soul. The difference that exists among men is not so much in their nature, not so much in their intrinsic power, as in the power of communication. To some it is given to unbosom and embody their thoughts; but all men, more or less, feel those thoughts. The very glory of genius, the very rapture of piety, when rightly revealed, are diffused and spread abroad and shared among unnumbered minds. When eloquence, and poetry speak; when the glorious arts, statuary and painting and music; when patriotism, charity, virtue, speak to us, with their thrilling power, do not the hearts of thousands glow with a kindred joy and ecstasy? Who's here so humble, who so poor in thought, or in affection, as not to feel this? Who's here so low, so degraded, I had almost said, as not sometimes to be touched with the beauty of goodness? Who's here with a heart made of such base materials, as not sometimes to respond through every chord of it, to the call of honour, patriotism, generosity, virtue? What a glorious capacity is this! a power to commune with God and angels! a reflection of the brightness of heaven, a mirror that collects and concentrates within itself all the moral splendours of the universe; a light kindled from heaven, that is to shine brighter and brighter for ever! For what then, my friends, shall we care as we ought to care for this? What can man bear about with him; what office, what array, what apparel, that shall beget such reverence as the soul he bears with him? What circumstances of outward splendour can lend such imposing dignity to any being, as the throne of inward light and power, where the spirit reigns for ever? What work of man shall be brought into comparison with this work of God? I will speak of it in its simplest character. I say, a thought, a bare thought; and yet I say, what is it; and what is its power and mystery? Breathed from the inspiration of the Almighty; partaking of infinite attributes: comprehending, analyzing, and with its own beauty clothing all things; and bringing all things and all themes, earth, heaven, eternity, within the possession of its momentary being; what is there that man can form, what sceptre or throne, what structure of ages, what empire of wide-spread dominion, that can compare with the wonders and the grandeurs of a single thought? Of all things that are made, it is that alone that comprehends the Maker of all. That alone is the key, which unlocks all the treasures of the universe. That alone is the power that reigns over space, time, eternity. That, under God, is the sovereign dispenser to man, of all the blessings and glories, that lie within the compass of possession, or within the range of possibility. Virtue, piety, heaven, immortality, exist not, and never will exist for us, but as they exist, and will exist in the perception, feeling, *thought* —of the glorious mind.

Indeed, it is the soul alone that gives any value to the things of this world; and it is only by raising the soul to its just elevation above all other things, that we can look rightly upon the purposes of this life. This, to my apprehension, is not only a most important, but a most practical view of the subject.

I have heard men say that they could not look upon this life as a blessing. I have heard it more than insinuated, I have known it to be actually implied in solemn prayers to God, that it is a happiness to die in infancy. And nothing, you are aware, is more common than to hear it said, that youth, unreflecting youth, is the happy season of life; and when, by reason of sickness or the infirmities of age, men outlive their activity and their sensitive happiness, nothing is more common than to look upon the continuance of life, in these circumstances, as a misfortune.

Now I do not wonder at these views so long as men are as worldly as they usually are. I wonder that they do not prevail more. "Oh! patient and peaceable men that ye are!" I have been ready to say to the mere men of this world—"peaceable men and patient! what is it that bears you up? What is it but a blind and instinctive love of life, that can make you content to live?" But let the soul have its proper ascendancy in our judgments, and the burthen is relieved. Life is then the education of the soul, the discipline of conscience, virtue, piety. All things, then, are subordinate to this sublime purpose. Life is then one scene of growing knowledge, improvement, devotion, joy and triumph. In this view, and in this view only, it is an unspeakable blessing; and those who have not yet taken this view, who have not given the soul its just pre-eminence, who have not yet become spiritually-minded, are not yet prepared to live. It is not enough to say, as is commonly said, that they are not prepared to die; they are not prepared to *live.*

I would not address this matter, my friends, merely to your religious sensibility; I would address it to your common sense. It is a most serious and practical matter. There are many things in this world, as I have more than once said, which are called interests. But he who has not regarded his soul as he ought, who has gained no deep sense of things that are spiritual, has neglected the main interest, the chief use of this life, the grand preparation for living calmly, wisely, and happily. It is a thousand times more serious for him, than if he had been negligent about property, about honour, or about worldly connections and friendships.

With this reasonable subjection of the body to the soul, with this supreme regard to the soul as the guiding light of life, every man would feel that this life is a blessing; and that the continuance of it is a blessing. He would be thankful for its continuance with a fervour which no mere love of life could inspire; for life to him, and every day of it, would be a glorious progress, in things infinitely more precious than life. He would not think the days of unreflecting youth the happiest days. He would not think that the continuance of his being upon earth, even beyond active usefulness to others, was a misfortune or a mystery. He would not be saying, "Why is my life lengthened out?" He would feel that every new day of life spread before him glorious opportunities to be improved, glorious objects to be gained. He would not sink down in miserable ennui or despondency. He would not faint or despair, or be overwhelmed with doubt, amidst difficulties and afflictions. He would feel that the course of his life, even though it pass on through clouds and storms, is glorious as the path of the sun.

Thus have I endeavoured to show that the care of the soul is the most essential of all human interests. Let no worldly man think himself wise. He might be a wise animal; but he is not a wise man. Nay I cannot admit even that. For, being what he is—animal or man, call him what you will—it is as truly essential that he should work out the salvation of his soul, as it is that he should work with his hands for his daily bread. How reasonable, then, is our Saviour's exhortation, when he says, "Labour, therefore, not for the meat which perisheth but for that which endureth unto everlasting life."

II.

ON RELIGIOUS SENSIBILITY.*

AND I WILL GIVE YOU A HEART OF FLESH.—Ezekiel, xxxvi. 26.

THE subject to which I wish to invite your thoughts in this discourse, is that religious sensibility, that spiritual fervour, in other words, that "heart of flesh," which is spoken of in the text.

To a sincere, and at the same time, rational cultivator of his religious affections, it seems, at first view, a thing almost unaccountable, that Christians, apparently serious and faithful, should everywhere be found complaining of the want of religious feeling; that the grand, universal, standing complaint of almost the entire body of Christians, should be a complaint of dullness. To one who has studied the principles of his own nature, or observed its tendencies—who knows that, as visible beauty is made to delight the eye, so moral beauty is made to delight the mind; it seems a tremendous moral solecism, that all the affections of this nature and mind, should become cold and dead, the moment they are directed to the Infinite Beauty and Glory. It will not solve the problem to say that human nature is depraved. If, indeed, the depravity of men were such, that all enthusiasm for excellence had died out in the world, the general reason assign-

* The substance of the two following discourses was addressed to the graduating class, in the Theological Department of Harvard University, in 1834. This circumstance will account for the form that is given to some of the topics and illustrations.

ed might satisfy us. But what is the fact? What is the beauty of nature, but a beauty clothed with moral associations? What is the highest beauty of literature, poetry, fiction, and the fine arts, but a moral beauty which genius has bodied forth for the admiration of the world? And what are those qualities of the human character which are treasured up in the memory and heart of nations, the objects of universal reverence and exultation, the themes of celebration, of eloquence and of festal song, the enshrined idols of human admiration and love! Are they not patriotism, heroism, philanthropy, disinterestedness, magnanimity, martrydom?

And yet the Being, from whom all earthly beauty and human excellence are emanations, and of whom they are faint resemblances, is the very Being whom men tell us that they cannot heartily and constantly love: and the subject which is held most especially to connect us with that Being, is the very subject in which men tell us they cannot be heartily interested. No observing pastor of a religious congregation who has been favoured with the intimacy of one mind awaking to this subject, can fail to know that this is the grand complaint. The difficulty about feeling, is the first greatly difficulty; and it is one which presses upon every after step of the religious course. Few arrive at that point where they can say with the apostle, "I *know* in whom I have believed." The common language and tone in which even religious confidence is expressed, do not go beyond such distrustful and desponding words as these; "I hope that I love God; I hope I have an interest in religion;" alas! how different from the manner in which friendship, love, domestic affection, breathe themselves into the ear, and thrill through the heart of the world!

It seems especially strange, that this complaint of dulness should be heard in places devoted to the acquisition of religious knowledge, and the cultivation of religious affection; and yet it is, perhaps, nowhere more common or emphatic. And it is confined to no one species of religious seminaries; it is confined, I mean, to no one sect. I have heard it in tones as emphatic from Catholic and Calvinistic seminaries, as from any other. I have heard it as strongly expressed in other lands, as in our own. But is it not very extraordinary? We hear it not from the studios of artists. We hear it not from the schools of law and medicine. There is no complaint of dulness, there is no want of enthusiasm, about their appropriate objects in any of these. He, whose mind is occupied with the most abstruse questions of science or of the law; he, who gazes upon a painting, or upon a statue; ay, and he who gazes upon a skeleton, does not complain that he cannot be interested in them. I have heard such an one say, "Beautiful! beautiful!" in a case where admiration seemed almost absurd; where it provoked a smile from the observer. And yet in schools, in schools of ardent youth, where the subject of attention is the supreme and infinite glory, if we may take confession for evidence—all is cold and dead.

But I *must* here, and before I go any further, put forward one qualification. I do not think that confession *is* to be taken for evidence, altogether and without any qualification. One reason doubtless, why Christians complain so much of the want of feeling, is to be found in the very sense which they entertain of the infinite value and greatness of the objects of their faith. And it is unquestionably true that there is often a great deal of feeling in cases where there are very sad lamentations over the want of it. Lamentation certainly does not prove total insensibility.

Still, however, there is an acknowledged deficiency; not appertaining to any one class or condition, but to the entire body of Christians. And it is especially a deficiency of *natural*, *hearty*, *genuine*, *deep* sensibility. And once more, it is deficiency, sad, strange and inexcusable, on a subject more than all others claiming our sensibility. And yet again, it is a deficiency which, when existing on the part of the clergy, is most deplorable in its consequences. It is therefore everybody's interest, and that for every reason, to consider what are the causes and what are the remedies of this peculiar, prevailing, religious insensibility.

I have some question, indeed, whether this demand for sensibility—the popular rage that is to say for feeling, feeling alone—is not, in some views, mistaken, excessive and wrong. But let me admit, for I cannot resist the strength, the supremacy of the claim, which religion has on our whole heart. The first and lawful demand of the mind awakened to religion, is to feel it. The last attainment is to feel it deeply, rationally, constantly. Of the awakened mind, the first consciousness always is; "I do not feel; I never did feel this subject as I ought. It claims to be felt. The solemn authority and the unspeakable goodness of God; the great prospect of immortality; the strong bond of duty upon my nature: the infinite welfare of my soul; these are themes, if there be any such, upon which I ought to feel." The mind, thus aroused from worldly neglect to the greatest of subjects, will feel its coldness, its indifference to be a dreadful burthen; and it will sigh for deliverance: and the preacher who has never such a mind to deal with, may well doubt whether he is preaching to any purpose. And in all its after course, it will hold a fervent religious sensibility to be indispensable to its peace. If its prayers are formal and heartless, if its love waxes cold, if its gratitude and humility are destitute of warmth and tenderness, it cannot be satisfied.

And it ought not to be satisfied. This demand for feeling in religion, I say, is right; it is just; and I am desirous, in this discourse, to meet it and to deal with it as such. And yet I am about to say in the first place, that there are mistakes about it, and that in these mistakes are to be found some of the causes of the prevailing religious insensibility.

I. Is there not something wrong, then, in the first place; is there not something prejudicial to the very end in view, in this vehement demand of feeling? I have said that it is mainly right, and that I intend so to regard it. But may there not be some mistake in the case? May not the demand for feeling sometimes be made to the prejudice of feeling, and to the prejudice also, of real, practical virtue? I confess that I have been led at times to suspect, that the craving of some for great religious feeling in the preacher, though right in fact, yet was partly wrong in their minds. A person conscious of great religious deficiency, conscious of weekly and daily aberrations from the right rule and the religious walk, will be glad, of course, to have his feelings aroused on the Sabbath; it gives him a better opinion of himself; it puts him on a better footing with his conscience; it, somehow, brings up the moral account, and enables him to go on, as if the state of his affairs were very well and prosperous. This perhaps explains the reason, if such indeed be the fact, why in some cases a very pathetic and fervent preacher seems to do less good, than a man of much inferior endowments. In this latter case, the congregation cannot depend upon the periodical and passive excitement, and is obliged to resort to something else, to some religious activity of its own.

It appears to me also that the great religious excitements of the day answer the same purpose, however unintentionally, of keeping the people satisfied with general coldness and negligence.

But I was about to observe that this urgent demand for feeling, is probably one of the causes of religious insensibility. That is to say, the directness, urgency, and reiteration of the demand, are unfavourable to a compliance with it. This importunity with regard to feeling, does not allow it to spring up in the natural way. If it were applied to feeling on any other subject, to friendship, filial attachment, or parental affection; how certainly would it fail of success; Human feeling, in its genuine character, can never be forced, urged, compelled or exhorted, into action. The pulpit, I believe, has occasion to take a lesson from this principle of analogy. It is not the way to make the people feel, to be constantly telling them that they *must* feel, to be complaining continually of their coldness, to be threatening them perpetually with heaven's judgments upon their insensibility. And he who has used only these methods of awakening emotion, need not wonder that the people have no feeling about religion. No, let the preacher himself feel; let him express his feeling, not as if he had any design upon the feelings of others, but as if he could not help it; let him do this, and he will find hearts that sympathize with him. The chill of death may have been upon them, it may have been upon them for years; the rock may never have been smitten, the desert never cheered; but there is a holy unction, a holy unction of feeling, which is irresistible. It is like the rod of miracles in the hand of Moses; the waters will flow at its touch, and there will be life and luxuriance and beauty, where all was barrenness and desolation before.

I do not say that there will, of necessity, be actual regeneration, in the heart where this feeling is excited; I do not say that there will certainly be fruit, where all this verdure and beauty are seen: for the importance of feeling is often exaggerated to that degree that it is made a substitute for practical virtue. And thus the mistake we are considering, is made unfavourable to religious sensibility in another way. For, although, at first view, it seems to favour sensibility to make so much of it; although in fact it exaggerates its importance; yet, as the nature of the exaggeration is to make feeling all-sufficient of itself, the effect of course, is to draw off attention from that basis of principle and habit, which are essential to the strength and permanency of feeling. This is—so much to admire the beauty and luxuriance of vegetation in one's field, as to forget and neglect the very soil from which it springs. Of course the luxuriance and beauty will soon fade away. And so the common religious sensibility, is like the seed which was sown upon stony places; forthwith it springs up because it has no deepness of earth; and because it has no root, it withers away. Or, it is like the torrent after a shower. There has been a commotion in the moral elements of society; there have been thunderings in heaven, and an outpouring from the skies; and fresh streams are gushing forth and flowing on every side; and how many in their agitation, their enthusiasm, and their zeal, will mistake these noisy freshets, for the deep, pure, silent, ever-flowing river of life!

Nay, this vehement demand for feeling tends to

throw an interested and mercenary character over it, which are also extremely unfavourable to its cultivation. There is that trait of nobleness still left in human nature, that it will not barter its best affections for advantage. He who is striving with all his might to feel, only because feeling will save him, is certain to fail. This is the reason why none are ever found so bitterly complaining of the want of feeling, as men often are, in the midst of a great religious excitement. They see the community around them, aroused to great emotion; they are told that this is the way to be saved; the fear of perdition presses upon them; under this selfish fear, they strive, they agonize, they goad themselves, they would give the world to feel; and the result is, that they can *feel nothing!* Their complaint is, and it is true, that their heart is as cold as a stone. No; men must feel religion, if at all, because it is right to feel it. The great subject of religion must sink into their hearts; in retirement, in silence, without agitation, without any thought of advantage. They must feel if at all, involuntarily; they must feel, as it were, because they cannot help feeling.

This, too, is one of the reasons, as I believe, why there is so little religious sensibility, in theological seminaries. There is a perpetual demand for sensibility; society demands it; religious congregations demand it; the student is constantly reminded by his fellows, by everybody, that he cannot succeed without it, that his eloquence, his popularity depends upon it; and every such consideration tends directly to chill his heart. He is ashamed to cultivate feeling under such influences. Let him, then, forget all this; let him forget that it is his interest, almost that it is his duty, to feel; let him sit down in silence and meditation ; let him spread the great themes of religion before him, and with deep attention, ay, with the deep attention of prayer, let him ponder them ; and he will find that which he did not seek ; he will find that feeling is the least thing, the easiest thing, the most inevitable thing, in his experience.

II. In the second place, there are mistakes, and they arise in part from the one already stated, concerning the characteristics and expressions of religious sensibility ; and these mistakes, too, like the former, are unfriendly to its cultivation.

I shall not think it necessary to dwell long upon this topic ; or, at least, not upon its more obvious aspects. Every one, unhappily, is but too familiar with the extravagancies, and the extravagant manifestations, of religious feeling. They are as public as they are common. Their effect, in repelling and estranging the feelings of multitudes from religion, is no less clear.

In a celebrated volume of Essays published some years ago, you will remember one, "On the aversion of men of taste to Evangelical religion." The aversion is there taken for granted ; and, indeed, it is sufficiently evident. Whether the taste be right, or the religion be right, the fact of their contrariety is indisputable. The whole body of our classic English literature, that literature with which the great mass of readers is constantly communing and sympathizing, is stamped with nothing more clearly, than an aversion to what is called Evangelical religion. The peculiarities of its creed, of its feelings, of its experiences, of its manners, of its tones of speech, have all been alike offensive to that taste, which is inspired by the mass of our best English reading.

But the effect unhappily does not stop with repelling the mind from religion in the Evangelical form.

It repels the mind from religion in every form. And more especially it begets a great distrust of all religious earnestness. Hence all the solicitude there is, especially among the cultivated classes, to have every thing sober, calm, rational in religion. Hence the alarm that is so easily taken, at every appearance of zeal and enthusiasm. It seems to be thought by many that there *can* be no religious earnestness, but what breaks out into extravagance and fanaticism. If they had not identified two things essentially different, they would be no more afraid of enthusiasm in religion, than they are afraid of enthusiasm in science, in literature, in the arts. It would be, in their account a noble and beautiful thing. But now, the very description of a person as "zealous in his religion," carries with it a kind of imputation upon his understanding and liberality. Hence, in the train of consequences, it comes to pass that many are cold in religion. "For this cause, many sleep." They apparently think it better to *sleep* in security, than to wake in distraction; they prefer stupor to madness; they had rather perish in their senses, than in a fit of insanity; this, at least, is the light in which matters appear to them; and how is it strange, that repelled by the ordinary forms of religious emotion, and identifying all religious feeling with these, they should sink down into a cold, chilling, cheerless insensibility.

But I must not leave it to be supposed, that men of taste and refinement alone, are exposed to this result. The truth is that the popular sensibility on this subject, has been itself deficient in real strength and true fervour; it has been remarkable thus far, for wanting those qualities, which were necessary to give it depth and impressiveness in its own sphere: and from no quarter have there been more bitter complaints of coldness, than from the very sphere of fanaticism. The observation may seem to be a singular one, perhaps, and the fact scarcely credible. But if you will take the pains to observe, I am confident you will find it to be true, that the wildest sects and the wildest excitements are precisely those, from which there come from time to time, the deepest confessions of coldness and stupidity. Yes, in the bosom of fanaticism is harboured the deepest and most painful doubt, about the truth and reality of all religion. And the reason is, that neither there, nor in any of the modifications of spiritual extravagance, has religion been familiar enough to have become an easy, natural, abiding guest; nor reflective enough to have settled down into a principle and habit; nor has it long enough rested in the soul, amidst quietness and silence, to have become incorporated with its nature.

And thus it comes to pass, that in many, perhaps, in most minds, where religion gains admission, it is felt to be a strange, mysterious, extraordinary thing. I think, indeed, that the religious experience of the world, generally, has not got beyond this point; it is still *an extraordinary thing*. And it is obvious, that this sense of its being extraordinary, will not be favourable to composure, steadiness and permanency of feeling, but rather to excitement, wonder, delight and all those tumultuous emotions that speedily pass away.

I am afraid, too, that this consciousness of religious experience as being something extraordinary, has another injurious and repulsive effect: that is to say, that it gives birth to that religious vanity, that spiritual pride, that sense of personal importance, which is so apt to spring up with religious zeal. I know, indeed, that the Gospel demands humility; and I know that

Christians have been much given to self-disparagement; but I know, too, that no sooner does a man "obtain religion," to use the common phrase, than his own sense of the great and wonderful thing which he conceives has happened to him, and the attentions of those around him, usually contribute to invest him with a very disagreeable air of self-importance. There is a strange delusion, by which a man contrives to think himself very humble, and to be very proud, at the same time. He says that he is the greatest of sinners, a most wonderful instance of the triumph of divine grace; and perhaps he is never so proud as when he says it. His confession is made, with a saving clause; and the saving clause is very likely to be more with him, than the confession. He is the greatest of sinners; but then he is rescued. He is a most extraordinary instance of grace; but then it follows certainly, that he is himself a very extraordinary person.

Whether this be a just account of the matter or not, it is certain that spiritual vanity has been, thus far in the world, one of the prevailing forms of religious experience. And since this quality, I mean, vanity, whether religious or otherwise, is always one the most offensive and insufferable; since it always brings more unpopularity upon its possessor, I had almost said, than all other bad qualities put together; it is not strange that it should have brought some discredit upon religion, and especially upon religious zeal and earnestness. There are, there *must* be, not a few, who will stand aside and aloof, and say, "Let me have no religion rather than that:" and one of the most important duties of religious teaching is, to show them that they *may* have religion without presumption, pride or ostentation; nay. and that the religion, which they hold in simplicity, modesty and singleness of heart, with no thought of themselves, will be far more deep, thorough and fervent, as well as far more graceful and beautiful.

There is one effect of this sense of religion as some thing very extraordinary, which I must mention before leaving this topic: and that is upon the manifestations of religious sensibility. The sense of the extraordinary tends to give expansion and exuberance to the expression of religious feeling—tends, if the phrase will be understood, to too much manifestation. Our sensibility always takes arms against an appearance of this sort. This explains the reason, why some religious conversation and some preaching, which seems to be charged and overcharged with religious fervour, which vents itself, perhaps, in a passion of tears, which is full of exclamations and entreaties, and exhorts us to feel with every moving interjection in the language, yet never moves us at all. The precise reason is, that the expression is overcharged. We wonder at our insensibility perhaps; we think it is very wicked in us not to feel; but the fact is, we are, all this while, true to nature. Possibly some might think, though I will not suspect any one who hears me of holding the opinion, that this apology ought not to be stated; that self-reproach is so rare a thing and so good a thing, that men should be left to accuse themselves as much as ever they will. I confess that I can understand no such reasoning as this. On the contrary, I have regretted to hear the language of self-reproach in such cases; because I do not think it just, and because I know that every false self-accusation, tends to blunt the edge of the true self-accusation. Doubtless men should always feel religion if they can; but the question is now, about being made to feel it, by a particular manifestation. And, I say, if the manifestation be overcharged; if it go beyond the feeling, rather than come short of it; if there be more expression, vociferation, gesture, than genuine emotion, it will inevitably, with the discerning, have an effect the very contrary of what was intended. No; let one speak to us by our fireside, or in the pulpit, with an emotion which he is obliged to restrain; let it appear evident, that he lays a check upon his feelings; let one stand before us, I care not with what varied expression; with the cheek flushed or blanched, with the tear suppressed or flowing, with the voice soft or loud, only so that the expression never seem to outrun, to exceed the feeling; and he is almost as sure of our sympathy, as that we are human beings.

The observation I have made on this point cannot be useless to any one, if it teaches only this, that nothing forced or factitious will answer any good purpose in religion; that if we would accomplish anything for ourselves or others in this great cause, we must engage in it with our whole heart; that the sources of real religious influence, are none other than the fountains of the heart, the fountains of honest, earnest, irrepressible sensibility.

III. I must now add, in the third place, that there are mistakes, as in the vehement demand for religious sensibility, and concerning its nature and expressions, so also with regard to its Supreme Object.

We must allow indeed that on this point there are some intrinsic difficulties. There are difficulties attending the love of an Infinite, Eternal, Invisible, Incomprehensible Being. Our love of him must be divested of many of those sympathies and supports, which enkindle and strengthen in us the love of one another. We feel obliged to guard every word in which we speak of him, and of our connection with him. We must not say that our communion with him, is sympathy; or that our love of him is attachment.

We may not with propriety, say that he is "dear" to us. Many, indeed, of those phrases, many of those modes of expression, in which we testify the strength and charm of our social affections, sink into awe and are hushed to silence, before that Infinite and Awful Being. So, at least, does the subject of devotion appear to me; and I must confess that the familiarity of expression which is sometimes witnessed in prayer, is extremely irreverent and shocking.

But those difficulties which it is the tendency of ignorance and fanaticism to overlook, it is the tendency of immature reflection and philosophy to magnify. Reflection has gone just so far with some minds as to make it more difficult for them, than it ought to be, to approach their Maker. They regard his exaltation above them, as distance; his greatness, as separation from them. They look upon the very phrases, "love of God," "communion with God," as phrases of daring import, and doubtful propriety. They shrink back from the freedom of popular language, and this perhaps, they rightly do; but they retreat too far; they retreat to the opposite extreme of coldness, and cold abstractions. They are sometimes almost afraid to address God as a Being; they worship some mighty abstraction; they are like those ancient philosophers who worshipped the light; they worship "an unknown God." I do not know that anything but the teachings of Jesus, could ever have cured this error; the error at once of ancient philosophy and modern refinement. He "has brought us nigh to God." He has taught us that God is our Father. He has taught us to worship him, with the profoundest reverence indeed, but with boundless confidence and love. He has taught us that God does regard us; that he does look down from the height of his infinite heavens; that he does look down upon us, and upon our world—not exclusively, as some religionists would teach, not as if there were no other world—but still that he does look down upon *us*, and *our* world, with paternal interest and kindness.

The mistake now stated is one which lies at the very threshold of devotion. But when we enter the temple of our worship, how many errors are there, that darken its light and disfigure its beauty! The veil of the Jewish peculiarity is indeed rent in twain; but theology has lifted up other, and many, and darkening veils, before "the holy of holies." Our sins, too, have separated between us and God, and our iniquities have hidden his face from us. Unworthy, afraid, superstitious, erring, grovelling in the dust, how can we love God, purely, freely, joyfully? How, even, can we *see* the perfection of God, as we ought?

This, indeed, is the point upon which all difficulty presses. *Men do not* SEE *the perfection of God.* They do not identify that perfection, with all that is glorious, beautiful, lovely, admirable, and enrapturing, in nature, in character, in life, in existence. God's glory, they conceive to be something so different from all other glory; God's goodness, so different from all other goodliness and beauty, that they find no easy transition from one to the other. They mistake—and perhaps this is the most fatal part of the error—they mistake the very demand of God's goodness upon their love. They conceive of it, as if there were something arbitrary and importunate and selfish in the demand. Demand itself repels them; because they do not understand it. They think of the Supreme Being in this attitude, somewhat as they would of man, if he stood before them, saying, "Love me; give me your heart; upon pain of my displeasure, and of long-enduring penal miseries for your disobedience." Divine goodness thus regarded, does not and cannot steal into the heart, as the excellence of a human being does. And this, I say, is a mistake. Divine goodness, thus regarded, is mistaken, misapprehended altogether. There is not so much that is personal in God's claim for our hearts, as there is in man's claim. It does not so much concern him, if I may speak so, that we should love him personally, as it concerns man, that we should love him personally. He is not dependent on our love, as man is dependent upon it. The command which he lays upon us to love him, is but a part of the command to love all goodness. He equally commands us to love one another. Nay, he has graciously represented the want of love to one another, as the evidence of want of love to him. He has thus, in a sense, identified these affections; and thus taught us, that an affection for excellence, whether in himself or in his creatures, is essentially the affection that he demands. The demand for our love, which the infinite Being addresses to us, is infinitely generous. He requires us to love all goodness, to love it alike in himself and in others; to love goodness, for goodness' sake; to love it because it is just that we should love it, because it is right, because it is for our welfare, because, in one word, it is all our excellence and all our happiness.

I must not dwell longer upon these mistakes; but, in leaving this topic, let me exhort every one to endeavour to correct them. With many, this will require a frequent, an almost constant effort. The influence of early education or of later error; theology, superstition and sin, have so overshadowed their path, that they must not expect to see the light, without much faithful endeavour. Let them be entreated by everything most precious to them, to make it. And *thus* let them make the endeavour. *Let them see*

God in every thing that they lawfully admire and love. If there be any goodliness and loveliness in the world ; if there be anything dear and delightful in the excellence of good men ; if heaven from its majestic heights, if earth from its lowly beauty, sends one sweet, or one sublime thought into your mind ; think, that this is a manifestation of the ever-beautiful, ever-blessed perfection of God. *Think*, I say emphatically, and let not your mind sleep—think for ever, that the whole universe of glory and beauty, is one revelation of God. Think thus, I say,—thus faithfully and perseveringly; and you will find, that no strength nor freedom of emotion in the world, is like the freedom and strength of devotion; that no joy, no rapture on earth, is like the joy, the rapture of piety!

III.

ON RELIGIOUS SENSIBILITY.

AND I WILL GIVE YOU A HEART OF FLESH.—Ezekiel, xxxvi. 26

My object in the present discourse, is to offer some remarks upon the remedies for the want of religious sensibility; or upon the means and principles of its culture.

And in entering upon this subject, I would observe that much is to be done by a correction of those mistakes which have been already mentioned. Let then something, I would venture to say, of this vehement demand for feeling be abated. Let not the feeling of religion be subjected to perpetual importunity, any more than the feeling of friendship, or of family affection. Let not feeling be made to occupy a place in religion that does not belong to it, as if it were the only thing and everything; thus drawing away attention from the principles that are necessary to give it permanency, from the soil that must nourish and the basis that must support it. Let not religious feeling be appealed to in a way to impair its simplicity, disinterestedness and purity.

In the next place, let the common mistakes about the nature and signs of religious sensibility be corrected. Let all excess and extravagance be checked as much as possible; and especially let those who would cultivate a fervent piety, make the necessary discriminations between religion and fanaticism. Let them not conclude that abuses are the only forms, under which the religious principle can appear; that, in order to be zealous Christians, it is necessary to part with their modesty or their taste. In fine, let religion become so familiar that it shall cease to be, in their minds, or in their thoughts of it, anything extraordinary; and then let its manifestations be, like the expressions of all other high and pure feeling, unforced, natural, manly, strong, graceful, beautiful and winning. Thus let our light shine before men, not as the glaring meteor, but as the common light of day, attractive and cheering and constant.

And once more, let an honest and persevering endeavour be made, to correct those mistakes that prevail about the Supreme Object, to which religious sensibility is chiefly directed. Let not God be regarded as some unintelligible abstraction, or inaccessible majesty. Let the *Christian* teaching be welcomed; which instructs us to believe and to feel that He is our Father. Let an effort be made by every mind to break through the clouds of superstition and sin, and to perceive what the divine perfection is. Let not God's command that we should love him be mistaken for anything more arbitrary or importunate or personal, than is the claim of disinterested human excellence to be loved. Let not the divine demand for our love, be so construed as to chill or repel our love. In fine, let no thought be suffered to enter our minds that shall detract from the infinite generosity, the infinite dignity, the infinite beauty, of the divine perfection. How shall God be truly loved, if he is not rightly known? Let him be rightly known; and love will as certainly follow, as it will follow the knowledge of any other, of any human or angelic excellence. I do not say that it will certainly follow, but *as* certainly. Nay, why, if we rightly understood the subject, should it not be easier to love God, than to love man? For man is full of imperfection that offends us, and with him too we are liable to have questions and competitions. But God is all-perfect; and with him, our affections have reasonably nothing to do—but to love him.

Let me now proceed to offer a few suggestions more directly, upon the remedy for religious insensibility. And here let me say at once, that I have no specific to offer in the shape of a remedy; no new and before unheard-of method to propose. I have no set of rules to lay down, a mere formal observance of which will certainly bring about the desired result. Religious sensibility is to be cultivated like all other sensibility; i. e. rationally. And since it is impossible within my present limits to discuss the subject in all its parts and bearings, I shall confine myself to the defence and application of the rational method. And the rational method is *the method* of attention, in the forms of meditation, reading, hearing, prayer; the method of association, which pays regard to the indirect influences of places, times and moods of mind; and finally, it is *the method* of consistency, by which no feeling is expected to be strong and satisfactory, but as the result of the whole character.

My remedy, then, for religious insensibility, under the blessing of heaven—it might sound strangely in the ears of some—but I boldly say, that my remedy is reason. *It is thought*; it is reflection; it is attention; it is exercise of reason in every legitimate way. The true method, I say, is purely and strictly rational. And I say, moreover, that it is not that Christians have used their reason so much, but so little, that they have been so deficient in real feeling.

Reason and feeling if they be not the same thing in different degrees of strength, are yet so intimately connected, that no man may ever expect, on any subject, to feel *deeply and habitually*, who does not feel rationally. The slight sometimes thrown upon reason in religion, is an invasion of the first law of the mind, the first law of heaven. This law is "elder scripture," and no more designed to be abrogated by the written word, than the law of gravitation is designed to be abrogated by the written word. The word proceeds upon the assumption, that the intellect is to be addressed: it actually, and everywhere, addresses it. The whole theory of human affections proceeds upon it. The grandest theoretical mistake of all in religion, is that by which feeling is separated from the intellect.

Nor am I at all sure, my brethren, little liable as it may be thought we are to make this mistake, that we have altogether escaped it. When it is said, as it sometimes is said, that certain preaching is too intellectual for a plain congregation, or too rational for an humble congregation, I must think, either that the meaning is false, or that the terms are used in a false sense. There never was too much intellect, there never was too much reason, yet put into a sermon. There may have been too little feeling; but it does not follow, that there was too much reason. There may have been too much barren and useless speculation, but not too much intellect. Some of the most practical and devotional books in the world—such as Law's Serious Call, Baxter's Saints' Rest, the Sermons of Butler and Paley, and the works of Jonathan Edwards, are specimens of the closest reasoning. A genuine, just, and powerful moral discourse has need to be one of the keenest, closest, and most discriminating compositions in the world. Such were the discourses of our Saviour. Nothing could be farther from loose, rambling, common-place exhortations. Nothing could be farther from that style, which says, "Oh! my hearers, you must be good; you must be pious men; and you must feel on this great subject." No, the hearers, by close, cogent, home-put argument, were made to feel; and they said, "never man spake like this man."

I may be thought singular, but I verily believe, that in most moral discourses at this day, the grand defect is not so much a defect of feeling, as it is a defect of close and discriminating argument; and that higher powers of argumentation are precisely what are wanted, in such sermons, to make them more weighty, practical and impressive. And it is not the intellectual hearer, who can perhaps supply the deficiency, that most needs this; but the plain hearer who is mystified, misled and stupified, by the want of clear and piercing discrimination. I have that respect for human nature in its humblest forms, as to think that the highest powers of man or angel, would not be thrown away upon it: and I cannot believe that nothing but truisms and common-places, vague generalities and unstudied exhortations, are required in teaching religion to such a nature.

It is required of a man, to be sure, according to what he hath, and not according to what he hath not. But if it be thought that the utmost, and far more than the utmost measure of human talent, may not be well employed in religious discussion, how, let me ask, is that opinion to be defended against the charge of doing dishonour to religion? There is no other interest which is not held to be worthy of the profoundest discussion. He who is to plead the cause of some earthly right or property before the judges of the land or its legislators, will, by deep study, prepare himself to give the most able and elaborate views of the subject; be it of a title or a tariff, a bond or a bank. It is a great occasion, and must task all the powers of the mind to do it justice. But "a little plain sense,"—is not this the thought of some? "a little plain sense, a little common-place thought, is good enough for religion!"

There are tasks for the religious teacher; and to name no other, that of disembarrassing religious experience from the many mistakes in which it is involved, is one that must carry the preacher far enough beyond the range of common-place truths, valuable as they may be; and one that is very necessary to the promotion of a just and healthful religious sensibility. And this only amounts to saying, that there are new things to be said, new views to be given in religion; that, not plain and obvious things only are to be said, but that there is to be something to be told to many which they did not think of before. And what though the preacher *feel* his subject, and the people be impressed; yet after all, the impression, the feeling may have much in it that is wrong. The whole subject of religious sensibility, its sources and the methods of its culture, may be very ill understood; and there is no little evidence that it is ill understood, from the fact, that most religious feeling is so artificial, so mechanical, so periodical, and fluctuating, and uncertain, instead of being habitual and healthful and strong. A man may feel very much, within a very narrow compass of thought. Who has not often observed it? But who that has observed it, would not think it desirable to carry him beyond this little mechanism, by which he contrives from time to time, (if I may speak so) to grind out a certain amount of feeling,—to carry him beyond, I say, to those wide and generous views of religion, to that intelligent culture of his nature, from which religious feeling will spring naturally and freely, and flow abundantly, and in a full and living stream. There is all the difference here, and only of infinitely greater importance, that there is between the slavish artisan, governed by rules, and the intelligent machinist, discovering principles, constantly inventing and improving, and ever going on to perfection.

But it is time that I should proceed from the defence to the more particular application of my proposition. The proposition is, that feeling in religion, to be deep and thorough, to be habitual, to be relied on to spring up with unvarying promptitude at every call of religion, *must be rational*, perfectly rational; rational in its nature, its methods of culture, its ends. You ask how you shall learn to feel on the subject of religion, —with spontaneous freedom, with unaffected delight, and with true-hearted earnestness; how you shall learn to feel in religion as you do in friendship, and in the family relations; and I answer, *rationally*. And I say, moreover, that provided a man really and honestly desires and strives to feel, the reason why he fails, is, that there is something irrational in his views, irrational in his seeking, irrational in the whole method of his procedure. He has irrational views of the nature of religious feeling. He expects it to be some strange sensation, or something supernatural, or some hallucination, or something, he knows not what. Or he has wrong views of God. He does not see the glory and loveliness of his perfection. Or he has wrong ideas of the methods of obtaining religious feeling. He is indolently waiting for it, or irrationally expecting it to come upon him in some indescribable manner, or unreasonably looking for an influence from above, which God has never promised. For although he has promised help, he has not proffered in that help, anything to be substituted for our own efforts: and our efforts are to be every way just as rational, as if he had promised nothing. Or, the seeker of religion has irrational views of the end. He does not distinctly see, that his perfection, his happiness is the end. If he did, he would be drawn on to seek it, with a more willing and hearty earnestness. No, but he feels as if the demand for his heart in this matter, were a mere arbitrary requisition, as if it were the bare will of some superior Being, without any reason for it. He seeks religion, because he vaguely and blindly apprehends that it is something—that it is the prominent idea of thousands something which he *must have.*

I say that the process of obtaining a high and delightful religious sensibility, that sensibility which makes prayer always fervent and meditation fruitful and satisfying, must be rational, and nothing but rational. And I do not say this, in any spirit of defiance towards that prevailing opinion which has fastened on this word, rational, the idea of coldness and indifference. I say it, because in sober truth and earnestness, I know of no other way to feel the deep sense of religion, but to feel it rationally. It is out of my power—is it *within* any man's power?—to conceive of any other way to awaken emotion, but to fix the mind on those objects that are to awaken it. If I would feel the sentiment of gratitude and love to my Creator, I can conceive of no way of doing so, but to think of his goodness, his perfection; to spread before my mind, all the images and evidences of his majesty, his perfection, his love. If I would feel the charms of virtue, I must contemplate her; I must *see* "virtue in her shape, how lovely." If I would love good men, which is a part of religion, I must know them, and mingle with them; I must talk with them, or read of them, and spread the story of their generous and blessed deeds before me. And thus also, and for the same reason, if I would love God, I must not only contemplate him, as has been already said, but I must be familiar with the contemplation of his being and perfection. Earth through all her fair and glorious scenes, must speak to me of *Him*. The sacred page, with all its gracious words of teaching and promise, must speak to me of *Him*. And I must listen with gladness, with a sense of my high privilege, and with joy must I commune with all the teachings of God to me, as I would commune with the words of a friend. This is the rational process.

But this, my friends, is not to say, that "we hope we shall some time or other, attain to the love of God," or that "we desire it," or that, "it is difficult," or that "we fear we never shall reach it;" it is not saying, and saying, this or that, in a sort of ideal, or idle speculation; but it is doing something. It is seeking to feel the power of religion, as we seek to feel the power of other things; of the arts, of philosophy, of science, of astronomy, or of music; attentively, sedulously, with a careful use of opportunities, with a heedful regard to circumstances. The rational method, then, is the method of attention.

But in the next place, the rational method is the method of association; or, in other words, it is a method, which regards that great law of the mind, the law of association. It pays regard to places and times and seasons, and moods of mind. It is partly an indirect method. It is, to put ourselves *in the way of* obtaining a sense of religion.

The direct effort is to be valued for all that it is worth. And its value, indeed, is such that it is indispensable. Certainly, where the religious character is to be formed, after our arrival at the period of adult years, periodical and private meditation and prayer seem to be essential aids. There is much to learn, and much to overcome, and there should be definite seasons and direct efforts, for these purposes. But it would be irrational to make these seasons and efforts the only means. If we should attempt to form a friendship for a human being, by such a series of fixed and direct contemplations alone, it is easy to see that they would be very likely to be injurious, to create in our minds a set of repulsive or irksome associations with the human being in question, however amiable and excellent he might be. It would require the effect of many indirect influences to blend with these, and give them their proper character. So in the cultivation of a devotional spirit, it is not safe to trust to prayers and meditations *alone*. Many wise and good men, in their writings, have recommended that the most special heed be given to those visitations of tender and solemn emotion, those touches of holy sensibility, those breathings of the Spirit of all grace, which steal into the heart unsolicited, and offer their heavenly aid unsought. Let not him who would catch the sacred fervour of piety, venture to neglect these gracious intimations. Let him not neglect to put himself in the way of receiving them. Let him not willingly invade the holy Sabbath hours with business or pleasure, or forsake the assemblies where good men meditate and pray, or resist the touching signs of nature's beauty or decline, or turn away from the admonition of loneliness and silence, when they sink deep into the heart. Or, if he does turn away, and avoid and resist all this, let him not say that he seeks or desires the good gift of the grace of God, the gift of light and love and holy joy.

Finally, the rational method is a method of consistency. Religious feeling to be itself rational, and to be rationally sought, must not be expected to spring up as the result of anything else, than the whole character. You desire to feel the power of religion. Do not expect, do not desire to feel it, but as an impression upon your whole mind and heart, the general tone and tenor of all your sentiments and affections, the consenting together of all your reflections and actions, and habits. If you feel it, as some peculiar thing, something singular in you, and technical in your very idea, of it, as something apart from your ordinary self; if it is either a flame of the imagination or a warmth of the affections, or a splendour of sentiment, one of them alone and not all of them together; it will certainly lead you astray: it will be but a wavering and treacherous light. It may appear to you very bright. It may lead you to think well of yourself; far better than you ought to think. But it will be only a glaring taper, instead of the true light of life.

An irrational fervour is often found to stand in direct contrast to the rest of the character; to general ignorance, to want of moral refinement and delicacy, and of daily virtue. There is not only a zeal without knowledge, but there is a zeal which seems to thrive exactly in proportion to the want of knowledge; that bursts out, from time to time, like a flame from thick smoke, instead of shining with any clear radiance, any steady light. But it is the distinctive mark of rational feeling, that it rises gradually, and steadily gains strength; like the spreading of daylight upon the wakening earth. Hence, it rises slowly; and no one should be discouraged at small beginnings; and no one should expect or wish to rush into the full flow of religious sensibility at once.

I repeat it; this sensibility, if rational, must be felt as the spirit of the whole character: and he would do well to tell us nothing of his joys, of whom nothing can be told, concerning his virtues, his self-denials, his general and growing improvement, the holy habits and heavenly graces of his character and life. Dost thou love good men, and pity bad men; is thy heart touched with all that is generous and lovely around thee; is thine eye opened to all that is like God in his creatures and works? Then, and not till then, am I prepared to hear of thy love to God. Dost thou, indeed, love that great and kind Being? Dost thou, indeed, love that intrinsic, infinite, eternal, inexpressible beauty and glory of the divine perfection? Then, truly, art thou prepared rightly to love all who bear his image, and to pity and pray for all who bear it not; then, does thy social and religious sensibility flow on in one stream, full and entire, steady and constant, a living stream; a stream like that which floweth fresh, full, perennial, eternal, at the right hand of God!

My brethren! it *is* constant: so far at least as anything human can bear that character, it *is* constant. He who will rationally cultivate the sense of religion, both directly and indirectly, and as the consent and tendency of all his habits, may be just as certain of feeling it, as he is certain of loving his friend, his child, his chief interest. It is one of the irrational aspects of the *common* religious sensibility, that its possessors have usually spoken of it, as if it were totally uncertain whether, on a given occasion, they should feel it or not. They have gone to church, they have gone to their private devotions, with a feeling, as if it were to be decided, not by the habits of their own minds, but by some doubtful interposition of divine grace, whether they were to enjoy a sense of religion or not. But, my friends, nothing can be more certain to him who will rationally, heartily, and patiently cultivate the religious sensibilities of his soul, than that he shall, on every suitable occasion, feel them. It is to him, no matter of distressing doubt and uncertainty. He knows in whom he has believed. He knows in what he has confided. He knows by sure experience, that as certainly as the themes of religion pass before him, they will, physical infirmity only excepted, arouse him to the most intense and delightful exercise of all his affections. He is sure, when the fulness of the blessing of the Gospel of Christ is presented before him; he is like Paul, *sure* that he shall enter into it. Not that this is any boasting assurance of the devoted Christian. God forbid! He knows his weakness. But he knows, that by the very laws of the divine goodness and grace, if he will be faithful, no good thing shall be wanting to him.

Christian brethren! we hear much, in these days, about excitement. Why, every prayer—of a Christian at once perfectly rational, and perfectly devoted—every prayer is an excitement; and every religious service, every sermon, is an excitement as great as he can well bear; and every day's toil of virtue, and contemplation of piety, is a great and glorious excitement. Excitements! Is a man never to be moved by his religion but when some flood of emotion is sweeping through society; when agitation and disorder and confusion are on every side of him? Is it only when the tenor of quiet life, the pursuits of industry, the pleasures of relaxation, are all broken up, that he is to feel the power of religion? I do not say that this is any body's theory; but if this is the fact that results from any form of religious teaching, then I ask, for what end was the whole tenor of life, for what end were the pursuits of industry and the pleasures of society ordained? For what was the whole trial of life, so exquisitely moral, so powerfully spiritual—for what was it appointed, if the seasons for obtaining religious impressions are so ordered by human interference, that they come only in idleness, disorder, and a derangement of the whole system of life? Excitements in religion! Are they to be things occasional, and separated by the distance of years? Is a man to be excited about religion, only in a certain month, or in the winter; and when that month, or that winter is past, yes, when all nature is bursting into life, and beauty, and songs of praise, is the religious feeling of the people to be declining into worse than wintry coldness and death? Is this religion?—the religion whose path shineth brighter and brighter to the perfect day?

Let us have excitements in religion; but then let them be such as may be daily renewed, as never need to die away. Any excitement in society that can bear this character, I would heartily go along with. The Christian religion, I am sure, was designed powerfully to excite us; nothing on earth so much; nothing in heaven more. It was designed to arouse our whole nature, to enrapture our whole affection; to kindle in us a flame of devotion, to transport us with the hope and foretaste of heaven. But its excitements, if they be like those that appeared in the great teacher, are to be deep, sober, strong, and habitual. Such excitements may God ever grant us; not periodical, but perpetual; not transient, but enduring; not for times and seasons only, but for life; not for life only, but for eternity!

IV.

THE LAW OF RETRIBUTION.

BE NOT DECEIVED; GOD IS NOT MOCKED: FOR WHATSOEVER A MAN SOWETH, THAT SHALL HE ALSO REAP.—Galatians vi. 7.

I UNDERSTAND these words, my brethren, as laying down in some respects, a stricter law of retribution than is yet received, even by those who are considered as its strictest interpreters. There is much dispute about this law at the present day; and there are many who are jealous, and very properly jealous, of every encroachment upon its salutary principles. But even those who profess to hold the strictest faith on this subject, and who, in my judgment, do hold a faith concerning what they call the infinity of man's ill-desert, that is warranted neither by reason nor scripture; even they, nevertheless, do often present views of conversion and of God's mercy, and of the actual scene of retribution, which in my apprehension detract from the wholesome severity of the rule by which we are to be judged. Their views may be strong enough, too strong; and yet not strict enough, nor impressive enough. Tell a man that he deserves to suffer infinitely, and I am not sure that it will by any means come so near his conscience, as to tell him that he deserves to endure some small but specific evil. Tell him that he deserves an infinity of suffering, and he may blindly assent to it; it is a vast and vague something that presses upon his conscience, and has no edge nor point: but, put a sword into the hand of conscience, and how might this easy assenter to the justice of infinite torments, grow astonished and angry, if you were to tell him that he deserved to suffer but the amputation of a single finger! Or tell the sinner that he shall suffer for his offences a thousand ages hence, and though it may be true, and will be true, if he goes on offending till that period, yet it will not come home to his heart with half so vivid an impression, or half so effectual a restraint, as to make him foresee the pain, the remorse and shame, that he will suffer the very next hour. Tell him, in fine, as it is common to do—tell him of retribution in the gross, and however strong the language, he may listen to it with apathy; he often does so; but if you could show him what sin is doing within him at every moment; how every successive offence lays on, another and another shade upon the brightness of the soul; how every transgression, as if it held the very sword of justice, is cutting off one by one, the fine and invisible fibres that bind the soul to happiness; then, by all the love of happiness, such a man must be interested and concerned for himself. Or tell the bad man that he must be converted, or he cannot be happy hereafter, and you declare to him an impressive truth; but how much would it add to the impression, if, instead of leaving him to suppose that bare conversion, in the popular sense of that term—that the brief work of an hour, would bring him to heaven, you should say to him, "You shall be just as happy hereafter, as you are pure and upright, and no more; just as happy as your character prepares you to be, and no more; your moral, like your mental character, though it may take its date or impulse from a certain moment, is not formed in a moment; your character, that is to say, the habit of your mind, is the result of many thoughts and feelings and efforts; and these are bound together by many natural and strong ties; so that it is strictly true, and this is the great law of retribution; that all coming experience is to be affected by every present feeling; that every future moment of being must answer, for every present moment; that one moment, sacrificed to sin or lost to improvement, is for ever sacrificed and lost; that one year's delay, or one hour's wilful delay, to enter the right path is to put you back so far, in the everlasting pursuit of happiness; and that every sin, ay, every sin of a good man, is thus to be answered for, though not according to the full measure of its ill-desert, yet according to a rule of unbending rectitude and impartiality. This is undoubtedly the strict and solemn Law of Retribution: but how much its strictness has really entered—I say not now into our hearts and lives; I will take up that serious question in another season of meditation—but how much the strictness of the principle of retribution has entered into our theories, our creeds, our speculations, is a matter that deserves attention.

It is worthy of remark, indeed, that there is *no* doctrine which is more universally received, and at the same time, more universally evaded, than this very doctrine which we are considering. It is universally received, because the very condition of human existence involves it, because it is a matter of experience; every after period of life being affected, and known to be affected by the conduct of every earlier period; manhood by youth, and age by manhood; professional success, by the preparation for it; domestic happiness, by conjugal fidelity and parental care. It is thus seen, that life is a tissue, into which the thread of this connection is everywhere interwoven. It is thus seen that the law of retribution presses upon every man, whethe he thinks of it or not; that it pursues him through all the courses of life, with a step that never falters nor tires, and with an eye that never sleeps nor slumbers. The doctrine of a future retribution has been universally received, too, because it has been felt that in no other way, could the impartiality of God's government be vindicated; that if the best and the worst men in the world, if the ruthless oppressor and his innocent victim, if the proud and boasting injurer and the meek and patient sufferer, are to go to the same reward, to the same approbation of the good and just God; there is an end of all discrimination, of all moral government, and of all light upon the mysteries of providence. It has been felt, moreover, that the character of the soul carries with it, and in its most intimate nature, the principles of retribution, and that it must work out weal or wo for its possessor.

But this doctrine so universally received, has been, I say, as universally evaded. The classic mythologies of paganism did, indeed, teach that there were infernal regions; but few were doomed to them: and for those few, who failing of the rites of sepulture, or of some other ceremonial qualification, were liable to that doom, an escape was provided by their wandering on the banks of the Styx awhile, as preparatory to their entering Elysium. So too, the creed of the Catholics, though it spoke of hell, had also, its purgatory to soften the horrors of retribution. And now there are, as I think, among the body of Protestants, certain speculative, or rather may I say, mechanical views of the future state, and of the preparation for it, and of the principles of mercy in its allotments, that tend to let down the strictness of that law, which for ever binds us to the retributive future.

Is it not a question, let me barely ask in passing,

whether this universal evasion does not show that the universal belief has been extravagant; whether men have not believed too much, to believe it strictly and specifically to its minutest point? It certainly is a very striking fact, that while the popular creed teaches that almost the whole living world is going down to everlasting torments, the popular sympathy interposes to save from that doom, almost the whole dying world.

But, not to dwell on this observation, I shall proceed now briefly to consider some of those modern views, which detract from the strictness of the law of retribution.

I. And the first which I shall notice, is the view of the actual scene of retribution, as consisting of two conditions, entirely opposite and altogether different. Mankind according to this view, are divided into two distinct classes; the one of which is to enjoy infinite happiness, and the other to suffer infinite misery. It is a far stronger case, than would be made by the supposition, that man's varied efforts to gain worldly good, were to be rewarded by assigning to one portion of the race, boundless wealth, and to the other, absolute poverty; for it is infinite happiness on the one hand, and, not the bare destitution of it, but infinite misery on the other.

Let me observe, before I proceed farther to point out what I consider to be the defect which attends this popular view of retribution, that the view itself is not warranted by scripture. The Bible teaches us that virtue will be rewarded and sin punished; that the good shall receive good, and the evil shall receive evil; and that is all that it teaches us. It unfolds to us this simple and solemn and purely spiritual issue, and nothing more.

All else is figurative; and so the most learned interpreters have generally agreed to consider it. It is obvious, that representations of what passes in the future world, taken from the present world, must be of this character. When heaven is represented as a city, and hell as a deep abyss, and Christ is described as coming to judgment on a throne, with the state and splendour of an Oriental monarch, and separating, *in form and visibly* separating the righteous from the wicked, we know, that these representations are figurative descriptions of a single and simple fact; and this fact is, and this is the whole of the fact that is taught us, that a distinction will be made between good men and bad men: and that they will be rewarded or punished hereafter, according to the character they have formed and sustained here.

It is to be remembered, too, in appealing to the Scriptures, that there are other teachings in them than those which are figurative, and teachings which bind us far more to the letter. It is written, that whatsoever a man soweth, that shall he also reap; and that God will render unto every man according to his deeds; i. e. according to his character, as by deeds is doubtless meant in this instance.

But now to return to the view already stated, I maintain, that the boundless distinction which it makes in the state of the future life, is *not* rendering unto men according to their deeds; that is to say, according to their character. Because, of this character, there are many diversities, and degrees, and shades. Men differ in virtue, precisely as they differ in intelligence; by just as many and imperceptible degrees. As many as are the diversities of moral education in the world, as numerous as are the shades of circumstance in life, as various as are the degrees of moral capacity and effort in various minds, so must the results differ. If character were formed by machinery, there might be but two samples. But if it is formed by voluntary agency, the results must be as diversified and complicated as the operations of that agency. And the fact, which every man's observation must show him, undoubtedly is, that virtue in men differs just as intelligence does; differs, I repeat, by just as many and imperceptible degrees. But now suppose that men were to be rewarded for their intelligence hereafter. Would all the immense variety of cases be met by two totally different and opposite allotments? Take the scale of character, and mark on it, all the degrees of difference, and all the divisions of a degree. Now what point on the scale will you select, at which to make the infinite difference of allotments? Select it where you will, and there will be the thousandth part of a degree above, rewarded with perfect happiness, and a thousandth part of a degree below, doomed to perfect misery. Would this be right, with regard to the intelligence, or virtue of men?

We are misled on this subject by that loose and inaccurate division of mankind, which is common, into the two classes of "saints and sinners." We might as well say that all men are either strong or weak, wise or foolish, intellectual or sensual. So they are, in a general sense; but not in a sense, that excludes all discrimination. And the language of the Bible, when it speaks of the good and bad, of the righteous and wicked, is to be understood with the same reasonable discrimination; with the same reasonable qualification of its meaning, as when it speaks of the rich and poor. The truth is, the matter of fact is, that from the highest point of virtue, to the lowest point of wickedness, there are, I repeat, innumerable steps; and men are standing upon all these steps; they are actually found in all these gradations of character. Now to render to such beings according to their character, is not to appoint to them two totally distinct and opposite allotments, but just as many allotments as there are shades of moral difference between them.

But does not the Bible speak of two distinct classes of men as amenable to the judgment, and of *but* two; and does it not say of the one class, "these shall go away into everlasting fire," and of the other, "but the righteous into life eternal?" Certainly it does. And so do we constantly say, that the good shall be happy, and the bad shall be miserable in the coming world. But do we, or does the Bible, intend to speak without any discrimination? Especially, can the omniscient scrutiny and the unerring rule be supposed to overlook any, even the slightest differences and the most delicate shades of character? On the contrary, we are told that "one star, differeth from another in glory;" and we are told that there is a "lowest hell:" and we are led to admit that in the allotments of retributive justice, the best among bad men, and the worst among good men, may come as near to each other in condition, as they come in character.

I am not saying, let it be observed, that the difference even in this case, is unimportant; still less that it is so, in general. Nay, and the difference between the states of the very good man and of the very bad man, may indeed be as great as any theory supposes; it may be much greater, in fact, than any man's imagination conceives; but this is not the only difference that is to be brought into the final account; for there are many intermediate ranks between the best and the worst. I say, that the difference of allotment may, nay, and that it must be great. The truly good man, the devoted Christian, shall doubtless experience a happiness beyond his utmost expectation. The bad man, the self-indulgent, the self-ruined man, will doubtless find his doom severer than he had looked for. I say not what it may be. But this at least, we may be sure of, that the consequences both of good and bad conduct, will be more serious, will strike deeper, than we are likely, amidst the gross and dim perceptions of sense, to comprehend.

But this is not the point which I am at present arguing. It is not the extent of the consequences; but it is the strict and discriminating impartiality which shall measure out those affecting results; it is the strict law by which every man shall reap the fruits of that which he sows. And I say that the artificial, imaginative, and, as I think, unauthorized ideas which prevail with regard to a future life, let down the strictness of the law.

Let me now illustrate this by a single supposition. Suppose that you were to live in *this* world one thousand or ten thousand years; and suppose, too, that you felt that every present moment was a probation for every future moment; and that in order to be happy, you must be pure; that every fault, every wrong habit of life or feeling, would tend and would continue to make you unhappy, till it was faithfully and effectually corrected; and corrected by yourself, not by the hand of death, not by the exchange of worlds. Suppose yourself to entertain the conviction, that if you plunged into self-indulgence and sin, diseases and distempers and woes would accumulate upon you—with no friendly interposition or rescue, no all-healing nostrum, no medicine of sovereign and miraculous efficacy to save—that diseases, I say, and distempers and woes would accumulate upon you, in dark and darkening forms, for a thousand years. Suppose that every evil passion, anger or avarice or envy or selfishness in any of its forms, would, unless resisted and overcome, make you more and more miserable, for a thousand years. I say that such a prospect, limited as it is in comparison, would be more impressive and salutary, a more powerful restraint upon sin, a more powerful stimulus to improvement, than the prospect, as it is usually contemplated, of the retributions of eternity! Are we then making all that we ought to make, of the prospect of an eternal retribution? God's justice will be as strict there, as it is here. And although bodily diseases may not accumulate upon us there, yet the diseases of the soul, if we take not heed to them, will accumulate upon us; and he who has only one degree of purity, and ten degrees of sin in him, must not lay that flattering unction to his soul, that death will "wash out the long arrears of guilt." I know that this is a doctrine of unbending strictness, a doctrine, I had almost said, insufferably strict; but I believe that it is altogether true.

"But," some one may say, "if I am converted; if I have repented of my sins, and believed on the Lord Jesus Christ, then I have the assurance, through God's mercy, of pardon and heaven."

This statement embraces the other doctrinal evasion of the law of retribution which I proposed to consider. And I must venture to express the apprehension that, by those who answer thus to the strict and unaccommodating demand of inwrought purity, neither conversion, nor repentance, nor the mercy of God, are understood as they ought to be.

A man says, "I am not to be judged by the law, but by the Gospel." But when he says that, let me tell him, he should take care to know what he says and whereof he affirms. The difference between the Law and the Gospel, I believe, is much misapprehended in this respect. The Gospel is not a more easy, not a more lax rule to walk by, but only a more encouraging rule. The Law demands rectitude, and declares that the sinner deserves the miseries of a future life; and there it stops, and of course it leaves the offender in despair. The Gospel comes in, and it did come in, with its teaching and prophetic sacrifices, even amidst the thunders of Sinai, saying, If thou wilt repent and believe, if thou wilt embrace the faith and spirit of the all-humbling and all-redeeming religion, the way to happiness is still open. But does the Gospel anything more than open the way? Does it make the way more easy, more indulgent, less self-denying? Does it say, You need not be as good as the Law requires, and yet you shall be none the less happy for all that? Does it say, You need not do as well, and yet it shall be just as well with you? "Is Christ the minister of sin? God forbid!" Nay, be it remembered that the solemn declaration upon which we are this day meditating—"whatsoever a man soweth that shall he also reap"—is recorded not in the law, but in the Gospel.

"But if I repent," it may be said, "am I not forgiven entirely?" If you repent entirely, you are forgiven entirely; and not otherwise. What *is* repentance? It is a change of mind. That, as every scholar knows, is the precise meaning of the original word in the Scriptures, which is translated repentance. It is a change of mind. If, then, your repentance, your change of mind is entire, your forgiveness, your happiness is complete; but on no other principle, and in no other proportion. Sorrow, is only one of the indications of this repentance or change of heart; though it has unfortunately usurped, in common use, the whole meaning of the word. Sorrow is not the only indication of repentance; for joy as truly springs from it. It is not therefore the bare fact, that you are sorry, however sincerely and disinterestedly sorry for your offences, that will deliver you from all the suffering which your sins and sinful habits must occasion. You may be sorry, for instance, and truly sorry, for your anger; yet if the passion breaks out again, it must again give you pain; and it must for ever give you pain, while it lives. You may grieve for your vices. Does that grief instantly stop the course of penalty? Will it instantly repair a shattered constitution? You may regret, in declining life, a state of mind produced by too much devotion to worldly gain, the want of intellectual and moral resources and habits. Will the dearth and the desolation depart from your mind, when that regret enters it? Will even the tears of repentance immediately cause freshness and verdure to spring up in your path?

"But," it may be said, once more, "does not all depend on our being converted, or being born again? And is not conversion, is not the new birth, the event of a moment?

I answer with all the certainty of conviction that I am capable of—no; it is not the event of a moment. That conversion which fits a soul for heaven is *not* the event of a moment. And, my brethren, I would not answer thus in a case, where there is controversy, if I did not think it a matter of the most serious importance. Can anything be more fatal; can any one of all loose doctrines be more loose, than to tell an offender who is going to the worst excesses in sin, that he may escape all the evil results, all the results of fifty, sixty, seventy years of self-indulgence, by one instant's experience? Can any one of us believe, dare we believe, that one moment's virtue can prepare us for the happiness of eternity? Can we believe this, especially when we are, on every page of the Bible, commanded to watch, and pray, and strive, and labour, and by patient continuance in well-doing, to seek for glory, and honour, and immortality; and this, as the express condition of obtaining eternal life or happiness?

No, Christians! subjects of the Christian law! No conversion, no repentance, no mercy of heaven, will save you from the final operation of that sentence, or should save you from its warning now; "Be not deceived"—as if there was special danger of being deceived here—"be not deceived; God is not mocked; for whatsoever a man soweth, that shall he also reap; he that soweth to the flesh, shall of his flesh reap corruption; but he that soweth to the spirit shall of the spirit reap life everlasting."

It is a high, and strict, I had almost said, a terrible discrimination. Yet let us bring it home to our hearts; although it be as a sword to cut off some cherished sin. Oh! this miserable and slavish folly of inquiring whether we have enough piety and virtue to save us! Do men ever talk thus about the acquisition of riches or honours? Do they act as if all their solicitude was to ascertain and to stop at, the point that would just save them from want, or secure them from disgrace? "Enough virtue to save you," do you say? The very question shows that you have not enough. It shows that your views of salvation are yet technical and narrow; if not selfish. It shows that all your thoughts of retribution yet turn to solicitude and apprehension.

The law of retribution is the law of God's goodness. It addresses not only the fear of sin, but the love of improvement. Its grand requisition is that of progress. It urges us at every step to press forward. And however many steps we may have taken, it urges us to take still another and another, by the same pressing reason with which it urged us to take the first step.

Yes, by the same pressing reason. Let him who thinks himself a good man, who thinks that he is converted and on the right side and in the safe state, and who, nevertheless, from this false reasoning and this presumptuous security, indulges in little sins, irritability, covetousnes, or worldly pride; let him know that his doom shall be hereafter, and is now a *kind of hell*, compared with the blessedness in store for loftier virtue and holier piety; and let him know too, that compared with that loftier standard, he has almost as much reason to tremble for himself, as the poor sinner he looks down upon. For if woes are denounced against the impenitent sinner, so are woes denounced, in terms scarcely less awful, against the secure lukewarm negligent Christian. God is no respecter of persons nor of professions. It is written that he will render to *every* man, according to his deeds." It is written, too, that "*whatsoever* a man soweth, that shall he also reap."

I repeat that language of fearful discrimination, "*whatsoever*—a man *soweth, that,* not something else —*that*, shall he also *reap*." That which you *are doing;* be it good or evil, be it grave or gay; that which you are doing to-day and to-morrow, each thought, each feeling, each action, each event; every passing hour, every breathing moment, is contributing to form the character by which you are to be judged. Every particle of influence that goes to form that aggregate, your character, shall, in that future scrutiny, be sifted out from the mass, and shall fall particle by particle, with ages perhaps intervening—shall fall a distinct contribution to the sum of your joys or your woes. Thus every idle word, every idle hour, shall give answer in the judgment. Think not, against the closeness and severity of this inquisition, to put up any barrier of theological speculation. Conversion, repentance, pardon—mean they what they will—mean nothing that will save you from reaping, down to the very root and ground of good or evil, that which you have sowed. Think not to wrap that future world in any blackness of darkness, or any folding flames; as if, for the imagination to be alarmed were all you had to feel or fear. Clearly, distinctly shall the voice of accusation fall upon the guilty ear; as when upon earth, the man of crime comes reluctantly forth from his hiding place, and stands at the bar of his country's justice, and the voices of his associates say, "thou didst it!" If there be any unchangeable, any adamantine fate in the universe, this is that fate; that the future shall for ever bring forth the fruits of the past.

Take care, then, what thou sowest, as if thou wert taking care for eternity. That sowing, of which the scripture speaketh, what is it? Yesterday, perhaps, some evil temptation came upon you; the opportunity of unrighteous gain, or of unhallowed indulgence, either in the sphere of business, or of pleasure, of society or of solitude. If you yielded to it, then and there did you plant a seed of bitterness and sorrow. To-morrow, it may be will threaten discovery; and agitated, alarmed, you will cover the sin, and bury it deeper in falsehood and hypocrisy. In the hiding bosom, in the fruitful soil of kindred vices that sin dies not, but thrives and grows; and other, and still other germs of evil gather around the accursed root, till from that single seed of corruption, there springs up in the soul all that is horrible in habitual lying, knavery, or vice. Long before such a life comes to its close, its poor victim may have advanced within the very precincts of hell. Yes, the hell of debt, of disease, of ignominy, or of remorse, may gather its shadows around the steps of the transgressor even on earth; and yet these,—if holy scripture be unerring, and sure experience be prophetic—these are but the beginnings of sorrows. The evil deed may be done, alas! in a moment, in one fatal moment; but conscience never dies; memory never sleeps: guilt never can become innocence; and remorse can never, never whisper peace. Pardon may come from heaven; but self-forgiveness, when will it come?

Beware then, thou who art tempted to evil—and every being before me is tempted to evil; beware what thou layest up for the future; beware what thou layest up in the archives of eternity. Thou who wouldst wrong thy neighbour, beware! lest the thought of that injured man, wounded and suffering from thine injury, be a pang which long years may not deprive of its bitterness. Thou who wouldst break into the house of innocence and rifle it of its treasure, beware! lest, when many years have passed over thee, the moan of its distress may not have died away from thine ear. Thou who wouldst build the desolate throne of ambition in thy heart, beware what thou art doing with all thy devices, and circumventings, and selfish schemings! lest desolation and loneliness be on thy path as it stretches into the long futurity. Thou, in fine, who art living a negligent and irreligious life, beware! beware how thou livest; for bound up with that life is the immutable principle of an endless retribution; bound up with that life are elements of God's creating, which shall never spend their force; which shall be unfolding and unfolding with the ages of eternity. Beware! I say once more, and be not deceived. *Be not deceived;* God is not mocked; God who has formed thy nature thus to answer to the future, is not mocked; his law can never be abrogated; his justice can never be eluded; beware, then, be forewarned; since, for ever, and for ever will it be true, that whatsoever a man soweth, that shall he also reap!

V.

THE LAW OF RETRIBUTION

BE NOT DECEIVED; GOD IS NOT MOCKED: FOR WHATSOEVER A MAN SOWETH THAT SHALL HE ALSO REAP.—Galatians vi. 7.

THE views which are usually presented of a future retribution, are characterized, as I have observed in my last discourse, rather by strength than by strictness of representation. The great evil attending the common statements of this doctrine, I shall now venture to say, is not, that they are too alarming. Men are not enough alarmed at the dangers of a sinful course. No men are; no men, though they sit under the most terrifying dispensation of preaching that ever was devised. But the evil is, that alarm is addressed too much to the imagination, and too little to the reason and conscience. Neither Whitfield, nor Baxter, nor Edwards,—though the horror produced by his celebrated sermon "on the justice of God in the damnation of sinners," is a matter of tradition in New England, to this very day—yet no one of them ever preached too much terror, though they may have preached it too exclusively; but the evil was that they preached terror, I repeat, too much to the imagination, and too little to the reason and conscience. Of mere fright, there may be too much; but of real, rational fear, there never *can* be too much. Sin, vice, a corrupt mind, a guilty life, and the woes naturally flowing from these, never can be too much dreaded. It is one thing, for the preacher to deal in mathematical calculations of infinite suffering, to dwell upon the eternity of hell-torments, to speak of literal fires, and of burning in them for ever; and with these representations, it is easy to scare the imagination, to awaken horror, and a horror so great as to be at war with the clear, calm and faithful discriminations of conscience. With such means, it is easy to produce a great excitement in the mind. But he who should, or who *could*, unveil the realities of a strict and spiritual retribution, show what every sinner loses, show what every sinner must suffer, in and through the very character he forms, show, too, how bitterly every good man must sorrow for every sin, here or hereafter, show, in fine, what sin is, and for ever must be to an immortal nature, would make an impression more deep, and sober, and effectual.

It is not my purpose at present to attempt any detail of this nature, though I shall be governed by the observations I have made, in the views which I *am* to present, and for which I venture to ask a rational, and calm, and most serious consideration.

The future is to answer for the present. This is the great law of retribution. And so obviously necessary and just is it; so evidently does our character create our welfare or wo; so certainly must it give us pain or pleasure, as long as it goes with us, whether in this world or another world, that it seems less requisite to support the doctrine by argument, than to save it from evasions.

There are such evasions. No theology has yet come up to the strictness of this law. It is still more true, that no practice has yet come up to it. There are theoretical evasions; and I think they are to be found in the views which are often presented, of conversion and repentance, and of God's mercy and the actual scenes of retribution; but there is one practical evasion, one into which the whole world has fallen, and so dangerous, so momentous in its danger, that it may well deserve, for one season of meditation, I believe, to engross our entire and undivided attention.

This grand evasion, this great and fatal mistake, may be stated in general terms to be, *the substitution of something as a preparation for future happiness, in place of devoting the whole life to it;* or to a course which is fitted to procure it. This evasion takes the particular form perhaps, of an expectation that some sudden and extraordinary experience may, at a future time, accomplish what is necessary to prepare the mind for happiness and heaven; or that certain circumstances, such as sickness and affliction, may, at some subsequent period of life, force the growth of that, which is not cultivated now, and may thus remedy the fearful and fatal neglect; or it is an expectation—and this is the most prevalent form of the error,—that old age or death, when it comes, will have power to penetrate the heart with emotion, and subdue it to repentance, and prepare it for heaven. The subject, yet, it must be feared to be the victim, of this stupendous error, is convinced that in order to be happy eventually, he must become pure; there is no principle of indulgence, there is no gospel of mercy, that can absolve him from that necessity; he must become pure; he must be pious; his nature must be exalted and refined. It is his nature, his mind, that is to be happy; and he is convinced by experience, that his mind must be cultivated, purified, prepared, for that end. But he is not doing this work to-day, nor does he expect to do it to-morrow; he is not doing it this month, nor does he expect to do it next month; he is not doing it this year, nor does he in particular expect to do it next year; and thus, month after month and year after year are passing, and one season of life after another is stealing away: and the only hope is, that in some tremendous exigency, or by some violent paroxysm, when fear and remorse and disease and death are darkly struggling together, *that* may be done, for which the whole previous course of life has not been found sufficient.

But is it true—for I am willing to pause at this point, and deliberately to consider the question—is it true, can it be true, some one may ask, that a mistake so gross, so irrational, so at war with all that we know about character, about its formation, and its necessary results—can it be true, that such a mistake, about the whole vast concern of our happiness, is actually made by any of us? Can it be, you will say, that men, with reason and experience and Scripture to guide them; can it be that men, in their senses, are substituting in place of that deliberate formation of their character for happiness for which life is given, some brief preparation for it, at a future period, and especially at the last period of their lives?

I am persuaded that it is true, my brethren, however strange; and these are the considerations that convince me of it.

In the first place, there are multitudes around us, that hope and expect to be happy hereafter, who are conscious, that they are not preparing for it; who acknowledge at every successive stage of life, that if they were instantly to die, without any further opportunity to prepare for it, there would be little or no hope for them; who feel that, if the very character which they are now, every day forming, were to go to the judgment, their case would be desperate; who hope therefore, most evidently, not to be judged by the prevailing tenor of their lives, but secretly expect to do something at last, to retrieve the errors, the follies and sins, which they are now daily committing.

Again; although it is a common impression, that but *few* LIVE in an habitual preparation for heaven, the impression is almost *as* common, that but few ac tually *die* unprepared. Of almost every individual who leaves the world, something is told, which encourages the hopes of survivors concerning him. I stand before you, my brethren, as a Christian minister, and I solemnly declare, that familiar as I have been with that sad and mournful scene, the death of the wicked, it has almost invariably left this strange and delusive hope behind it. Indeed, the extreme solicitude with which every symptom of preparation is marked in these circumstances, the trembling anxiety with which every word, every look is caught, but too plainly indicate the same impression. What the amount of this proof is, we will presently consider. It is sufficient at this point of the inquiry to state, that it is collected and arranged as carefully, and offered as confidently, as if it were material; that it encourages those who repeat and those who hear it; that the instance of death is very rare, in which surviving friends do not tell you that they trust and believe that all is well. Even when a man has led an eminently pious life, many are apt to feel as if the proof of his piety was not consummated, unless he had died a happy and triumphant death; as though it were to be not only desired, but demanded as a matter of course, that in feebleness and distress of body and mind, and the sinking of all the faculties, the mind should exhibit its utmost energy; as if, amidst the cold damps of death, the expiring flame of sensibility should rise the highest. It is to be feared that good men, and with the best intentions no doubt, have yet given great distress to many faithful Christians and done great injury to others, by countenancing this unreasonable notion. The great question is, not how a good man dies, but how he has *lived*.

The third and final reason, which convinces me of the prevalence of this mistake, which I am considering, is the almost universal dread of sudden death. It is not to be denied, indeed, that a change so great as that of death, and so mysterious too, is in itself and naturally, fitted to awaken a feeling of apprehension. But I maintain, that the principal reason for this apprehension, is the fear of consequences, "the dread of something *after* death;" and that there is a vague hope in almost every mind, that some preparation could be made at the last, if only a little time were granted for it. And indeed, if we all entertained a settled conviction that we are to reap as we have sowed; that we are to be miserable or happy in the other world, according to the character we have formed in this; that we are to be judged by the life we live, and not by the death we die; what would it import to us, whether we fell suddenly, in the paths of life, or slowly declined from them; whether we sunk at once beneath the stroke of an apoplexy, or more slowly under the attack of a consumption? Something, it would import to us no doubt, as friends; for we should wish to give our dying counsels; but as expectants of retribution, what could the time of a week or a month's last sickness avail us? I will answer: and I say, as much, by the most favourable supposition,—as much as such a space of time, in any part of life could avail us; and no more.

Such then and so fearful, and proved to be so fearful by the plainest indications, is the moral state of multitudes. Life is given them for the cultivation of a sacred virtue, of a lofty piety, of pure and godlike affections, as the only way to future improvement and happiness. They are not devoting life, to this end; they know they are not; they confess they are not; and their hope is—yes, the hope, on which they rest their whole being is, that by some hasty effort or paroxysm of emotion, in the feeble and helpless time of sickness, or in the dark day of death, they shall be able to redeem the lost hope of a negligent life. If only a week or a month of health were offered them to prepare; if that specific time, a week or a month, were taken out from the midst of life, and they were solemnly told that this must be all the time they can have to prepare for eternity, they would be in despair; and yet they hope to do this, in a month or a week of pain and languishment and distracting agitation. It is, as if the husbandman should sport away the summer season, and then should think to retrieve his error, by planting his fields in the autumn. It is as if the student should trifle away the season appointed for his education, and then, when the time came for entering upon his profession, should think to make up for his deficiencies, by a few weeks of violent, hurried and irregular application. It shows, alas! that the world, with all its boasts of an enlightened age, has not yet escaped the folly of those days of superstition, when the eucharist was administered to dying persons, and was forcibly administered, if the patient had no longer sense to receive it; or when men deferred their baptism till death; as if the future state were to depend on these last ceremonies. And as well depend on ceremonies—and more consistently could we do so.—as depend on any momentary preparation for happiness. As well build a church or a monastery to atone for our sins, as to build that fabric of error in our imagination.

It is not for us, I know, to limit the Almighty! It is not for us to say, that he cannot change the soul in the last moments of its stay on earth. But this we may fearlessly say; that he does it, if at all, by a miraculous agency, of whose working we can have no conception, and of whose results, by the very supposition, we can have no knowledge.

I desire, my brethren, to state this point with all sufficient caution. I not only do not deny, that God has power to convert the soul in the last moments of life, but I do not absolutely deny that there may be some such instances in the passing away of every generation. I do not know, and none of us can know, whether such miracles are performed or not. It is commonly thought that the case recorded in Luke's Gospel, of the thief on the cross, is an instance of this nature. But I do not think it can be pronounced to be such. We know not how much time he may have had, to repent and form a new character. He says, "we indeed suffer justly;" but the act for which he suffered, may have been a single act, in which he had fallen from a generally good life. But admit that such interpositions do take place; is it safe to rely upon them? We do not know that they do. We do not know, that in the passing away of all the generations of mankind, there has been one such instance. Is it safe to rely, in so tremendous a case, upon what we do not know, and upon what, after all, may never be? My object is to show that it is not safe; and for this purpose, I shall reason upon the general principle. The general principle is, that the future must answer for the present; the future of this life, for the present of this life; the next month, for this month; the next year for this year; and in the same way the next life for this life. I say, then, that the expectation of any hasty retrieving of a bad month, of a bad year, of a bad life, is irrational, and unwarrantable, and ought to be considered as desperate.

I. And for the purpose of showing this, I observe, in the first place, that the expectation of preparing for futurity hastily, or by any other means, than the voluntary and deliberate formation of right and virtuous habits in the mind; or that the expectation of preparing for death when it comes, is opposed to the professed import of that Sacred Volume, which gives law alike to our hopes and our fears.

It is opposed to the obvious, and the professed, and the leading character of the Bible. What is that character? What is the Bible? It is a revelation of laws, motives, directions and excitements, to religious virtue. But all of these are useless, if this character is to be formed by a miraculous energy, at a perilous conjuncture, or in a last moment. Motives must be contemplated, directions must be understood, excitements must be felt, to be effectual; and all this must be done deliberately, must be many times repeated, must be combined with diligence and patience and faith, and must be slowly, as everything is slowly wrought into the character, in order to be effectual.

But it may be said, "If the rule is so strict, where is the *mercy* of the Gospel?" I answer, that its very mercy is engaged to make us pure; that its mercy would be no mercy, if it did not do this: and that, of becoming pure and good, there is but one way; and that is the way of voluntary effort; an effort to be assisted by divine grace, indeed, but none the less, on that account, an effort and an endeavour, a watching and a striving, a conflict and a victory. I answer, again; that the mercy of the Gospel is a moral and rational, a high and glorious principle. It is not a principle of laxity in morals. It is not a principle of indulgence to the heart. It is a moral principle, and not a wonder-working machinery, by which a man is to be lifted up and borne away from guilt to purity, from earth to heaven, he knows not how. It offers to fabricate no wings for the immortal flight. It is a rational principle; and is not based upon the subversion of all the laws of experience and wisdom. The Gospel opens the *way* to heaven, opens the way to poor, sinful, ill-deserving creatures. Is not that, mercy enough? Shall the guilty and lost spurn that, and demand more? It opens the way, I repeat; but then, it lays its instructions, commands and warnings, thickly upon that way. With unnumbered directions to faith, and patience, and prayer, and toil, and self-denial, it marks out every step of that way. It tells us, again and again, that *such* is the way of salvation, and no other. In other words, it offers us happiness, and prescribes the terms. And those terms, if they were of a meaner character, if they were low and lax, would degrade even our nature, and we could not respect them. It would, in fact, be no mercy to natures like ours, to treat them in any other way.

In speaking of the scriptural representations on this subject, the parable of "the labourers in the vineyard' may probably occur to you; in which he who came at the eleventh hour, received as much as he who had borne the heat and burthen of the day. I suppose the parable has no relation whatever to this subject. It cannot intend to teach that he who is a Christian during his whole life, is no more an object of the divine approbation and is to be no more happy, than he who is so for a very small part of it. It evidently refers to the introduction of the Christian dispensation; it relates to the Jews and Gentiles, as nations: meaning that the Gentiles, who came later into covenant with God, would be as favourably received as the Jews.

To interpret this parable as encouraging men to put off their preparation for futurity till death, if there were no other objection, would contradict, I repeat, all the scriptural information we have on this subject. This would appear, if you should carry to the oracles of divine truth, any question whatever, about piety, or virtue, or the qualification for heaven. What is piety itself? A momentary exercise; or a habit? Something thrown into the heart in a mass; or a state of the heart itself, formed by long effort and care? Does the great qualification for heaven consist in one, two or ten good exercises; or in a good character? And to what is that judgment to relate, which will decide our future condition? "Who will render," says the sacred record, "to every man according to his deeds!"

But still further to decide the question, if it can be necessary, let it be asked, what *is* that heaven of which we hear and say so much? What is heaven? Are we still, like children, fancying that heaven is a beautiful city, into which one needs only the powers of locomotion to enter? Do we not know that heaven is in the mind; in the greatness and purity and elevation of our immortal nature? If piety and virtue then are a habit and state of mind expressed and acted out in a life that is holy; if the judgment has relation to this alone; if heaven consist in this; what hope can there be in a brief and slight preparation?

II. No, my friends, the terms on which we receive happiness—and I now appeal to reason in the second place—the terms on which we receive true, moral, satisfying happiness, cannot be easy. They are not;

experience shows that they are not; life shows that they are not; and eternity will but develop the same strict law; for it is a part of our nature; it is a part of the nature and reason of things. The senses may yield us such pleasure as they can yield, without effort; taste may delight us, and imagination may minister to us, in careless reverie; but conscience does not offer to us its happiness on such terms. I know not what may be the law for other beings, in some other sphere; but I know that no truly, morally happy being was ever made here, but through much effort, long culture, frequent self-denial, and abiding faith, patience and prayer. To be truly happy—what is so difficult? What is so rare? And is heaven, think you, the blessed consummation of all that man can ask, to be obtained at less expense than it will cost to gain one pure, calm day upon earth? For even this comparatively trifling boon, one blessed day, one day of religious joy, one day of joy in meditation and prayer, one day of happiness that is spiritual, and not physical nor circumstantial—even this comparatively slight boon, I say, cannot be gained without long preparation of mind, and heart, and habit. There are multitudes around us and of us, to whom, at this moment, one such day's happiness is a thing just as impossible, as it would be in that day to make a world! And shall they think to escape this very law of happiness under which they are actually living, and to fly away to heaven on the wings of imagination?—to pass at once from unfaithfulness to reward, from apathy to ecstasy, from the neglect and dislike of prayer to the blessed communion of heavenly worship, from this hour of being, absorbed in sense and the world, to an eternity of spiritual glory and triumph? No; be assured that facts are here, as they are everywhere, worth more than fancies—be they those of dreaming visionaries or ingenious theologians; if you are not now happy in penitence, and humility, and prayer, and the love of God, you are not in fact prepared to be happy in them hereafter. No; between the actual state of mind prevailing in many, and the bliss of heaven, "there is a great gulf fixed," over which no wing of mortal nor angel was ever spread. No; the law of essential, enduring, triumphant happiness, is labour and long preparation for it; and it is a law which will never, never—never be annulled!

There is a law, too, concerning habits. It is implied in the following language. "Can the Ethiopian change his skin, or the leopard his spots? Then may those who are accustomed to do evil, learn to do well." Habit is no slight bond. Slightly at first, and gently afterwards, may it have drawn its silken cords around us; but not so are its bonds to be cast from us; nor can they, like a green withe, be broken by one gigantic effort. No, the bonds of habit are chains and fetters, that must be worn off. Through the long process of slow and imperceptible degrees, they must be severed with weariness, and galling, and bitter anguish.

"Can it be supposed," says an eloquent writer and preacher, "that, where the vigour of life has been spent in the establishment of vicious propensities; where all the vivacity of youth, and all the soberness of manhood, and all the wisdom of old age, have been given to the service of sin; where vice has been growing with the growth, and strengthening with the strength; where it has spread out with the limbs of the stripling, and become rigid with the fibres of the aged—can it, I say, be supposed, that the labours of such a life, are to be overthrown by one last exertion of the mind, impaired with disease; by the convulsive exercise of an affrighted spirit; or by the inarticulate and feeble sounds of an expiring breath?"

Besides, the rule is as equitable, as in the divine ordination of things, it is necessary. The judgment which ordains that whatsoever a man soweth, that shall he also reap, is a righteous judgment. It is easy no doubt, to regret a bad life when it is just over. When death comes, and the man must leave his sinful indulgences and pleasures; or, when he has no longer any capacity for enjoying them; when sickness has enfeebled the appetites, or age has chilled the passions, then, indeed, is it but a slight sacrifice, and a yet poorer merit in him, to feel regret. But regret, let it be considered, is not repentance! And while the former may be easy and almost involuntary, the other, the repentance, may be as hard, as the adverse tendencies of a whole life can make it. Yes, the hardest of all things then, will be to repent. Yes, I repeat, that which is relied upon to save a man, after the best part of his life has been lost, has become by the very habits of that life, almost a moral impossibility.

And the regret, the selfish regret, can it be accepted? I ask not if it can be accepted by our Maker; I doubt not his infinite mercy; but can it be accepted by our own nature? Can our nature be purified by it? Can the tears of that dark hour of selfish sorrow, or the awful insensibility which no tear comes to relieve —can either of them purge away from the bosom the stains of a life of sin? Let us never make the fearful experiment! Let us not go down to the last tremendous scene of life, there, amidst pain and distraction, with the work of life to do! Let us not have to acquire peace from very terror, and hope from very despair; let us not, thus, trust ourselves to a judgment," that will render unto us according to our deeds; that will render,—mark the explanation—to them, who by patient continuance in well-doing, seek for glory, honour and immortality, eternal life; but tribulation and anguish to every soul that doeth evil."

III. From these views of our subject, drawn from scripture and reason, let me, in the third and last place, refer to a no less decisive consideration which is independent of them; a consideration fully borne out by melancholy facts. It is this: that every man will die, very much as he lives: I mean, that in his character, his habits of feeling, he will. There is not this wide difference, between the living world and the dying world, which is generally supposed. Character, as I have contended, and as we all see, indeed, is not formed in a moment; it cannot upon any known law or principle—it cannot, but in contradiction to every known law and principle, be changed in a moment. Christianity has introduced no law, in subversion of the great laws of experience, and rational motive, and moral action, or of its own established principles. Its doctrine of conversion is only misunderstood when it is supposed to provide a briefer and easier way of preparation for heaven, than watching and striving, and persevering in virtue, and patient continuance in well-doing. I say, therefore, and repeat the certain and solemn truth, that every man will die the same, essentially the same, that he has lived.

For the correctness of this conclusion, I have soon to refer to a single, and as it seems to me, momentous fact. But in the meantime, let me remark that there is one question here, which I view with a kind of apprehension I scarcely know how to express; with almost a dread, for once, to ask what the simple truth is.

My brethren, we are sometimes called upon to pray for a change of heart, in the sinful and negligent man, as he is drawing nigh, in horror and agony, his last hour! It is an awful situation even to him, who only ministers at that dying bed. What shall he *do?* what *can* be done?—I have asked myself. Shall I discourage prayer, even in the uttermost extremity? Can I, when I hear from those lips that are soon to be sealed in death, the pathetic entreaty, "Oh! pray;" can I refuse to pray? I do not; I cannot. Prayer is our duty; events are with God. But I must say, I will say—I will tell the negligent man beforehand—what I fear. I fear, I do fear, that such praying is nothing better than the supplication of our terror and despair! I fear, that it is altogether an irrational and unauthorized praying! I fear that it is like praying, that guilt, and even a whole life of it, may feel no enduring remorse; that sin may not be followed by sorrow; that vice may leap at once to the rewards of virtue; that the sword which a man has plunged into his bosom, may not wound him, or that the envenomed draught he has taken, may not poison! I fear that it is, as if we should take our station on the banks of the mighty river, that is pouring its accumulated waters into the ocean, and pray that they may turn back to their fountain-head; or as if we should gaze upon the descending sun in heaven, and pray that he may stand still in his course! I tremble with a strange misgiving, as if it were a praying not to God, but against God!

For, what *is* this prayer? It cannot harm us to make the inquiry now, before that crisis comes. What *is* this prayer? It *is* a prayer that the flow of moral habits may turn back to its source: that the great course of moral causes and effects may all be stopped; that the great laws of the moral universe may all be suspended. It *is* praying against many a solemn declaration of Holy Writ. And will it—I ask—will the prayer he heard? Again, I tremble, at that question, again, my misgivings come over me; I ask; but I know not what to answer. I know in fact—I may conjecture, and hope—but I *know* of no answer to that awful question, unless it be in this more awful language. "Be not deceived"—it sounds like a warning in my ear—"be not deceived: God is not mocked:" man's indulgence may flatter him; plausible systems of his own devising may encourage him to venture his soul upon an easier way of salvation; and weaker bands than those of almighty justice might have been escaped, but—"God is not mocked; for whatsoever a man soweth"—not what he wishes, when the seeds of sin are implanted, and have sprung up, have grown to maturity—I cannot read it so—but, "whatsoever a man soweth, *that* shall he also reap."

Tell me not the oft-repeated tale, of a death-bed repentance. I turn to it an incredulous ear. What does it amount to, even when it comes with the kindest testimony of partial affection? Alas! it is doubtful, even in its utmost latitude, and in the moment when it claims our utmost sympathy. For what is it? It is, that the subject of this charitable judgment, was willing to die, when to die was inevitable; that he sought for pardon, when he felt that he must be pardoned or perish in his sins: that he prayed, but it was when *Atheists* have prayed; that he hoped; ah, he hoped, when it had become too terrible to despair!

And now what is the result? What is it, that the issue of all this fearful, I cannot call it flattering, experience tells us? What is the fact, on which this solemn conclusion, concerning the inefficacy of a death-bed repentance, rests? In many cases it is revealed only in another world, and is beyond our scrutiny. But when it is known, I beg it may be solemn-

.y considered what it is, and what is its bearing on the hopes of a death-bed repentance. The result is—and I speak, let it be repeated, of a fact—the result is almost without exception, in cases where the subject of such experience recovers, that he returns to his old habits of living, without any, or any but a very slight and temporary change. In many such instances, where the experience has been very bright and convincing, the individual retains no recollection of any thing he said, or was supposed to have felt. It was all a delirium. The moral state as well as the mental state, was all delirium. And there is too much reason to fear that all such experience is a moral delirium, at best. I would not willingly disturb, for one moment, the peace of a fond and anxious friendship. I will not speak of the state of those, who are dead; but I must speak of the dangers of those, who are living. And surely, if there are any, this side of the retributions of eternity, who could most fearfully warn us not to postpone religion to a dying hour, it would be those, who have hung with anxious watchings around the last hours of the disobedient and irreligious, and have trembled, and prayed, and wept, for their welfare!

My friends, I have only time to present to you and to myself, one practical question; *are we habitually ready to die?* The question, my brethren, is not, whether we expect to be ready at some future time. It is not whether we mean to be ready. It is not whether we are making the most solemn promises to ourselves that we will, some time, set about the preparation for that great hour. But the question is, are we ready for it now? Are we habitually ready? Are we convinced that we are to be judged, not by some imaginary life which we intend, and intend, and for ever intend to lead, and which we never do lead, because we are always intending it;—are we convinced, I say, that we are to be judged not by that imaginary life which we are for ever intending to lead, but by the life which we are now actually living? Have we given up the folly of expecting to do anything in future, which we will not do now; of expecting to do that in sickness, which we cannot do in health; of expecting to do that in death, which we cannot do in life? Are we doing just as much to prepare as if the judgment were to depend on what we are doing; for it is to depend on what we are doing, and doing, and doing, through the whole of life: as much, I say, as if the judgment were to depend on these hourly deeds which we are now performing, on these momentary feelings which we are now cherishing? If not, then, there ought to be a revolution in our lives—call it conversion, regeneration, a change of heart, I care not by what name—but, I say, that there ought to be a revolution in our lives, of such magnitude and moment, that the eternal judgment only can declare it! Are we, then, habitually ready to die? If not habitually, we never are, for religion is a habit. If not habitually; if not, at least, habitually *making* ourselves ready, there is reason to fear that we never shall be; for life—do you not perceive?—is a tissue of thoughts, purposes, and feelings, which is growing stronger as it lengthens; so that the disinclination to prepare for death is growing every moment, while, every moment the time for it lessens.

There is a vague notion—for it is the hope of all that death will not break into the midst of life—a vague notion, with many, of retiring in advancing years from the cares and business of life to make this preparation, which involves a great and hazardous mistake.

They seem to think that the heart will become pure and spiritual and heavenly, as the state of life becomes quiet and free from the urgency of worldly cares. Delusive expectation! as if all growth in nature were not most vigorous amidst calm and silence: as if, in like manner, the rooted passions of the soul were not likely to grow stronger and more stubborn, amidst the silence and quietude of declining years! What is the fact? Did you ever *see* selfishness, or avarice, or a worldly mind, lose its accustomed power in such circumstances? On the contrary, we know—who has not witnessed sad and striking instances of it?—we know, that nothing is more common, than for avarice and worldliness to find strength in leisure and freedom in retirement; that they fix a stronger grasp upon the decaying faculties, and fling their icy bonds over the soul amidst the winter of age. As well might the Ethiopian change his complexion, by retiring from the scorching sun, to his shaded hut: as soon might the leopard lose his spots, barely by plunging into the solitudes of the wilderness: when the flood could not wash them away. The waters of death are not waters of ablution, but rather do they give the colouring and complexion to our destiny. They are not a slow and oblivious stream; but rather a rushing torrent that bears us away, before we are aware. Death comes suddenly to all. It does break sooner or later into the midst of life. It comes at a time when we think not. It comes, not when all our plans are ready for it; not with harbingers and prophecies and preparations; not with a heart-thrilling message, saying, "set thy house in order, for this year thou shalt die;" no voice is in the infectious breath of the air that brings contagion and death with it; no coming step startles us when disease is approaching; no summoning hand knocks at the gate of life, when its last dread foe is about to enter its dark and guarded passages; no monitory conviction within, says, "this month, this week I shall die!" No, it comes at a time when we think not; it comes upon an unprepared hour, unless our life be preparation; it finds us with all our faults, with all our sins about us; it finds us, that which life has made us—finds us such as the very action, habit, and spirit of life, have made us; and bids us die, such as we lived!

Who of *you* will meet his end when he expects it? Perhaps not one. Or if you should, how solemn a message would you address to the living! Who of us has, in our own apprehension, been brought to such a crisis, but has had thoughts, which no language can utter, on this momentous concern? We felt that then was not the time to prepare. "Oh! not now—not here!" is the language of the dying man, as with broken utterance and the failing and faltering breath of life, he testifies his last conviction, "not now—not here, is the place or the time, to prepare for death!" And he feels too, that all which the world contains, vanishes into nothing, compared with this preparation! Are we, then, prepared?—not by a preternatural or extravagant state of feeling; not by glooms, nor by raptures; nor by any assurance, nor by any horror of mind; but by the habitual and calm discharge of our duty, by labours of kindness, by the spirit of devotion?—by a temper of mind, kindred to that heaven which we hope to enter? Are we thus ready, every day, every hour? On the exchange, in the office, in the study; in the house and by the way; in the work-shop and in the field; are we ever ready? "Blessed are those servants, whom the Lord when he cometh shall find watching: and if he shall come, in the second watch, or in the third watch, and find them so, Blessed are those servants."

VI.

COMPASSION FOR THE SINFUL.

AND WHEN HE HAD LOOKED ROUND ABOUT HIM WITH ANGER, BEING GRIEVED FOR THE HARDNESS OF THEIR HEARTS, HE SAID UNTO THE MAN, STRETCH FORTH THY HAND.—Mark iii. 5.

THAT part of this passage, only, which relates to the moral temper of our Saviour, is proposed for your present meditations. It is, in other words, and especially, the compassion of Jesus.

In reading the first clause of the sentence—he "looked round about him with anger"—I suppose that many may have felt an emotion, a thrill almost, of pain and doubt; they have felt that these words, by themselves, and in their simple meaning, were in painful contrast with all their ideas of our Saviour's meekness and patience; they have been ready to doubt whether the words *could* have been correctly translated. But how entirely and delightfully is the mind relieved by the words that follow—"being grieved for the hardness of their hearts!" He was indignant as he looked around him, and witnessed the bitter enmity and the base hypocrisy of the Jews; but his indignation instantly softened into pity; he was grieved at the hardness of their hearts.

This is one instance of that sublime moral harmony, that union in which the most opposite qualities met and mingled, that so entirely singles out from all other models, the character of our heavenly Teacher and Master. We recognise the same spirit with that which was so pathetically manifested, in his appeal to Jerusalem. "O Jerusalem! Jerusalem!—thou that killest the prophets and stonest them that are sent to thee,"—here is the tone of indignation and reproach; but mark, how instantly it is redeemed from the ordinary character of those sentiments—"thou that killest the prophets and stonest them that are sent unto thee; how often would I have gathered thy children even as a hen gathereth her brood under her wing, but ye would not!"

The spirit with which we should regard the faults and sins of mankind is nearly a neglected subject in morals; and it had been well for moral reformers and preachers of righteousness, if they had more thoroughly considered it. It is, moreover, a very practical subject to all men. For we are constantly brought into contact with the faults and transgressions of mankind; every day offers, from this cause, some annoyance to our feelings, or some injury to our interests; every newspaper, that is taken in our hand, is burthened with the recital of crimes—robberies, murders, piracies, wars. Indeed, this constant experience of injustice or exasperation in some or other of their forms, and this extensive observation of human wickedness, are a part of our moral discipline; and it becomes us, to consider how we should meet it, and be made better by other men's faults. It is, indeed, in its mildest form, a sad and grievous discipline, from which, no one should be willing to come out, unprofited.

There is another general observation applicable to this subject. As we advance in our moral discriminations, we shall always find that things before indifferent, become interesting; and things distant, it may be added, become near. A war, for instance, breaks out between distant nations. A man may say—what is that to me? What is the case of the French and the Austrians, of the Russians and the Poles, to me? I answer, it is much to you. For every time you read an account of a battle; every time you read of the prowess of armies, of blood and carnage, of blazing battlements and groaning hospitals, you have certain feelings; and they are marked with a strong moral complexion. You are pleased or pained; you exult or you regret; or you are indifferent; and to any refined moral sensibility, these states of mind will not be unimportant. Or, an extensive fraud in some public institution, although it may not touch you in your interests, does touch you in your feelings; and therefore, does concern, though not your pecuniary, yet, your moral welfare. And while others think that they have nothing to do but with words, nothing to do but to talk, and speculate, and wonder, and rail; a thoughtful man will feel that he has much to do with his own heart. Or, when the poor miserable victim of vice, the shattered wreck of a man, appears before the public eye, he may be contemplated with laughter or scorn; but from a man, who breathes the spirit of the Christian Master, that spectacle will draw forth deeper sentiments. It is the form of sacred humanity that is before him; it is an erring fellow-being; it is a desolate, forlorn, forsaken soul; and the thoughts of good men, that gather around that poor wretch, will be far deeper than those of indifference or scorn. And in fine, all human offences,—that whole system of dishonesty, evasion, circumventing, forbidden indulgence and intriguing ambition, in which men are struggling together, will often be looked upon, by a thoughtful observer, not merely as the sphere of mean toils and strifes, but as the solemn conflict of minds immortal, for ends vast and momentous as their own being. Sad and unworthy strife indeed! and let it be viewed with indignation; but let that indignation too, melt into pity.

Such, indeed, is the spirit recommended in our text, a spirit of indignation at human faults and follies, but a spirit too, which leans to pity: a feeling which although it begins often with indignation, always, by the aids of reflection and piety, *ends* in pity.

There *is* a portion of indignation in the right temper. The right feeling is not a good natured easiness at the transgressions of men, nor a worldly indifference, nor a falsely philosophic coldness, that puts on an air of reasoning and says, "it must be so," and "men were made so," and "this is what we must expect." Neither is it a worldly laxity of conscience, that accounts every thing well, that passes under the seal of public opinion. It is a decided and strong moral feeling, that ought to be awakened by human wickedness. It is indignation.

But, then, it is not a harsh and cruel feeling. It is not peevishness nor irritation. It is not hasty nor angry reproach. It is not a feeling that delights in denunciation. No; but the words of warning fall, as they did from the lips of Jesus, mingled with lamentation. Or, the words of reproach are uttered as they were by Paul, when he told the Philippians, and told them *even weeping*, that some among them, were enemies of the cross of Christ.

There are other mistakes which we are liable to commit, and other wrong feelings, which we are prone to cherish, towards the erring and guilty.

Good men—shall I say it?—are too proud of their goodness. Here are you, a respectable individual in society. Dishonour comes not near you. Your countenance has weight and influence. Your robe is unstained. The poisonous breath of calumny has never been breathed upon your fair name. Ah! how easy is it to look down with scorn upon the poor, degraded offender; to pass by him with a lofty step; to draw up the folds of your garment around you, that it may not be soiled by his touch! Yet the great Master of virtue did not so; but he descended to familiar intercourse with publicans and sinners.

There is a feeling, I say, not only of scorn but of triumph, often springing up from the survey of other men's faults. Many seem to think themselves better, for all the sins they can detect in others. And when they are going over with the catalogue of their neighbour's unhappy derelictions of temper, or conduct, there is often, amidst much apparent concern, a secret exultation, that poisons and blasts all their pretensions to wisdom and moderation, and their claims even to virtue itself. Nay, this feeling goes so far, that men take actual pleasure in the sins of others. It is not the corrupt man, only; it is not the seducer into the path of evil only, that does this; but it is every man, whose thoughts are often employed in agreeable comparisons of his virtues, with the faults of his neighbour.

The power over men's faults, which is lost by a harsh or haughty treatment of them, would of itself, form a great subject; and one that much needs to be commended to all those who would exert any moral influence over their fellow-beings. The power of gentleness, the subduing influence of pity, the might of love, the control of mildness over passion, the commanding majesty of that perfect character which mingles grave displeasure with grief and pity for the offender; these things have been too little seen in the world. I believe that our pulpits, and our tribunals of justice, and parental authority among us, must put on a new aspect, before they will appear in all their dignity, their venerableness, their power, and beauty. We scarcely know, as yet, what we might do with men's passions and vices. They are commonly reputed, and some of them in particular, to be untameable, incorrigible, and fated to procure the ruin of their victims; and they are in part made so, by our wrong treatment of them. The human heart cannot yield to such an influence as we too often endeavour to exert upon it. It was not made to bow willingly to what is merely human; at least, not to what is *infirm* and *wrong* in human nature. If it yields to us, it must yield to what is divine in us. The wickedness of my neighbour cannot submit to my wickedness; his sensuality, for instance, cannot submit to my anger against his vices. My faults are not the instruments that are to correct his faults. And it is hence, that impatient reformers, and denouncing preachers, and hasty reprovers, and angry parents, and irritable relatives, so often fail in their several departments, to reclaim the erring.

I would, therefore, remind them that they have a new lesson to learn, from the compassion of Jesus; and that is, while they permit in themselves the liveliest sensibility to the sins of men, to mingle with it the deepest commiseration for them.

I. And they may learn this lesson, they may find it enforced rather, first, by considering what it is, that their feelings and thoughts are exercised about.

It is sin. It is combined guilt and misery. It is the supreme evil. Whence shall we gather comparisons to set it forth? Shall we name sickness? Sickness belongs to the body; the corruptible and perishable body. Pain?—physical pain? The body is its instrument, and end. Loss, disappointment? They are worldly accidents. Dishonour? It is, comparatively, a shade upon a name. But a moral offence possesses all these characters, and it attaches them all to the soul. It is sickness, it is pain, it is loss, it is dishonour, in the immortal part. It is guilt; and it is misery added to guilt. It is calamity in itself: and it brings upon itself in addition the calamity of God's displeasure, and the abhorrence of all righteous beings, and the soul's own abhorrence. If you have to deal with this evil, deal faithfully, but patiently, and tenderly with it. This is no matter for petty provocation, nor for personal strife, nor for selfish irritation.

Speak kindly to your erring brother. God pities him; Christ has died for him; Providence waits for him; the mercy of heaven yearns towards him; and the spirits of heaven are ready to welcome him back with joy. Let your voice be in unison with all those powers that God is using for his recovery.

Parent! speak gently to your offending child. This trait of parental duty should be deeply pondered. A tone of grave rebuke should, indeed, be sometimes used: perhaps, occasion may require that it should be often used; but the tone of peevish complaint and anger, never. There is a different language; and how much more powerful! "Ah! my child!" might one say, in the manner, if not in language, "my child! what injury is all this doing you? This passion, this violence, or this vice, what a bitter cup is it preparing for you!" This language, this tone from the grave wisdom of a father, or the tender anxiety of a mother, might have saved some whom peevishness and provocation have driven farther and deeper into the ways of transgression.

But let us put the strongest case. Your neighbour

has done you grievous wrong. And he has the face to tell you so; and to exult in his dishonesty. What man is there whose countenance would not be flushed with momentary indignation, at being so confronted with one that had injured him, and that gloried in the injury! And *let* us concede thus much to the weakness of nature, or even to the first impulse of virtue. But the *next* feeling should be unfeigned regret and pity. Yes, the man who stands before you, triumphing in a prosperous fraud, and palpable wrong, is the most pitiable of human beings. He has done himself a deeper, a far deeper injury, than he has done to you. It is the inflicter of wrong, not the sufferer, whom God beholds with mingled displeasure and compassion; and his judgment should be your law. Where amidst the benedictions of the Holy Mount is there one for this man? But upon the merciful, the peacemakers, the persecuted, they are poured out freely; these are the sacred names, upon which the spirit and blessing of Jesus descend.

II. In the next place, it may temper the warmth of our indignation against sin, and soften it into pity; it may well bring us, indeed, to imitate the compassion of Jesus, for us to reflect, that what others are, and however bad, we, in other circumstances, might have been as they are.

We are all men of like passions, propensities, exposures. There are elements in us all, which might have been perverted, through the successive processes of moral deterioration, to the worst of crimes. The wretch whom the execration of the thronging crowd pursues to the scaffold or the gibbet, is not worse than any one of the multitude might have become, in similar circumstances. He is to be condemned, indeed; but how much he is to be pitied, let his burning passions, his consuming remorse, his pallid cheek, his sinking head, the mingled apathy and agony of his apprehensions; let these tell.

I feel that I am speaking of a case that is fully practical. There is a vindictive feeling in society, towards convicted and capital offenders, towards those who are doomed to abide the awful severity of the law, that does not become the frail and the sinful. I do not adopt the unqualified language, that it is nothing but the grace of God that saves us from being as bad as the worst of criminals. But it is certain that we owe much to the good providence of God, ordaining for us a lot more favourable to virtue. It is certain that we all had that within us, that might have been pushed to the same excess. And therefore, a silent pity and sorrow for the victim, should mingle with our detestation of the crime.

The very pirate, that dyes the ocean-wave with the blood of his fellow-beings; that meets with his defenceless victim in some lonely sea where no cry for help can be heard, and plunges his dagger to the heart which is pleading for life; which is calling upon him by all the names of kindred, of children and home, to spare; yes, the very pirate is such a man, as you or I, might have been. Orphanage in childhood; an unfriended youth; an evil companion; a resort to sinful pleasure; familiarity with vice; a scorned and blighted name; seared and crushed affections; desperate fortunes; these are steps that might have led any one among us, to unfurl upon the high seas the bloody flag of universal defiance; to have waged war with our kind; to have put on the terrific attributes, to have done the dreadful deeds, and to have died, the awful death of the ocean robber. How many affecting relationships of humanity plead with us to pity him!

That head, that is doomed to pay the price of blood, once rested upon a mother's bosom. The hand that did that accursed work, and shall soon be stretched, cold and nerveless, in the felon's grave, was once taken and cherished by a father's hand, and led in the ways of sportive childhood and innocent pleasure. The dreaded monster of crime, has once been the object of sisterly love, and all domestic endearment. Pity him, then. Pity his blighted hope, and his crushed heart. It is a wholesome sensibility. It is reasonable; it is meet for frail and sinning creatures like us to cherish. It foregoes no moral discrimination. It feels the crime; but feels it as a weak, tempted and rescued creature should. It imitates the great Master; and looks with indignation upon the offender, and yet is grieved for him.

III. In the last place I would set forth the intrinsic worth and greatness of this disposition as a reason for cherishing it. This rank does the virtue of compassion hold in the character of our Saviour.

How superior is the man of forbearance and gentleness to every other man, in the collisions of society! He is the real conqueror: the conqueror of himself; but that is not all; he conquers others. There is no dominion in the social world like this. It is a dominion which makes not slaves but freemen; which levies no tribute but of gratitude; whose only monuments are those of virtuous example.

No man may claim much merit, merely for being *indignant* at the faults and sins of those around him. It is better than indifference, better than no feeling; but it is only the beginning and youth of virtue. The youthful, untutored, unsubdued mind is *only* angry with sin; and thinks it does well to be angry. But when more reflection comes, and a deeper consciousness of personal deficiencies; and a more entire subjection to the meek and compassionate spirit of Jesus Christ is wrought out in the mind, a new character begins to develop itself. Harsh words, borne upon the breath of a hasty temper, do not ruffle the soul as they once did. Reproof is received with meekness and in silence. The tongue is not ever ready, as if it were an instrument made to ward off reproach. The peace of the soul does not stand in the opinion of others. Faults are estimated with forbearance. Mature and fixed virtue is too high and strong to think of building itself up, like a doubtful reputation, upon surrounding deficiencies. Sins are more immediately and habitually connected with the sufferings they must occasion; and therefore they more surely awaken pity. The man of advancing piety and virtue is growing in the conviction, indeed, that the only real, essential, immitigable evil is sin. He mourns over it in himself; he mourns over it in others. It is the root of bitterness in the field of life. It is the foe with which he is holding the long, and often disheartening conflict. It is the cloud upon the face of nature. That cloud overspreads his neighbour, with himself. And he pities, from his inmost soul, all who walk beneath it.

Patience with the erring and offending, is one of the loftiest of all the forms of character. "Compassion for souls," though the phrase is often used in a cant and technical manner, ought to be a great and ennobling sentiment. Compassion, indeed, for souls; how should it transcend all other compassion! Look over the world, and say, where are its sufferings? In the diseased body, in the broken limb, in the wounded and bruised organs of sense? In the desolate dwelling of poverty; in hunger, and cold and nakedness? Yes, suffering is there; and Providence has put a tongue in every suffering member of the human frame, to plead its cause. But enter into the soul; pass through these outworks, and enter the very seat of power; and what things are there; uttering no sound perhaps, breathing no complaint—but what things are there to move compassion? Wounded and bruised affections, blighted capacities, broken and defeated hopes; desolation, solitariness, silence, sorrow, anguish; and sin, the cause and consummation of all the deepest miseries of an afflicted life. If the surgeon's knife should cut the very heart, it would hardly inflict a sharper pang than anger, envy, smiting shame, and avenging remorse. Yet, happiness is near that heart; happiness, the breath of infinite goodness, the blessed voice of mercy, is all around it; and it is all madly shunned. Eternal happiness is offered to it; and it rejects the offer. It goes on, and on, through life, inwardly burthened, groaning in secret, bleeding, weltering in its passions; but it will not seek the true relief. Its wounds are without cause; its sufferings without recompense; its life without true comfort; and its end without hope. Compassion, indeed, for souls! who may not justly feel it for others, and for his own?

So Jesus looked upon the world—save that *he* had no compassion to feel for himself; and so much the more touching was his compassion for us. From the sublime height of his own immaculate purity, he looked down upon a sinful, and degraded, and afflicted race. "Weep not for me," he said, "but weep for yourselves and your children." So Jesus looked upon the world, and pitied it. He taught us, that we might be wise; he was poor that we might be rich; he suffered that we might be happy; he wept that we might rejoice; he died—he died the accursed death of the cross, that we might live—live for ever.

VII.

GOD'S LOVE; THE CHIEF RESTRAINT FROM SIN, AND RESOURCE IN SORROW.

GOD IS LOVE.—1 John iv. 16.

It was a saying of Plato, that "the soul is mere darkness, till it is illuminated with the knowledge of God." What Plato said of the soul is true of every-thing. Every thing is dark, till the light of God's perfection shines upon it. That "God is love," is the great central truth, that gives brightness to every other truth. Not only the moral system, but nature, and the science of nature, would be dark without that truth. I am persuaded it might be shown, that it is the great essential principle, which lies at the foundation of all interesting knowledge. It may not be always distinctly observed by the philosopher; but how could he proceed in those investigations that are leading him through all the labyrinths of nature, if it were not for the conviction secretly working within him, that all is right, that all is well! How could he have the heart to pursue his way, as he is penetrating into the mysteries, whether of rolling worlds or of vegetating atoms, if he felt that the system he was exploring, is a system of boundless malevolence! He would stand aghast and powerless, at that thought. It would spread a shadow, darker than universal eclipse, over the splendour of heaven. It would endow every particle of earth with a principle of malignity, too awful for the hardiest philosophic scrutiny !

The Scriptures assign the same pre-eminence to the doctrine of divine goodness, which it holds in nature and philosophy. It is never said, in Scripture, that God is greatness, or power, or knowledge ; but with a comprehensive and affecting emphasis, it is written that GOD IS LOVE ; not that he is lovely, not that he is good, not that he is benevolent, merely—that would be too abstract for the great, vital, life-giving truth—but it is written, I repeat, that GOD IS LOVE !

And it is not of this truth as an abstract truth, my friends, that I propose now to speak. I wish to consider chiefly its applications ; and especially its applications to two great conditions of human life ; to the conditions of temptation, and sorrow. Affliction, we know, is sometimes addressed with worldly consolations ; and sin is often assailed with denunciation and alarm ; yet for both alike, and for all that makes up the mingled conflict and sorrow and hope of life, it seems to me that a deep and affectionate trust in the love of God, is the only powerful, sustaining, and controlling principle.

Let me say again, an affectionate trust ; the faith, in other words, that works by love. It is not a cold, speculative, theological faith, that can prepare us to meet the discipline of life. It is the confidence of love only that can carry us through. Love only can understand love. This only can enable us to say "we have known and believed the love that God hath to us." We profess to believe in God ; to believe in the divine perfection. But I say, my brethren, that we do not properly know what we believe in, without love to it. Love only can understand love. Love only can give to faith in divine love, its proper character ;

and especially that character of assurance and strength, which will enable us to meet, unshaken and unfaltering, the temptations and trials of life.

The principle that is to meet exigencies like these, that is to hold the long conflict with sin and sorrow, that is to sustain triumphantly the burthen of this mortal experience, must be intelligent, active, penetrating, and powerful. For, the problem of this life, my brethren, is not readily, nor easily to be solved. I know that there is light upon it; welcome light. But it cannot be carried into the mazes of human experience, it cannot illuminate what is dark and clear up what is difficult, without much reflection—and reflection upon what, if not upon the character of the Ordainer of this lot?—without much reflection, I repeat, and care every way to the direction and posture of our own minds. It was not intended that our faith should be a passive principle; that all should be plain and easy to it; that moral light should fall upon our path, as clear, obvious and bright as sunshine. It pleases God to try the reliance of his earthly children. He would have their trust in him to be a nobler act than mere vision could be. He would have their faith grow and strengthen by severe exercise. He would say to them at last, not only "well done, good!—but, well done *faithful!*—enter ye into the joys of your Lord: enter into joys made dear by sorrow, made bright by the darkness you have experienced, made noble and glorious by the trying of your faith which is more precious than of gold."

I said, that the problem of this life is not readily nor easily to be solved. I can conceive that this may be an unmeaning declaration, to those who have not thought much of life, to those whose lot has been easy, and whose minds have partaken of the easiness of their lot. But there are those, to whom the visitation of life, to whom the visitation of thought and feeling, has been a different thing. I can believe that there are some to whom I speak, whose minds have been haunted from their very childhood, with that mournful and touching inquiry which we used to read in our early lessons, "Child of mortality, whence comest thou?" Man is, indeed, the child of a frail, changing, mortal lot; and yet the creature of an immortal hope. We are ready to ask such a being, at whom we must wonder as it seems to me, whence camest thou, and for what end? Didst thou come, frail being! from the source of strength and wisdom and goodness? Why then, so feeble, so unwise, so unworthy? Why art thou here, and such as thou art—so strong in grief, and so weak in fortitude! so boundless in aspiration, so poor in possession! Why art thou here?—with this strangely mingled being; so glad and so sorrowful; so earthly and so heavenly; so in love with life, and so weary of it; so eagerly clinging to life, and yet borne away by a sighing breath of the evening air! Whence, and wherefore, frail man! art thou such an one? All else is well; but with *thee* all is not well. The world is fair around thee; the bright and blessed sun shineth on thee; the green and flowery fields spread far, and cheer thine eye, and invite thy footstep; the groves are full of melody; ten thousand happy creatures range freely through all the paths of nature; but *thou* art not satisfied as they are; *thou* art not happy; thou art not provided for as they are: earth has no coverts for thy sheltering; thou must toil, thou must build houses, and gather defences for thy frailty; and in the sweat of thy brow, must thou eat thy bread. And when all is done, thou must die and thou knowest it. Death, strange visitant, is ever approaching to meet thee; death, dark gate of mystery, is ever the termination of thy path!

But, my brethren, is this all? To live, to toil, to struggle, to suffer, to sorrow, to die—is this all? No, it is not all; but it is God's love, and the revelation of God's love in the promise of immortality only, that can assure us that there is more. And so necessary do these seem to me, to bear up the thinking, feeling, suffering, hoping, inquiring mind; so necessary is it, that a voice of God should speak to the creatures of this earthly discipline; necessary, as that a parental voice, should be ready and near to hush the cry of infancy; that instead of stumbling at marvels and miracles, and interpositions and teachings, I confess I have sometimes wondered that there were not more of them. I have wondered that the manifestations of God, did not oftener appear in the blazing bush, and the cloud-capt mountain. I have wondered that the curtain of mystery, that hides the other world, were not sometimes lifted up; that the cherubim of mercy and of hope were not sometimes throned on the clouds of the eventide; that the bright and silent stars, did not sometimes break the deep stillness that reigns among them, with the scarcely fabled music of their spheres; that the rich flood of morning light, as it bathes the earth in love, did not utter voices from its throne of heavenly splendour, to proclaim the goodness of God. No, I wonder not at marvels and miracles. That scene on the Mount of transfiguration—Moses and Elias talking with our Saviour—seems to me, so far from being strange and incredible, to meet a want of the mind; and I only wonder, if I may venture to say so, that it is not sometimes repeated.

Yet why should I say this? The love of God to us, is sure; and it is a sufficient assurance. Trust in him is a sustaining principle; and it is sufficient strength. There *is* another state of being for us—perish all reason and all faith if it is not so!—there *is* another state of being for us; and though the eye hath not seen it, and the ear hath caught no sound from its wide realm, the great promise and hope are sufficient.

I say, the love of God is sure. He does love the moral beings whom he has made in his image; loves them, I doubt not, in their fears and doubtings and struggles and sorrows; loves them, I believe, even in their sins, nay, and has commended his love to them in this very character—has commended his love to them, in that while they were yet sinners, Christ died for them.

Can you doubt whether man is the object of God's love? Look at the feeble insect tribes, sporting in the beams of life, happy in their hour, perishing but to give life to others. Is he not a kind Being, who made even *these?* Is it not the breath of love, in which even *they* live? Look at the ranks and orders of irrational creatures, that inhabit the fields, the groves, the mountains, the living streams of ocean. Look at the free and fleet rangers of the forest. Go thou, and unfold the inward frame of such an one; trace every part of the wonderful mechanism; mark every sinew; follow the courses of its life-blood; see every skilful and exquisite adaptation for sustenance, for strength, for speed, for beauty. Is not this the workmanship of goodness? *Could* any but a kind and gracious Being have done this? "Ask, now, of the beasts, says Job, and they shall teach thee; and the fowls of the air, and they shall tell thee; or speak to the earth, and it shall teach thee; and the fishes of the sea shall declare unto thee."

But turn, now, from all these, and look—yes, look

at one human heart. How infinite the difference! The human heart—say what we will of it, let the cynic or the skeptic say what he will—but what a concentration of energies, what a gathering up of solemn thoughts, what a home of dear and gentle affections, what a deep fountain of tears and sorrows, is *there!* What strugglings are pent up within its narrow enclosure; what awful powers sleep within its folding bosom; what images of the grand, the godlike, the indefinite, the eternal, lie in its unfathomable depths! Doth not the Maker of that heart regard it with kindness? Doth he not pity a being that can *sorrow?* Doth he not love a being whom he hath made capable of love; of all its yearning, of all its tenderness? Doth he not care for a being, whom he hath made capable of improving forever?

Assuredly, if nature speaks truth, if revelation utters wisdom, he does love his rational offspring. How strong is the language of that revelation! "Can a mother forget her child? Yea, she may forget, yet will not I forget thee."

Let this, then, be settled in every heart as one of the great convictions of life; let it be taken to the soul as a part of the armour of God, to defend it against this world's temptations and calamities. We may not all, or we may not always feel the need of it; but we do all need it, and we need it always. Always, I say: for we are always exposed to sin, and we are always exposed to sorrow. Let us look at these conditions of human life for a few moments, to see how the apprehension of God's love to us is fitted to restrain us in the one case, and to comfort us in the other.

Nothing would be so effectual to restrain us from evil, if we felt it, as the love of God to us; nothing would be so effectual to recall us from our wanderings. It is a lofty conviction, of which I speak, my brethren, and not the ordinary and dull acknowledgment, the mere theological inference, that God is good. Let any one feel that God is as truly good to him, as truly loves him, is as really interested for his welfare, as his father, or his most devoted friend: that even when he is rebellious and disobedient, the good and blessed God pities him, and pleads with him to return, pleads with him even through the sufferings of Christ, his Son; let him feel that the kind and gracious CREATOR has fashioned that wonderful but abused mind within him, called forth those sweet, but neglected affections, provided dear objects for them, given him home, given him friends, showered mercies upon him; let him thus feel how ungenerous and ungrateful is the evil course; and surely all this, if any thing can, will touch him with conviction, and move him to repentance. Let it be so, that all other motives have failed; but who of us, if he rightly saw it, could lift his hand against that which is all love? Who of us, if he felt that love to him, and to all around him—who could be selfish, contemptuous, haughty, or hard-hearted towards his brother? Who of us, if he saw all the gifts of life to be the sacred gifts of that love, could abuse them to purposes of selfish ambition, or vicious indulgence?—The spirit of the sinner, the spirit of sin, I mean, so far as it goes, is a reckless spirit. The offender cares not, very much in proportion as he feels that nobody cares for him. He hardens himself against everything the more, because he supposes that everything is hardened against him. And when he goes to the worst excesses in vice, the manifest scorn of his fellow-creatures is the last influence, that steels his heart against every better feeling. And yet even then, there is sometimes left one thougnt, that moves him to tears. It is the thought of his mother, dwelling alone perhaps, in his far distant and forsaken home; it is the thought of his mother, who sighs in secret places for him; who still mingles his outcast name with every evening prayer, saying, "Oh! restore my poor child!" But let him remember, that even if his mother should forget, God does not forget him; does not forsake him; does not withdraw all his mercies from him. His friends may withdraw themselves; he may have no earthly bosom to lean upon!—but the elements embosom him around; the air breathes upon him a breath of kindness; the sun shines beneficently upon him; the page of mercy is spread for him; and it is written over with invitations and promises: it says, in accents that might break a heart of stone, "turn thou! turn, thou forsaken one! for why wilt thou die?"

So effectual, my brethren, did we rightly consider it, might be the love of God to restrain us from evil, and recall us to virtue and piety.

Equally might it avail, and equally indispensable is it, to comfort us in affliction. I have already spoken of the afflictions of life, and need not repeat what I then said. Suffice it, that every heart knows what it has to suffer, and to struggle with. But one thing I am sure of, that that heart can find no repose but in a firm trust in the infinite love of God. I speak now for a reasonable mind, for one that is not willing to suffer blindly as a brute suffers, for one that does not find it enough to conclude that it must suffer and cannot help it. I speak for one whom sorrow has aroused to consider the great questions, wherefore he is made, and why he is made to suffer; and I am sure that such an one must behold GOODNESS enthroned and reigning over all the events of time and the destinies of eternity; or, for his mind, there is no friend nor helper in the universe. Ah! there are questions, which nothing can answer, but God's love; which nothing can meet, but God's promise; which nothing can calm, but a perfect trust in his goodness. Speak to the void darkness of affliction, "the first dark day of nothingness" after trouble has come; speak to life, through all its stages and fortunes, from oftentimes suffering infancy to trembling age; speak to this crowded world of events, accidents, and vicissitudes; ay, or speak thou to the inward world of the heart, with all its strifes, its sinkings, its misgivings, its remembrances, its strange visitings of long gone thoughts,

"Touching the electric chain wherewith we are darkly bound,"

and none of these can answer us; we call as vainly upon them, as the priests of Baal upon their god. There is shadow and mystery upon all the creation, till we see God in it; there is trouble and fear, till we see God's love in it.

But give me that assurance; and though there are many things which I know not, many things which I cannot explain nor understand, yet I can consent *not* to know them. Enough, enough to know, that God is good, and what he does is right. This known; and the works of creation, the changes of life, the destinies of eternity, are all spread before us, as the dispensations and counsels of infinite love. This known; and then we know, that the love of God is working to issues, like itself beyond all thought and imagination, good and glorious; and that the only reason why we understand it not, is that it is too glorious for us to understand. This known: and what then do we say? God's love taketh care for all, nothing is neglected:

God's love watcheth over all, provideth for all, maketh wise adaptations for all; for age, for infancy, for maturity, for childhood in every scene of this, or another life; for want, for weakness, for joy, and for sorrow, and even for sin; so that even the wrath of man shall praise the goodness of God. All is good; all is well; all is right; and shall be for ever. This, oh! this is an inheritance, and a refuge, and a rest for the mind, from which the convulsions of worlds cannot shake it.

In what an aspect does this conviction present the scenes of eternity? We are placed here in a state of imperfection and trial, and much that seems like mystery and mischance. But what shall the future be, if the light of God's goodness is to shine through its ages? I answer, it shall be all bright disclosure, full consummation, blessed recompense. We shall doubtless *see*, what we can now only believe. The cloud will be lifted up, and will unveil—eternity! And what an eternity! All brightness; all beatitude; one unclouded vision; one immeasurable progress! The gate of mystery shall be past, and the full light shall shine for ever. Blessed change! That which caused us trial, shall yield us triumph. That which was the deeper darkness, shall be but the brighter light. That which made the heart ache, shall fill it with gladness. Tears shall be wiped away; and beamings of joy shall come in their place. He who tried the soul that he loved, shall more abundantly comfort the soul that he approves. That God, who has walked in the mysterious way, with clouds and darkness around about him, will then appear as the great Revealer: and he will reveal what the eye hath not seen, nor the ear heard, nor the heart conceived.

Let me insist, in close, as I did in the beginning, upon the necessity of this affectionate trust in God.

We cannot live as reasonable beings upon any conviction less lofty, less divine, less heartfelt than this. This is not a matter of will; it is a matter of necessity. Our minds cannot have a full and, at the same time, safe development; reflection and feeling cannot safely grow in us, unless they are guided, relieved and sustained by the contemplations of piety. The fresh and unworn sensibility of youth may hold on for awhile, and may keep its fountain clear and bright; but, by and bye, changes will come on; affliction will lay its chastening hand upon us; disappointment will settle, like a chilling damp, upon the spirits; the mind will be discouraged, if there is nothing but earthly hope to cheer it on; the reasonings of misanthropy and the misgivings of scepticism will steal into it, and blight its generous affections; morbid sensitiveness will take the place of healthful feeling; all this will naturally come on, with the growing experience of life, if the love of God be not our support and safeguard. Every mind may not be conscious of this tendency, but every mind that thinks much and feels deeply, will be conscious of it, and will feel it bitterly. Your body may live on; but your soul, in its full development, in its deep wants, in its "strong hour" of trial and of reflection, must pine, and perish, and die, without this holy trust. Let it not so perish. Creature of God's love! believe in that love which gave thee being. Believe in that love which every moment redeems thee from death, and offers to redeem thee from the death eternal. Believe in God's love, and be wise, be patient, be comforted, be cheerful and happy—be happy in time; be happy in eternity!

VIII.

THE DIFFERENCE BETWEEN SENTIMENTS AND PRINCIPLES.

AND DAVID'S ANGER WAS GREATLY KINDLED AGAINST THE MAN, AND HE SAID TO NATHAN, AS THE LORD LIVETH THE MAN THAT HATH DONE THIS THING SHALL SURELY DIE. AND NATHAN SAID TO DAVID, THOU ART THE MAN! 2 Samuel xii. 5, 7.

THE circumstances attending this celebrated reproof, require a brief notice, in order to unfold the instruction which it conveys to us. The charm, I may observe, of these old Bible stories is, that they are always records of the heart. Kings are but men, and palaces but common dwellings, beneath that eye that looks through all human disguises. The robe of sanctity itself does not hide the defects that lurk beneath it. Priest or patriarch, seer or saint, though the man be, yet the Bible will have us see him as he is.

When we consider what David *was*, in station, and repute, and actual piety; the King of Israel; "the man after God's own heart;" the writer of holy psalms which are sung in all Christian nations to this day; what *is it*, we are ready to exclaim, that we read here? Why is it that this man stands as a trembling culprit, before the searching eye of a prophet of his people? Alas! David, at this period of his life, was a fallen man. That which every good man should fear, had overtaken him; he had fallen! He had been guilty of deeds contrary to all his better thoughts. He had been guilty of crimes; of crimes which fell nothing short of actual murder; and murder committed with the most hateful intent and the most horrible deception.

For, observe what was done, in that ancient Hebrew court and kingdom. To possess the wife of Uriah, David wishes to rid himself of her husband; a devoted servant and a valiant warrior in his armies. And what now, think you, is the method he adopts to gain his purpose? He sends a letter by this same faithful servant, as if he would do him honour; he sends a letter by him to the captain of the host; and methinks the cheek of the hardened and unscrupulous Joab, must have turned pale as he read the words, "Set Uriah in the fore-front of the hottest battle, and retire from him that he may be smitten and die!" The cruel mandate is obeyed; and the man who for his sovereign, had bared his breast to the shock of battle where it raged the fiercest, falls a victim, not to the ordinary fate of war, but to the perfidy of the very master whom he served! The unhallowed design is accomplished; the object of guilty passion is obtained: David *possesses* the wife of Uriah!

But although conscience slept in the bosom of the king, it was not to sleep there forever. Time passed on; but time that bears in its bosom the burthen of guilt, is like no other time; heavy, dark, portentous. To the listening ear of the conscience-stricken man, something seems to be coming, he knows not what; some voice will break forth—he knows not where. And a voice *was* soon to fall on David's ear that should change the whole complexion of his guilty deed. For now in this awful crisis must not the prophet of God be idle. There is a stir in that world of conscience that surrounds the guilty king, of which he thinks not. Footsteps are heard approaching the royal apartments;

steps heavy and perhaps reluctant, but monitory and determined as the steps of Judgment. "And, the Lord," says the sacred record, "sent Nathan unto David."

Let us observe the manner of his proceeding. For it would be difficult to select a more beautiful example of ingenuity and fidelity united, than appeared in the address of the prophet on this trying occasion. He begins with a parable; yet a parable drawn with such masterly skill, that it has to the king all the appearance of reality. "There were two men in a city; the one rich, the other poor. The rich man had exceeding many flocks and herds; but the poor man," says this simple and beautiful parable, "had nothing, save one little ewe lamb; which he had bought and nourished up; and it grew up together with him and his children; it did eat of his own meat, and drank of his own cup, and was cherished in his bosom and was unto him as a daughter:" a familiar and striking description of the affection which a whole household often feels for a cosset, or pet animal, that is brought up at the farm-house door. "And there came a traveller unto the rich man, and he spared to take of his own flock and of his own herd, but took the poor man's lamb, and dressed it for the wayfaring man that was come unto him." Imagine now the grief of this poor family, as the cherished lamb is torn from their little enclosure and slaughtered before their eyes; and you have the whole picture which the prophet drew. It is a tale of humble, rural life indeed; but the royal justice is awakened and bursts out into strong indignation. "As the Lord liveth," says David—it is the form of a Jewish oath;—as if he had said, "By the justice of the living God, the man that hath done this thing shall surely die." Oh! then, with what eye was it, think you, that the fearless prophet looked into the very soul of his poor blinded master, and said, "Thou art the man!" I remember a picture of this scene, drawn by a master's hand. The prophet stands erect before the throned monarch, with pointed finger and an eye sad, but fixed and searching; and the majesty of an earthly kingdom cowers and shrinks away before the majesty of virtue!

We naturally ask how such a rebuke could have been received: and we are not only told that David said at the time, "I have sinned against the Lord;" but we are referred also to that unequalled penitential psalm, the 51st, which Jewish tradition has assigned to this period of David's life.

But the observation to which I wish now to draw your particular attention, is this: that the man who felt all this indignation at a certain act of baseness and injustice, was the very man that did it; or, to speak more accurately, who did the far worse act which was but shadowed forth in the parable. David abhorred a simple act of oppression. Of what was he guilty? Of oppression, treachery, adultery, murder—all consummated in one single tissue of crimes. His anger was greatly kindled against a certain supposed offender; he was even religious in his abhorrence; "As the Lord liveth," is his declaration, "the man that hath done this thing shall surely die;" and yet—and yet, David was the man who did it!

This is the point, then, to which I wish to bring your meditations: the difference, that is to say, between sentiments and principles. Let me attempt, first to define, next to illustrate it; and, finally, to consider the decision to which it must bring each mind with regard to itself.

1. There are two kinds of religion in the world;

and all other religious differences are trifling compared with this. There is a religion of imagination, and there is a religion of reality. There is an ideal and an actual religion; a religion of the head, and a religion of the heart. Or, to speak more exactly, there is a religion which is occasionally and transiently felt in the heart, but which does not constitute the character of a man; and there is a religion which dwells there habitually, and is the predominating disposition and mind of the man. This is the difference between sentiments and principles. Sentiments are temporary impressions of goodness and virtue; principles are abiding and controlling impressions of goodness and virtue. Sentiments are general and involuntary; they do not rise to the character of virtue; a man can scarcely help sometimes feeling them: they spring from the act of God's creation like bladed grass or opening flowers; and this is one sense in which God works within us, though I believe devoutly that he puts forth interpositions also, for our times and seasons of need. Principles, on the other hand, are personal, intentional, particular: they are brought home to the heart; they are acted out in the life; they are our own act; they are the very form of that act, through which, God helping, we work out our own salvation. We could do nothing without the help of God; but that supposed, we have a work to do; and it is the very work of virtue, the very work of our salvation. Now it is precisely short of this point, I fear, that most men stop. They have sentiments, but not principles. This is, for us at the present day, the very point of conversion. To pass over from sentiments to principles, is the very process of conversion. We are not utterly bad; we have some good feelings, some occasional religious emotions;

but in the eye of the Gospel, many of us fall short utterly, fatally. And when I utter this solemn word, fatally, I am not pronouncing some mere arbitrary pulpit decision; I am declaring the very laws of our nature. For without something more than sentiments, without principles of goodness and piety, we are not prepared to be happy here or hereafter. Happiness lies deeper than sentiments. In short, it is but the old story of human deficiency: we approve the right, but pursue the wrong. We may be bad men, with all our transient good feelings. When David said, "As the Lord liveth, the man that hath done this thing shall surely die!" that was an honest burst of indignation at wrong; and yet, at this very moment, he was in the commission of that very wrong; nay, of a far worse than that. You see, then, that although our discrimination is drawn from the unusual sphere of a monarch's life, it strikes far and wide, and deep; it strikes, in fact, at *the great religious defect of the world!* I solemnly believe that no point could be put forward for the consideration of a religious audience, more vital, more momentous than this.

2. Let us now endeavour to illustrate it.

The instance which is presented in the life of David, is not the only one to be found, of a total contradiction between a man's general sentiments and his particular conduct. We see the same thing around us every day. Who abets injustice, fraud, oppression, covetousness, revenge, envy, or slander? Not one. But are there no such things in the world? Are there not many to be found who are guilty of these things? Ay, guilty of these very things. And yet, I think, I could speak a parable upon any one of these vices; I could set forth in a story, the wickedness of injustice, or the cruelty of oppression, or the baseness of slander, or the miseries inflicted by unbridled indulgence; I could set before you the injured and ruined victims of wrong; I could make you hear the cry of their distress; yes, I could speak a parable at which the anger of every hearer should be greatly kindled; and yet to how many of these same hearers might I turn with the home-put rebuke of the prophet, and, even in the midst of his loudest exclamation, say to him, "Stop, good friend! hold back a little the edge of thy reproach; spare thyself a little; thou art the very man!" "What, I?"—might be his exclamation. Yes, thou. Thou art thyself in some relation unjust, or oppressive, or envious, or indulgent to thyself, or a careless talker of others. "Therefore, thou art inexcusable, O man, whosoever thou art that judgest," says St. Paul; "for wherein thou judgest another, thou condemnest thyself: for thou that judgest, doest the same things."

I believe, as we extend our observation of life, that we shall find it less and less safe to rely upon men's general sentiments and general conversation. More and more do we demand to know not what they say, but what they do. It is amazing to see how some men can talk of virtue and a virtuous parentage, whose life denies both. I have been struck sometimes with observing what a marvellous facility some bad men have, of quoting Scripture. It seems to comfort their evil consciences to use good words, and to gloze over bad deeds with holy texts, wrested to their purpose. Nay, there are not wanting instances, where the more a man talks about the Bible, the less he feels it; the more he talks about virtue, the less he has of it; and you may sometimes discover the very point of his deficiency by the extraordinary strength of his language about that very thing. Out of the abundance of the heart, it is true, the mouth speaketh; but it sometimes speaks the very contrary of what the man practices. When you are talking in general about religion and virtue, and find your neighbour ever drawing the conversation to a certain point, mark that point; it may be that he would make amends for some fault there, or he would spread out some flimsy veil of words, some subtle distinctions to shield his faults; or his guilty consciousness draws him to it with a kind of strange fascination. When you find a person very suspicious of others in some respects, look to it whether *he* be not an offender there. So the moment of a man's departure from his old faith, is often signalized by the most violent struggles and the loudest protests against heresy. And so a man may express the stongest disgust at sin, at self-indulgence, at sensuality in all its forms; nay, and in a sense, he may feel such disgust; and yet in some points, he may be—secretly if not openly, in a less measure if not in a greater, in one form if not in another, in imagination if not in act, in food if not in drink, in opium if not in alcohol, in indolence if not in passion, he may be a vicious man and a sensualist.

It is this contrariety which is often witnessed between what is felt at church, and what is done abroad in the world. Virtue and vice, in the ordinary sense of those terms, must, in this place, be mere matters of reflection and feeling. There is no opportunity for the practice of either. Men yield to the argument here, with most undesirable facility and readiness; because nothing is to follow. Nay, it is very easy and very safe while at church, to feel upon these matters. And a man shall to-day be wrapt in admiration of the noble and lovely virtues of Christianity; and yet to-morrow shall find him so different a man that he shall scarce know himself. When the sun shall rise again, that is to light him forth to his earthly pursuits, when the atmosphere of worldly gains and competitions grows warm about him, when the fervid courses of unlawful pleasure again bring on the fever of the passions, all his fine emotions, alas! about virtue, all his generous abhorrence of selfishness and sensual crime, shall be as the morning cloud that passeth away. That cloud may be tinged with colours of gold. It may be bright and beautiful, like the fine sentiments that we entertain about virtue. What do they avail, so long as they dwell in the airy regions of the imagination? We walk not on the cloud, but in the rugged path, where nothing but principles can sustain and bear us onward. I do not say that such emotions as I have described are necessarily false or fictitious. Nay, they may be quite sincere and real for the time; and this only increases the danger. A man may be really interested in religion in a certain way, while he is seriously, fatally deficient in virtue. I have known, perhaps you all have known instances of this, which are enough to overwhelm one with astonishment and dismay. It is common to resolve such cases into blank hypocrisy; but such, I confess, is not always my solution. Men have I known who have prayed most fervently, and I could not doubt most sincerely; and yet who have constantly been guilty of things, so bad and base, or so ungenerous and unrighteous, that robbery and murder, the crimes that fill the dockets of your criminal courts, could scarcely be more heinous! What an awful example of this is held up to us in the passage of Scripture history, from which I am discoursing! That the writer of the Psalms—the most perfect devotional compositions, inspiration apart, that the world ever saw; compositions which, considering the age in which they appeared, prove their own inspiration—that the writer of the Psalms could have been the seducer of Bethsheba, and the murderer of her husband, is a fact that may well put every man upon his guard! And indeed such is the inconsistency, and waywardness, and self-deception of the human heart, that I am tempted to think, it is scarcely too much to say, that a man may be quite a good man, or what the world calls quite a good sort of man in general, and yet a very bad man in particular; a good sort of man at church, and yet a bad man in the world; or a good sort of man in public, and yet a bad man in his family; or a good sort of man at home and on common days, but a very bad man on holidays, or a very bad man when he is on a journey, or a very bad man when he goeth to a strange city! And in how low a measure, in how doubtful a character, in what a dishonouring comparison, is he a good man, who is bad just when occasion offers or opportunity permits! He is not a good man at all!

At the risk of wearying you with multiplicity of illustration, I must invite your attention to another contrast; for the point is one of the most vital importance. And that is the contrast, not between the general feeling and the particular conduct, but between the general and the particular feeling. For we must go further, and say, that while a man's general feeling about abstract rectitude may be very correct, his particular feeling about the specific qualities that constitute rectitude, or the specific actions that it requires of him, may be decidedly wrong.

Have we never heard one say, that he wished he were a Christian, that he desired to be a good man? But, now do you take some pertinent occasion to remind him that goodness requires him to resist a certain passion, to sacrifice a certain indulgence, to control his appetite at a feast, or to keep his temper in a dispute; and then he will find that he does not wish to be good. Thus it was with the young man in the Gospel, who came to our Saviour to be instructed. So amiable and good did he appear, that Jesus, when he looked upon him, loved him. And yet, when he put that fair-seeming youth to the test, he was found utterly wanting. "Sell all that thou hast," he said, "and give to the poor, and come, follow me." When he heard that saying he was very sorrowful, for he was very rich. He could do many things; but he could not do that. Jesus at a distance seemed an attractive person, but he found it different when he came to understand him. Ah! how beautiful upon the *mountains* are the feet of them that "preach good tidings"; they are glorious forms as they stand on high, invested with the hues of distant scenery and clothed with the radiance of heaven; but let them come down, the plain and humble preachers of a cross, of self-renunciation; and then we find that they wear a rough garb and a stern face, and we like them not. No, we do not understand our Gospel when we merely admire it. Religion, a man says, is a good thing, and the Gospel is glad tidings, and the name of the Saviour is a gracious name, and he wonders that anybody can say that the human heart dislikes them; but let the Gospel say to him, as it said to Herod, "Thou must not have this woman; or thou must not have this cup of intoxication; or thou must not have this property which thou hast unjustly got;" and then he is ready to hate it for its interference with his pursuits and pleasures. Yes, the Gospel is then a different thing; no longer a speculative, but an experimental thing; no longer a sentimental, but a practical thing; no longer a lovely and a lulling song, of one that "hath a pleasant voice and can play well upon an instrument," but a harsh sound, and a word of rebuke and a stone of stumbling, and a rock of offence. So was it predicted of our Saviour, our embodied religion; so did he foresee that he would be regarded; so was he regarded; and why? Because, unlike the celebrated teachers of antiquity, he penetrated beyond the regions of vague sentiment—beyond the regions where moralizers and philosophers had woven their fine theories and spread out their beautiful maxims—penetrated, I say, to the depths of the heart, brought out its hidden iniquities, arraigned the cherished prejudices and darling passions of the very age and country, and of the very people amidst whom he lived. Therefore were they angry with him in the sanctuary, were ready to stone him in the street, hurried him to the brow of a precipice to cast him down, and finally bore him as a victim to the awful mount of Calvary. Yes, Calvary bears eternal witness to the sacrifice of one, whom men crucified, because, not content with delivering to them fine sentiments, he told them the cutting, keen-piercing, anger-provoking truth.

It is a tremendous thing to consider, that out of the bosom of a world of fine sentiments, such passions can spring. Had any one stood up in the synagogue at Jerusalem, the Sunday before the Crucifixion and discoursed eloquently on the beauties of virtue—of gentleness, candor and loving kindness—the people would have heard him with pleasure; the preacher would have been admired. On the Friday following, they hurried the living representative of all these virtues to death—to the ignominious death of the cross!

But the world is not essentially changed. That Jewish province is not, as we are wont to consider it, cut off from the great world of humanity. The same world *now* lives and breathes around us; a world of fine sentiments and foul practices, of good maxims and bad deeds; a world whose darker passions are not only restrained by custom and ceremony, but, strange to say, veiled over even from itself, by beautiful sentiments. I see this terrible solecism everywhere. I have seen it in Romish sentimentalism, covering infi delity and vice; in Protestant substitution, lauding spirituality and faith, and neglecting homely truth and candor and generosity; in ultra-liberal refinement, mounting to heaven in its dreams and wallowing amidst the mire of earth in its deeds. I see it in literature. *Bad* men and women can write good books —i. e. books in which virtue is praised. Nay, so excellent is public sentiment that they dare not write any other. And suppose a book of a different character to be written. Suppose that a book were written in praise of sin—i. e. in evident and unblushing praise of it. Why, the worst man among us would abhor the book—would throw it down in disgust. Find a man that is dishonest, and show him a book right heartily employed upon teaching men how to deceive and defraud; and he could not bear it. Find a cruel man—one who is every day saying and doing unkind, hard and bitter things—and show him this character spread out and eulogized in a book, and he could not suppress his indignation at it; his feelings would break out into speech; he would say it was a monstrous book. And yet some weak sufferer by his side, whose gentle and tender spirit was every day wounded by his violence or his satire, might turn to him astonished, and say, "It is thou!—it is thou!" Find the grossest sensualist, and open to him a work like some of the late French fictions, over whose pages is drawn the slime of every sensual vice, and drawn as if to paint and illuminate the page; and with an air of horror he would exclaim, that it was a work of the most shameless piofligacy that ever was seen. And yet some companion in evil might turn to him and say: "Why, I am surprised at this; I thought you would like this book. Why, thou art the very man!"

Well, it is fortunate, no doubt, that this sentiment lives; it is well that it is not dead and cannot easily die. But let us not mistake it for something better than it is; let us not be deceived by it; that is the only point about which I am anxious. Let us see and settle it with ourselves, that there may be a world of religious sentiment, and yet a world of little or no religion. The religious state of many minds, we must believe, alas! is no better than this; there is a vague and general sentiment of religion in them, but no particular devotion, no habitual piety. Religion plays about their minds, like the brilliant but cold lights that sometimes flash across the Northern sky. There are occasional splendours of thought about the man, and rich gleams of fancy, and transient corruscations that kindle the whole heaven of his imagination; but no vital warmth penetrates the heart; all is cold and sterile there as the regions of the Northern pole. He does nothing; he gains no victories over himself; he makes no progress; he is just where he was years ago; there is nothing about his cultivation of religion, de termined and resolute and regular, like his cultivation of anything else—his estate, his profession, his knowledge. His religion, the grand interest of his being, he leaves to take its chance in general and inefficient sentiment.

III. The defect is fatal; and it is this that I would insist upon for a moment in close: that no religion meets the Gospel demand, or the demand of our own nature for happiness, but that which passes from sentiment into principle.

The notions of religion that are floating loosely upon the mass of society, have indeed their uses. They bless society as a mass. So excellent a thing is religion that it can touch nothing which it does not in some respect benefit; that, even when it floats upon the surface, it is like a holy oil that tames down, to a certain extent, the waves of passion that are swelling beneath. But, my brethren, when I look into those deep waters beneath, when I look into the awful depths of a human heart, I see the need of a power that shall penetrate to the very abysses of that ocean, to which human nature may well be compared. To send down light, tranquillity, purity, into those deeps of the soul—no breeze upon the surface, nor brightening smile upon the face of life, can do that. That smile is lovely, that breeze is refreshing; but deep, oh! deep down in the heart, must stir the wrestling energies, the profound movements that will sway it to virtue and happiness. It is no vague sentimentalism that will save a man, but it must be a work, and a care, and a watching, and a striving, that, will save him.

Take the question for a moment out of the province of religion. Does an admiration for the fine arts, make any one an artist? Do just sentiments about trade, make any one a merchant? Do general maxims about industry, make any one an industrious man?

We do not understand the supreme, the unutterable interest embraced in religion, when we think to give less to it, than our whole heart. We do not understand our nature, when we think to shuffle off its stupendous charge as most men do. No interest on earth can so ill brook our levity or negligence. What is the matter with life but this? Why is it that so many, and so many who consider themselves quite good Christians too, are living such a poor, lame, halting life ; so ill-adjusted to the scene around them, so unhappy amidst craving wants, and disturbing passions, and pains of self-reproach ; but because they will not give their whole hearts to truth and purity, to goodness and to God ?

I think, too, that there must be special meditations and special resolves in this matter. I say not in what form : but the things must be. We want religion, indeed, to flow through the whole of life ; but it must have fountains and supplies, or it cannot flow on : it must have these, or it will be lost in the sands of vague and barren abstraction. In the vast and desolate wastes of Africa, travellers tell us of certain spectral illusion—the *mirage* of the desert—which spreads before them beautiful visions of fertility and verdure, that cheat the eye and mock the heart. Such, alas ! are piety and goodness to many a moral traveller. They are but visions ; ever in the distance ; never approached, never made realities. The fertility and verdure of a fruitful and beautiful piety are never seen in them ; and they never reach the land of that better life which they are forever going to lead. There, before them, is the gushing fountain, the cooling shade, the peaceful repose ; but they never reach it. In the barren waste of an unfaithful life, they die ; and never set foot on the promised land !

What a sad result, alas ! of so many good sentiments, so many good thoughts, of so many enthusiastic dreams of good, of so many solemn protests against evil ! When Hazael said, with indignant protestation, " But what ! is thy servant a dog, that he should do this thing ?" we read, and it is one of those touching traits of which the Bible is so full, that the man of God looked upon him and wept. And well might he weep. Well might any man weep, if he will ever weep over anything, at this sad contradiction in the lives of many. What a mournful thing it is, indeed, to contemplate—nothing on earth so mournful; on the one hand, sentiments noble, powers divine, a nature formed for immortal glory, and a preparation of means infinite as the grace of heaven; life given, and a Saviour dying to redeem!—and on the other hand, utter failure of the end, life spent in vain, the burial of the soul in sense and worldliness; existence, as to all spiritual purposes, a blank; the grand opportunity a defeat; the season gone, the harvest past, the summer ended, and the soul *not* saved!

If we would not have it so, permit me to make one suggestion in close. And permit me, too, to make it a word of exhortation. It is this. If any one here has a good feeling, let him go and *do* something; let him *do* some good thing. If your minds are at any time impressed with the contemplation of any virtue—be it prayer or watchfulness, or disinterestedness, or brotherly love, or the greatness and sanctity of a holy life—see that you immediately set about putting it in practice. Be sure that the occasion will soon enough come, if you will only watch for it. Thus fix and embody vague sentiment in distinct action. Thus let every week's practice carry out each Sunday's meditation. The preaching of angels will do you no good without this! So only can your Sabbaths help your week-days. So only can you make any day safe. You may say and think what you will, to-day; your meditations, I had almost said, may be lofty enough to be food for angels; your minds may be enraptured with themes that are divine; your hearts may melt in the tenderness of their religious emotions; but if you carry no holy thoughts with you into the scenes of business and care and temptation, to-morrow you may fall!—you may find the precipice of ruin to be but one step from the mount of meditation!

That which our present meditation demands of us, is the universal doing of what we feel to be right. It is to substitute doing, for our idle dreaming of right. It is to break up this eternal contradiction between our sentiments and principles. It is upon this that our Saviour ever laid the chief stress. Doing, doing, is ever the burden of his exhortation. "He that heareth my sayings, and doeth them"—is his constant language. As if he had known that men would admire the beauty of his character, and would be liable to stop there, ever does he press them to this point.

That which the present moment demands of us is a solemn determination so to do. Will you make it? Pardon this directness; I would use no improper freedom with you. I speak with deep respect to the mind, to the great nature that is capable of such a determination. *Will* you make it? I would press this question in no stern or repulsive manner. It is the most glorious determination that can be made on earth or in heaven. *Will* you make it?

You will; may I not say so? You will—you must. Good life, happy death, joy of heaven, blessed eternity, hangs upon the decision!—yes, hangs, it may be, upon the very decision that you shall form this day! For it is only going on and on in the same way, without any such decision, that leads men to perdition: that leads them to the failure of all high and sacred piety and virtue. Avoid it; I *must* press this point upon your consideration : avoid that way as you value your soul. In the name of reason, in God's name, set about the work of your salvation immediately. "Whatsoever thy hand findeth to do, do it quickly: for there is no work, nor device, nor knowledge, in the grave whither thou goest."

IX.

THE CROWN OF VIRTUE

BE THOU FAITHFUL UNTO DEATH, AND I WILL GIVE THEE A CROWN OF LIFE. —Rev. ii. 10.

THE image which is here employed to set forth the reward of Christian fidelity, is a crown. Now a crown is the symbol of the highest distinction. It is this circumstance that draws my attention in the passage of Scripture before us. For it is the crown of virtue, its unrivalled distinction, that I propose to you, Christian brethren, as the subject of this our present meditation.

And this idea of the grandeur of Christian virtue, let me observe—lest any one should think that it offends against the humility of the Gospel—is frequently introduced in the New Testament. Our Saviour says in his last prayer, "Father, the hour is come; glorify thy son, that thy son also may glorify thee." He desires to be vindicated: he desires to be honoured; and this that virtue, that Divinity may be honoured. Our text speaks of a crown. It is a familiar word in the Scriptures. It is frequently used to set forth the glory of virtue. We constantly hear of "a crown of righteousness, a crown of glory, an incorruptible crown." Often and emphatically is the very lowliest of the virtues, humility, represented as exalting its possessor to the highest honour. This feeling of the dignity of goodness, of the grandeur of the

Christian character, I may here observe, especially marks the writings of Paul. Goodness is always in his conception, something magnificent, God-like, glorious. When he says, "Whom he predestinated, them he also called, and whom he called, them he also justified;" he cannot stop, without adding, "whom he justified, them he also glorified." This idea of Christian virtue was pressed out into bolder prominence in his mind, perhaps, because he knew that the great and wise of this world, looked down upon him with scorn. Paul, as a man of learning and genius, might justly compare himself with the distinguished men of his time; and he was the more likely to be moved by their judgment; and he knew that that judgment was contemptuous. Therefore, glorying—not submitting to the reproach—was a very characteristic bias of his mind. "I glory," he says, "in tribulation;" I glory in the evil name and hard fortune that you despise. Paul was a true and magnanimous devotee to the only true worth; and sanctity, in the dust, was more magnificent in his eyes, than the throne of the world. He calls upon the Christians to think humbly, indeed, but yet to think loftily of themselves. He tells them that they are "the temples of God, sons of God, partakers of the Divine nature." And when he is speaking of his own noble strife after perfection, observe how his thoughts ascend to the highest climax. "I press forward," he says—it is an onward and an upward course—"I press forward towards the mark—for the prize—of the high calling—of God."

Such honour, then, my brethren, do I challenge for thie righteous course. I speak of the *crown* of virtue. True, it may overshadow a mortal brow, and men may not see its glory. True, it may overshadow a countenance pale and wasted, or marred with disease; it may be like the crown of thorns, which Jesus wore, stained with blood; but what earthly diadem was ever invested with such glory, as that crown of thorns? It was once indeed the badge of ignominy, the mark for scourging and spitting; but now, one of those thorns—I make the comparison reverently—one of those thorns, platted by the Roman soldiery for the head of the glorious Sufferer and Conqueror, would be dearer to us than the brightest gem, that ever shone on the brow of earthly monarch!

It is the CROWN of virtue then, my brethren, of which I will speak. And some need is there still in the world, to set forth its lofty distinction. Not only is the good man's honour often disesteemed, or less esteemed than it ought to be, but there are various other feelings in society, and especially strifes for worldly preference and preëminence, which commend this subject to our serious consideration. Let us then first enter for a moment into some of those prevailing states of mind, which makes this subject, the greatness of virtue, an interesting and practical topic of reflection.

All men desire distinction. All men feel the need of some ennobling object in life. These sentiments—the desire, that is to say, of eminence, and the desire of a worthy object—are indeed distinct in their character; but they often *combine* to produce a feeling of discontent with the ordinary lot of life. It may be remarked, indeed, independently of moral considerations, that those persons are usually most happy and satisfied in their pursuits, who have the loftiest ends in view. Thus I have observed that artists, mechanicians, and inventors, all those classes who are seeking to find principles or to develop beauty in their work, seem most to enjoy it. And just in proportion as *beau ideal* enters into any pursuit; for example, just in proportion as the farmer proposes, not mere subsistence as his end, but the beautifying of his estate, and the most scientific culture of it, is he likely to be happy amidst his labours. This, it appears to me, is one of the signal testimonies which all human employments give to the high demands of our nature. Avarice is said to be a very absorbing passion; but I do not think that the pursuit of wealth *as* wealth, ever gives such satisfaction, as it does to bring the humblest, although a comparatively useless piece of machinery, to *perfection*. If wealth, indeed, be sought for ends of philanthropy, or for the relief of kindred, or for the payment of just debts, it has a noble *beau ideal*, and a noble satisfaction; but exactly in proportion as the aims of the seeker run down on the scale of motive from the dearness of family and of principle, to the desire of display or of pleasure, does the pursuit become an unsatisfying drudgery.

This is felt to be too much the character of most human conditions and employments. There are doubtless many individual exceptions; but with the pursuits of multitudes there is connected a painful conviction. that they neither supply a sufficient object nor confer any satisfactory honour. "I live," says one, "I labour, I do business. What is it all for? What ultimate end am I to gain by it? I live; I die; the wave passes over me; and soon the world will not know that such a being ever existed. If I were an artist, and could paint the canvass or chisel the marble or lift the dome; or could write books of poetic inspiration, or of lofty morals and philosophy, or could establish a reputation for ability or eloquence, by any of which the world might know me, it would be with me an object and an ambition."

Now, to this state of mind it is, that I come to propose a yet nobler aim. To this man it is, that I come to speak of a crown; a crown of righteousness. For I say that in true and right living, in the imitation of Christ, in piety and self-culture, every man may attain the highest nobleness and grandeur known on earth or in heaven; that, in a higher sense than he thinks of, he may be an artist, and the greatest of artists—an author, and the greatest of authors; that more than his speech, his life may be eloquent. I say that every man has a work to do in himself, greater, sublimer than any work of genius; and that he works upon a nobler material than wood and marble—upon his own soul. I say to every man, thou shouldst be a greater than, as mere artist or author, was Homer or Shakspeare, Phidias or Raphael.

Let us see if this proposition is fairly chargeable with extravagance. What is it that the great author, or the great artist, does? I answer that, in the highest effort of his power, he but portrays what every man should *be*. That which in him is but conception, in us must be *action*. For what does he portray, and what is his conception? I answer again, it is nothing but moral beauty; magnanimity, or fortitude, or love, or forgiveness; the soul's greatness. If you look at the great paintings, what do they represent? The glory of the Christ, the loveliness of the Madonna, the penitence or love of some saint, the fortitude and forgiveness of the martyr, or some historic scene in which a noble action is celebrated. And what is all this but a portraying of virtues, commended to our admiration and imitation? To catch that almost living portraiture of horoism and goodness, to embosom it in our hearts, to embody it in our lives—this is the practical realization of those great ideals of art.

And so in all great writing; in the highest poetry, in the highest fiction, in the highest literature, the object of the writer is to present his loftiest ideal of all possible loveliness and grandeur. He is engaged in the work of nobly conceiving and describing what it is. But for us is reserved the higher work, of more nobly realizing it in our own character and life. And this, it is put within our power, with God's help, to do. The sphere of action may be different, but the thing to be attained—purity, sanctity, self-sacrifice, love—is essentially the same in all. The magnanimity of heroes, celebrated on the historic or poetic page; the constancy and faith of the martyr, or the beautifulness of saintly love and pity, glowing on the canvass; the delineations of truth and right that breathe life from the lips of the eloquent, are, in essence, only that which every man may feel and practice in the daily walks of life. If it is a nobler thing to be a hero than it is to describe one, to endure martyrdom than to paint it, to do right than to plead for it; then is the work of virtue nobler than any work of genius. In this view Sir Walter Scott's idea, had he applied it to this point, is a just one; that action is greater than writing. A good man is a nobler object of contemplation than a great author. To be is greater than to describe. It has been said that "there are but two things worth living for; to do what is worthy of being written, or to write what is worthy of being read." It is true; and I maintain that the greater of these is the *doing*.

I desire no one to give too easy an assent to this proposition. I seek rather for that difficult assent which yields to argument, which ripens into conviction, and results in action. If what I maintain is true, it is not an abstract theorem, nor an ingenious speculation. It takes hold of the entire principle and plan of a man's life. If it is true that *every* man has to do the noblest thing that *any* man can do or describe, what an appeal is this to the courage, cheerfulness, energy and dignity of human existence? Who, then, shall think his a a life doomed to mediocrity or meanness, to vanity or toil, or to any ends less than heavenly and immortal? Who shall say "the grand prizes of life are for others; I, alas! can be nothing." But is it *not* true? I have referred for comparison to what are considered as the noblest works of man; works of genius; works which draw universal attention and admiration; which fill the world with their renown; which give to successful authors and artists such an enviable position among men; and I say that there is something greater for every man to do than this. For suppose, now, that you were possessed of the loftiest power of unfolding that sense of beauty which dwells more or less in all minds; suppose that, in the high and solemn meditations of genius, you had portrayed scenes and characters of such moral beauty and sublimity, that they fired the breasts of millions, and drew tears of sympathy from the eyes of nations; and suppose, too, that the lofty feeling of your own heart, furnished the living portraiture. But, let me ask you, would it not be a still nobler thing for you to go and do that which you had described; to *be* the model that you drew? And, believe me—for this is a point on which I must insist, again and again—believe me, the loftiest action that ever *was* described, is not more magnanimous than that which we may find occasion to do, in the daily walks of life; in temptation, in distress, in bereavement, and in the solemn approach to death. 'n the great providence of God, in the great ordinances of our being, there is opened to every man a sphere for the noblest action. Nay, and it is not in extraordinary situations, where all eyes are upon us, where all our energy is aroused and all our vigilance is awake, that the highest efforts of virtue are usually demanded of us; but it is rather in silence and seclusion, amidst our occupations and our homes; in wearing sickness that makes no complaint; in sorely-tried honesty that asks no praise; in simple disinterestedness which hides the hand that resigns its advantage to another.

I seek, my friends, to ennoble common life. I know that it has been almost exclusively the office of the moral teachers of mankind to celebrate conspicuous virtue—virtue in extraordinary circumstances. Nay, even biography, though professing to give us the true life of a man, has mostly contented itself with giving us the life of a hero, a statesmen, an author, or a philanthropist. But there is still another work to be done; and that is to go down into the obscure and as yet unsearched records of daily conduct and feeling; to portray not the ordinary virtue of an extraordinary life, but the more extraordinary virtue of ordinary life. Yes, my brethren; what is done and borne in the shades of privacy, in the hard and beaten path of daily care and toil, full often of uncelebrated sacrifices; in the suffering, and sometimes insulted suffering, that wears to the world nothing but a cheerful brow; in the long strife of the spirit, carried on against pain, and penury, and neglect, carried on in the inmost depths of the heart; yes, I repeat, what is done and borne, what is wrought and won *here*, is a higher glory, and shall inherit a brighter crown. And I pray you to observe how emphatically this was the teaching of our Saviour. "Ye know," he says to his disciples, that "the princes of the nations exercise dominion over them; but it shall not be so among you. But whosoever will be great among you, let him be your minister, and whosoever will be chief among you, let him be your servant; even as the Son of Man came, not to be ministered unto, but to minister, and to give his life a ransom for many." And again he said, "Whosoever exalteth himself shall be humbled, and he that humbleth himself shall be exalted." Yes, humility, forgetfulness of self, self-sacrifice, these were in the mind of Jesus, the true distinctions.

I am sensible, I repeat, that the world has by no means yet arrived at this point of view. There is as yet, so little wisdom, so little spirituality, infused into the mass of public sentiment, that a thing to be admired must be conspicuous, must be surrounded with visible splendour, or invested with the halo of fame, must bear a title of honour or a name of greatness. A man to be honoured, must be a great general or statesman, a great author or artist. But I anticipate that the time will come, when it will be said to the greatest of these—yes, I repeat, when some one, pointing to a good man, will say to a man great as Shakspeare or Raphael, "you are but a describer; here is the doer; you have drawn or moulded a model of saintly beauty and goodness; here is the living original. Be thyself that same, and thou shalt be greater than thou now art. If thou wilt not, then do I venerate him more than I admire you. All the strugglings of genius in thee, have never equalled the strugglings of virtue in him. He is one who realizes all the beautiful conceptions of your art. If such as he had not existed—if such as he had not breathed out through form, and act, and countenance, the beauty of goodness, patience, and heroism, thine art had never existed. Thou art but a copyist; he is the original."

Yes, my friends, it is true. Goodness is the great inspirer, refiner, glorifier of the world. Let that be gone from the world, and the light of art, of literature, of history, is gone out entirely. The treasures of the world are its virtues—sanctity, self-sacrifice, patience, constancy, heroism, martyrdom. It is goodness only that we *love*—other things we may admire, beauty, wit, fortune—but it is goodness only that we love; and in the humblest shades of obscurity, we love it. It is this whose life we cherish more than our own life. It is this whose lonely grave we bedew with our tears, saying, "let us go and die with it."

I have thus attempted to assign to simple virtue the place that belongs to it. I call the quality of which I speak, virtue. I can well imagine that it may surprise, if not displease, some persons that I use this word so frequently. I suppose it sounds in their ears, as if it stood for a kind of heathenish excellence. I mean by it, then, let me say, all that I can mean by human excellence and sanctity; all that is meant by righteousness, holiness, spirituality. And I use it more frequently than I do some of these words, because they seem to me to be invested with false and blinding associations. I fear that we do but half feel the bond, when it is laid upon us by the words, holiness, godliness, grace. I fear that if I had spoken in this discourse of the grandeur, the supreme distinction of *holiness* or *spirituality*, though there might have been an easier assent, the truth would not have come home to us—home to our dwellings and our every-day lives. I may err on this point; but I certainly do use this word, virtue, from an anxiety to go down to the very grounds of a spiritual and good life. It seems to me peculiarly to appertain to the matured excellence of a human being. Infants may have innocence, and angels may have sanctity; but when I would describe the struggle of sacred principle in a man, the most comprehensive word, the word that reveals at once the character of the conflict, that bears the marks at once of the strife and victory upon it, is virtue; patient, courageous, enduring, victorious virtue!

But is all this which I have been saying, true? Or is it a mere fine theory! *Can* the routine and drudgery of life, be raised to heroism and grandeur? Is it true that common life opens a field for the noblest action of which a man is capable? Is it true that the artist's model, the poet's dream, the philosopher's theory, and more than all, the high teaching of the very Christ himself, may thus be realized in the daily walks of men? This is the grand assumption on which my discourse has proceeded; and now let me spend a few moments in close, in attempting to make this ground a little more apparent; and thus to bring what I have now been saying to a practical issue.

And in one word, is not all this proved to us Christians, by the example of our divine Master? It is an example in the sphere of common life—not on a throne nor in a palace, but in humble abodes, in daily intercourse. Now suppose that the story of his life had been a mere fiction:—that is to say, look upon it as a mere literary production; and would you not say, that it is the most beautiful conception ever embodied in the records of human speech? that such a divine ideal of life, such majesty, such loveliness was never before portrayed on any human page? But it is no fiction; it is reality. All the world has agreed that the reality alone, can account for the portraiture; that the Apostles never could have drawn such a life, if they had not seen it. Now after this reality, it is our duty and aim as Christians to follow. Was ever a higher aim than this proposed to mortal aspiration and effort?

But let us enter into this matter, a little in detail. Here opens to me a volume; and I can only touch upon two or three passages in this grandeur of the Christian life.

What is the bright word that is written on this volume of life, from which rays out on every side, an ineffable splendour? Duty! Not mean, cowering, slavish duty; but high, magnificent, glorious duty.

Let an instance suffice instead of precepts. A few years ago died in Portsmouth, (England,) a poor man, a crippled shoe-mender. A humble man of a humble calling; and yet around his gate when he died, is seen a collection of weeping children. Why is this? A few words will tell the story of a life unknown to fame, but beautiful, glorious, I had almost said, as the ministry of angels. This man—John Pounds was his name—of such humble and busy toils, and of such infirmity that he seemed destined to be a burden on charity, saw around him in the streets, poor neglected children, growing up to ignorance and vice; such as you may see, any day, around you. He had no money to give them; he had no time to give them; he had no spacious dwelling to receive them, even if he had had time. What then did he do? He gathered them around his knees as he sat and worked on his humble bench, and there he instructed them. For forty years, I think, he thus taught successive companies of poor children, and raised hundreds to virtuous, reputable and happy life. The tale speaks for itself. Is there no bright word written on the pages of common life—ay, and of the humblest life?

Again, what is the dark word that is written in this volume of life, spreading a shadow over all its pages? Temptation! It is no strange lot. It is the lot of common life. Every man is a tempted man. Every day we meet those awful hours, in which the great controversy between right and wrong, is pleaded in our bosoms. Then the senses' allurement steals upon us: then ambition, or anger, or envy invades the peace of our minds; then the world's great show, or "the world's dread laugh," demands our homage or threatens our freedom. Must we not fight every hour, with these besetting foes of the spirit? In the depths of the heart, in deepest silence where praise comes not; with solitary prayer and patience, must we not strive? And here in this post within, to be held against all the world, believe me, deeds are to be done and victories to be gained, compared with which the prowess of battles and the splendour of triumphs fade away! "Greater is he that ruleth his spirit," says the sacred proverbialist, "than he that taketh a city."

What is the power within, that holds this sublime conflict? It is God's vicegerent in the soul, the sovereign and majestic conscience. What on earth so noble! Lo! a man—"faithful found among the faithless;" and to this man the slightest whisper of his conscience, is more than the echoing fame of ages; the simple purpose of rectitude is more than all the blandishments of beauty and love; and the single, self-poised feeling of integrity in the heart, is more riches to him than the wealth of kingdoms. Ah! what an elevation is that! when the secret, invisible feeling in the heart, that says, "I will do right," weighs more, and is worth more with its possessor, than all the riches of the world; yes, when the whole accumulated magnificence of the world could not buy from him that simple feeling. I have seen the homage of loyalty to kings, the lowly and graceful prostration before the symbols of the majesty of earth; and I will confess that I thought it beautiful; the bare feeling of reverence, wins my sympathy; but what is it all, compared with the deep and lowly homage of a man to the awful sovereignty within him!

And so the righteous man liveth; pure, calm, strong; inwardly moved, and moved from within; self-subsisting, and dependent neither upon fashion, fortune, nor fame. Shall I say, it is the life of a sage, of a philosopher? It is more. It is the life of Christ in the soul; and it is the study and imitation of Christ that must lead us to it.

One more great hour there is, for the mind's trial; the hour that cometh to all; the time to die! Many a man has fought battles, who had no arms for the last conflict. Many a man has painted pain and agony, who could not endure them; and has described in thrilling terms and tones, the terrors of the last hour; whose spirit has sunk before those terrors when they came.

We speak of martyrdoms, and they are glorious. But there are long years of sickness and pain now conducting the steps of some we know to the grave, in which is endured the suffering of a hundred martyrdoms. But the briefer hours of mortal disease—what a spectacle do they present? The mind weighed down by infirmity, overshadowed by surrounding gloom, and upon the rack of pain; what a picture is it upon the dark curtain of death! I have seen it; in the silent and shaded chamber; amidst low and hushed voices, with sobs and tears around it; or amidst the awful stillness of constrained affection—no curtain fold disturbed, no sigh rising upon the breathless air;

and I have seen it thus encompassed, shining as the face of an angel! Oh! mortal languor and paleness, it is true, were there; marked and marred was that face with the hard buffetings of disease; but it was tranquil and resigned, and full of immortal trust. The righteous men that walked in the fiery furnace unhurt, shone not more gloriously, than did that Christian soul in its parting hour. How full of consideration was it, one while—speaking not much of itself, because others could not bear it!—how full of wisdom, at another time, uttering its calm, natural and rational meditations on life, and death, and the world unseen; speaking, indeed, with all the wisdom of Socrates; and more—how much more than all his trust!

My brethren, I have thus attempted to speak to you of the greatness of virtue. Does not the theme minister to the humblest life among us, a glorious encouragement. What would we greater than what, in opportunity, God hath given to us all? What? A brave apparel—a rich mansion—the circle of a golden crown? And for this is the crown of nobleness and sanctity to be accounted nothing? And shall we let poor, worldly discontent and base despite eat into that heart, where may be fashioned divine and immortal faculties? Shall we let the humbleness of earthly fortunes, shade the brow which may be radiant with the crown of virtue? What should we have thought of Raphael painting the Transfiguration, if he could have let the shadow of a Roman cloud disturb his equanimity? What should we have thought of Milton writing the Paradise Lost, if he could have let the flashing tinsel of a passing courtier's mantle, make him envious?

Ah! we believe not—here is the difficulty. We believe not in *ourselves*; we believe not in Christ; we believe not in God. Well may we pray the Lord evermore to increase our faith. Come, faith of Christ! faith of the crucified and the victorious! faith of him who said to the unjustly persecuted and suffering, rejoice and be exceeding glad!—come, and save us from our earth-born miseries, our miseries born of pride and ingratitude and worldliness.

Couldst thou, my friend, but once enter into thyself, and learn to be quiet, to know thyself, to commune with God, and to breathe the spirit of Jesus Christ; couldst thou learn to find thy kingdom, thy riches within, to explore and enjoy the treasures of a spiritual and immortal soul; couldst thou learn all the dignity, the calmness and blessedness of that inward life; how nobly shouldst thou then walk amidst the gauds and shows of this world! How shouldst thou walk, indeed, upon the high places of the world, and possess the earth, nature, life, being, anew. Thou shouldst be greater than the greatest of this world, wiser than the wisest, and only less blessed and glorious than the angels of heaven!

There is a crown of earthly royalty, that demandeth homage. There is another crown, too, which is of earth, but which is yet more glorious—the crown that genius wears—such as was once placed on the brow of Petrarch, amidst assembled multitudes, in the Eternal City. But know, O man of righteousness and fidelity and truth! thou who seekest a nobler prize—know that the time shall come when, amidst assembled worlds, a brighter crown shall be placed on the brow of virtue. "Be thou faithful unto death," saith the Judge of all hearts, "and I will give thee a crown of life."

ON COMMERCE AND BUSINESS.

X.

ON THE MORAL LAW OF CONTRACTS.

THAT NO MAN GO BEYOND AND DEFRAUD HIS BROTHER IN ANY MATTER.—1 Thessalonians, iv. 6.

I PROPOSE to invite your attention in a series of three or four Sabbath evening discourses, to the moral laws of trade, the moral end of business, and to the moral principles which are to govern the accumulation of property. The first of these subjects is proposed for your consideration this evening; and it is one, as I conceive, of the highest interest and importance.

This country presents a spectacle of active, absorbing, and prosperous business, which strikes the eye of every stranger, as its leading characteristic. We are said to be and we *are* a people, beyond all others, devoted to business and accumulation. This, though it is often brought against us as a reproach, is really an inevitable result of our political condition. I trust that it is but the *first* development, and that many better ones are to follow. It does, however, spring from our institutions: and I hold, moreover, that it is honourable to them. If half of us were slaves, that half could have nothing to do with traffic. If half of us were in the condition of the peasantry of Europe, the business transactions of that half would be restricted within a narrow sphere, and would labour under a heavy pressure. But where liberty is given to each one to act freely for himself, and by all lawful means to better his condition, the consequence is inevitably what we see; a universal and unprecedented activity among all the classes of society, in all the departments of human industry. The moral principles then, applicable to the transaction of buisness have strong claims upon our attention; and seem to me, very proper subjects of discussion in our pulpits.

There are moral *questions* too, as we very well know, which actually do interest all reflecting and conscientious men who are engaged in trade. They are very frequently discussed in conversation; and very different grounds are taken by the disputants. Some say that one principle is altogether right; and others, that another and totally different one is the only right principle. In such circumstances, it seems to me not only proper but requisite, for those whose office it is to speak to men of their duties, that they should take up the discussion of these, as they would of any other moral questions. I am obliged to confess that we are liable, scholastic and retired men as we are, to give some ground to men of business, for anticipating that our reasonings and conclusions will not be very practical or satisfatory. I can only say, for myself, that I have, for some time, given patient and careful attention to the moral principles of trade; that I have often conversed with men of business that I might understand the practical bearings and difficulties of the subject; that I have also read some of the books in which the morality of contracts is discussed; and although a clergyman, I shall venture, with some confidence as well as modesty, to offer you my thoughts on the points in question. I say the points in question; and I have intimated that there are points in debate, questions of conscience in business, which are brought into the most serious controversy. I have even known sensible men, themselves engaged in trade, to go to the length of asserting, not only that the principles of trade are immoral and unchristian, but that no man can acquire a property in this commerce without sacrificing a good conscience; that no prosperous merchant can be a good Christian. I certainly think that such casuists are wrong; but whether or not they are so, the principles which bring them to a conclusion so extraordinary, evidently demand investigation.

In preparing to examine this opinion, and indeed to discuss the whole subject, it will not be improper to observe in the outset, that trade in some form, is the inevitable result of the human condition. Better, it has been said, on the supposition already stated—better that commerce should perish than Christianity; but let it be considered whether commerce can perish. Nothing can be more evident than that the earth was formed to be the theatre of trade. Not only does the ocean facilitate commerce, but the diversity of soils, climes and products, requires it. So long as one district of country produces cotton, and another corn; so long as one man lives by an ore-bed which produces iron, and another, on pasture-lands which grow wool, there must be commerce. In addition to this, let it be considered that all human industry inevitably tends to what is called "the division of labour." The savage who roams through the wilderness, may possibly, in the lowest state of barbarism, procure with his own hand all that suffices for his miserable accommodation; the coat of skins that clothes, the food that sustains, and the hut that shelters him. But the moment society departs from that state, there necessarily arise the different occupations of shepherd, agriculturist, mechanic, and manufacturer; the products of whose industry are to be exchanged; and this exchange is trade. If a single individual were to perform all the operations necessary to produce a piece of cloth, and yet more a garment of that cloth, the process would be exceedingly slow and expensive. Human intelligence necessarily avails itself of the facility, the dexterity, and the advantage every way, which are to be obtained by a division of labour. The very progress of society is indicated by the gradual and growing development of this tendency.

Besides, it has been justly observed by a celebrated writer on this subject, that "there is a certain propensity in human nature to truck, barter, and exchange one thing for another. It is common to all men," he says, "and to be found in no other race of animals, which seem to know neither this nor any other species of contracts. Nobody," he observes, "ever saw a dog make a fair and deliberate exchange of one bone for another, with another dog. Nobody ever saw one animal by its gestures and natural cries signify to another, this is mine, that yours; I am willing to give this for that."*

Trade, then, being a part of the inevitable lot of cultivated humanity, the question is, not about abolishing, but about the moral principles that are to regulate it.

Let us first inquire, how we are to settle this question? What is the process of mind by which we are to ascertain and establish the moral laws of trade?

Does the natural conscience declare them? Is there any instinctive prompting of conscience, that can

* Adam Smith.

properly decide each case as it arises in the course of business? Is there any voice within, that says clearly and with authority, "thou shalt do thus and so?" I think not. The cases are not many, in any department of action, where conscience thus reveals itself. But in business they are peculiarly rare, because the questions there, are unusually complicated. You offer to sell to your neighbour an article of merchandise. You are entitled of course, i. e. in ordinary circumstances, to some advance upon what it cost you. But what that is, depends on many cirumstances. Conscience will hardly mark down the just price in your account-book. Conscience, indeed, commands us to do right; but the question is, what *is* right? This is to be decided by views far more various and comprehensive, than the simple sense of right and wrong.

The Scriptures, like conscience, are a general directory. They do not lay down any specific moral laws of trade. They command us to be upright and honest; but they leave us to consider what particular actions are required by those principles. They command us to do unto others as we would have them do to us; but still this is not specific. A man may unreasonably wish that another should sell him a piece of goods at half its value. Does it follow that he himself ought to sell on those terms? The truth is, that the golden rule, like every other in Scripture, is a general maxim. It simply requires us to desire the welfare of others, as we would have them desire ours. But the specific actions answering to that rule, it leaves us to determine by a wise discretion. The dictates of that discretion, under the governance of the moral law, are the principles that we seek to discover.

Neither, on this subject, can I accept without question the teachings of the common law; because, I find, that its ablest expounders acknowledge that its decisions are sometimes at variance with strict moral principle. I do not think it follows from this, that the general principles of the common law, are wrong, or abet wrong. Nay, I conceive that they may approach as near to rectitude as is possible in the circumstances, and yet necessarily involve some practical injustice in their operation. This results, in fact, from their very utility, their very perfection, as a body of laws. For it is requisite to their utility, that they should be general, that they should be derived from precedents and formed into rules; else, men will not know what to depend upon, nor how to govern themselves; and there would neither be confidence, nor order, nor society. But general rules must sometimes bear hard upon individuals; the very law which secures justice in a thousand cases, may, and perhaps must, from the very nature of human affairs and relationships, do injustice in one. Indeed, the law of chancery, or of equity, has been devised on purpose to give relief. But even chancery has its rules which sometimes press injuriously upon individual interests; and no human laws can attain to a perfect and unerring administration of justice. For this perfect justice, however, we seek. We are asking what it is to do no wrong to our fellow-man, whether the law permits it or not. We are asking how we shall stand acquitted, not merely at the bar of our country, but at the bar of conscience and of God.

I must add, in fine, that questions about right and wrong in the contracts of trade, are not to be decided by any hasty impulses of feeling, or suggestions of a generous temper. I have often found men, in conversation on this subject, appealing to their feelings; but however much I have respected those feelings, it has seemed to me, that they were not the proper tribunal. Nay, they have often appeared to me to mistake the point at issue. If a merchant has a large store of provisions in a time of scarcity, would it not be a very noble and praiseworthy thing, it is said, for him to dispose of his stock, without enhancing the price? But the proper question is not, what is generous, but what is just. And besides, he cannot be generous, or what is the same thing in effect, he cannot establish a generous principle in the distribution of his store. For if he sells in large quantities, selling, that is, at a low rate, it will avail nothing, because the subordinate dealers will raise the price. Or, if he undertakes to sell to each family what it wants; any one of them may take the article to the next warehouse, and dispose of it at the enhanced price. On the contrary, there are circumstances, undoubtedly, in which a man may take undue advantage of a monopoly; but this will be a case for future consideration. For the present, it is sufficient to observe, what I think must be obvious, that the great questions before us are to be decided, not by any enactments of law, nor any immediate dictate of conscience, or specific teaching of Scripture, or single impulse of good feeling, but by broad and large views of the whole subject. Conscience, and Scripture, and right feeling are to govern us; but it is only under the guidance of sound reasoning.

Let me beg your indulgence to one or two further preliminary observations. The questions to be discussed are of great importance, and scarcely of less difficulty. It is hardly possible to overrate the importance of a high, and at the same time, just tone of commercial morality. I am addressing merchants and young men, who are to be the future merchants of this city and country. I am addressing them on the morality of their daily lives, on the principles that are to form their character for time, and eternity; and while I task myself to speak with the utmost care and deliberation, I shall not be thought unreasonable, I trust, if I invite the patient attention of those who hear me, to share in the task.

There is then, on this subject, a distinction to be made between principles and rules. Principles, the principles that is to say, of truth, justice and beneficence, are clear and immutable; the only difficulty is about the application of them, i. e. about rules. Principles, I say, are to be set apart, at once and entirely, from all doubt and uncertainty. They hold their place on high, like unchanging lights in the heavens. The only question is, how, in obedience to their direction, we are faithfully and surely to work our traverse across the troubled ocean of business. Here, I say, is all the difficulty. Rules, I repeat, result from the application of principles to human conduct, and they must be affected by the circumstances to which they relate. Thus, it is an immutable principle in morals, that I should love my neighbour, my fellow-being, and desire to promote his happiness. This principle admits of no qualification; it can suffer no abatement in any circumstances. But when I come to consider what I shall *do* in obedience to this principle; what I shall do for the poor, the sick, or the distressed; by what acts I shall show my kindness to my neighbour, or my interest in the welfare of the world; when, in other words, I come to consider the *rules* of my conduct, I am obliged at once to admit doubts and difficulties. The abstract principle cannot be my law, without any regard to circumstances, though some moral reformers would make it such. I must go on the right line of conduct, it is true, but where that line shall lead me, is to be determined by a fair consideration of the cases that come before me. If it is not, I shall contravene the very principle on which I am acting. If, for instance, I do nothing but give, give to the poor, I shall be doing them an injury, not a kindness. The great law of benevolence, in fact, as truly requires discretion as it enforces action.

This distinction fully applies to the subject we are about to examine. Rectitude, justice, benevolence, truth-telling, are immutable laws of trade, as they are of all human conduct. There is no *certain extent* to which they go; they apply without limit to every department and every transaction in business; they are never to be contravened. But in laying down practical rules for traffic, we immediately meet with difficulties, and are obliged to leave a great deal to the honest judgment of the trader. He must do right, indeed; that is the great law; but what *is* right? Let us now more nearly approach this question, having narrowed it down to a question about rules, and more closely apply ourselves to the difficulties involved in it.

And here, I must ask you to consider as a further and final preliminary topic, the language of the legal writers on this subject. It is common with those writers to make a distinction between moral and legal justice; or, in other words, between the demands of conscience and the decisions of their courts. Conscience, for instance, demands that a certain contract shall be annulled, because there was some concealment or deception; but the courts will not annul it, unless the injury be very great. In short, it is a matter of degrees. Up to a certain extent, the law will, in fact, protect a man in doing what is wrong, in doing that which violates his conscience; beyond a certain extent, it will not protect him. This distinction is founded on the policy of the law, and the policy of trade. "In law," says Pothier, "a party will not be permitted to complain of slight offences, which he, with whom a contract is made, has committed against good faith; otherwise there would be too many contracts to be rescinded; which would open the way for too much litigation, and would derange commerce."* And again, "the interests of commerce will not easily permit parties to escape from bargains which they have concluded: they must lay the blame to their not having been better informed concerning the defects of the article sold."† And again he says, "this rule is wisely established for the security and freedom of commerce, which demand that no one should easily be off from his bargains; otherwise men would not dare to make contracts, for fear that he with whom they had bargained, should imagine that he was injured, and upon that ground (of mere imagination or pretence) should commence an action." Hence, Pothier says, that the wrong of which the courts will take cognizance, must be an enormous wrong.‡

Now there is, doubtless, a certain expediency here; a certain policy of trade, a certain policy of the law. It is expedient that a fair field be opened in business for ingenuity, sagacity, and attention; and that ignorance, indolence, and neglect, should meet with loss. "The common law," says Chancellor Kent, "affords to every one, reasonable protection against fraud in dealing; but it does not go the romantic length of giving indemnity against the consequences of indolence and folly, or a careless indifference to the ordinary and accessible means of information."§

* Traité des Obligations, Part. I. ch. 1. Sec. 1. Art. 3. § 3.

† Traité du Contrat de vente, Part. II. ch. 2. Art. 2.

‡ Traité des Obligations, Part. I. ch. 1. Sec. 1. Art. 3. § 4.

§ Commentaries.

What is the nature, and what is the amount of this concession to expediency? Let us carefully consider this question, for much depends upon it.

Legal expediency, then, is not to be so construed as to warrant the supposition, that it lends a *sanction* to what is wrong. It may, from necessity, permit or protect fraud, but does not abet it. A man is not to consider himself an honest man, simply because the law gives him deliverance. For the law *cannot* take cognizance of the secret intentions, nor of slight deviations from truth. If every man who says he has got a bad bargain, and who thinks he has been cheated, could be heard in court, our tribunals would be overwhelmed with business. No human tribunal can descend to the minutiæ of injustice. But the law, I repeat, does not sanction what it does not undertake to prevent, any more than the infinite providence sanctions those abuses which arise from its great law of freedom.

This being the nature of the concession to expediency, no principle being compromised, we may say, that the extent of the concession must be considerable It is certainly expedient that every man be put upon his own discretion, sagacity and attention, for success. In business, as in everything else, a premium is set upon these qualities by the hand of providence. It is expedient, in other words, that every man should take care of himself. Others are not to step forward at every turn to rescue him from the consequences of his indolence or inattention. The seller is not required to give his *opinion* to the buyer. If he *knows* of any defect in his merchandise, not apparent to the buyer, he is bound to state it: but he is not required to give his opinion. The buyer has no business to ask it of him; he is to form an opinion for himself. If he is relieved from doing this, he will always remain in a sort of mercantile childhood.

Nor do I know that there is any thing in Scripture, or in the laws of human brotherhood, that forbids this honest, not fraudulent, but honest competition between men's exertions, faculties and wits. We are indeed to do to others as we would have them do to us; but we ought not to wish them to do anything to us, which is inconsistent with the general welfare of the community, with the lawful and necessary stimulants to action. We may have unreasonable desires: we would, perhaps, that our rich neighbour should present us with half of his fortune; but unreasonable desires are not the measure of our duties. Not *whatever* we wish, but what we *lawfully* wish from others, should we do to them. And lawfully, we can no more wish that they should give to our indolence and negligence, the benefit of their sagacity and alertness in making a contract, than that they would give to our poverty the half of that wealth, which their superior industry or talent had earned for them. Thus, too, when it is said that we ought to treat all men as brethren; it is true, indeed, so far as that relation is expressive of the general relationships of society. But while there should be a brotherly community of feeling, there cannot be a brotherly identity of interests between the members of society; and, therefore, they are not bound to deal with one another as if they belonged to a community of Shakers, or of New Harmony men. We are not to break down the principle of individuality, of individual interests, of individual aims; while at the same time, we are to hold it in subjection to the laws of sacred honesty, and of a wise philanthropy.

Besides, it is not only expedient and right, but it is inevitable, that individual power and talent should come into play in business. A man's sagacity, it is obvious, he must use; that is to say, his mind he must use; for he has nothing else to go by. He may use it unjustly, to the heinous injury of his weaker neighbour; but still he must use it. So also with regard to the power acquired by a large property, or by a monopoly, it is inevitable that it should be used. To some extent, the possessor canot help using it. Wealth has credit; and monopoly, usually implying scarcity, carries an enhanced price with it; and such results are unavoidable. Finally, superior actual knowledge, may, and must be used, to some extent. In every department of business, superior knowledge is gained by attention, and it may and must be acted upon; albeit to the hurt or injury of those who know less, or have devoted less time and thought to the subject. A man has made an improvement in some machinery or manufacture, and he is entitled to some reward for the attention he has given to it; the goverment will give him a patent. A man has been to India or to South America, to acquaint himself with a certain branch of business; and he comes home and acts upon his knowledge, and he has a perfect right to do so. He is not bound to communicate his knowledge to his brother merchants who are engaged in the same trade; and, perhaps, his knowledge so much depends upon actual observation and experience, that he cannot communicate it. In like manner, a trader may obtain a superior knowledge of business and of the facts on which it depends, by a close observation of things immediately around him, and he must act upon it; he cannot employ himself in going about to see whether other men have got the same enlarged views. Nor have other men any right to complain of this. The unskilful painter or sculptor, the ignorant lawyer or physician, might as well complain, that their more distinguished brethren were injuring their business, and taking all the prizes out of their hands.

I have thus attempted to set forth the claims of individual enterprise, as having a useful, a beneficent tendency. These claims, I have all along implied, are subject to certain limitations. And these limitations are set by the laws of honesty and philanthropy. That is to say, a man may pursue his own interest; he may use his endeavour, sagacity, ability; but in the first place, he shall not pursue any traffic or make any contract to the injury of his neighbour; unless that injury is one that inevitably results from a general and good principle—that is to say, from the healthful action of business; and, in the next place, he shall not pursue his own ends to the extent of committing any fraud.

This last limitation is the one of the most palpable importance, and demands that we should distinctly mark it. What then is a fraud in contracts? In order to answer the question, let us ask what is a contract? A contract is a mutual engagement, to exchange certain goods for other goods, or certain goods for money; and the essence of the engagement lies in the supposed equivalency of the things that are exchanged. This results from the very nature of the case and of the human mind. For it is not the part of a rational being to give more for less. If you bargain away anything to your neighbour, you, of course, seek from him what to you is equivalent. But how are you to judge of this equivalency; of the value, that is to say, of the article offered to you? There are two grounds on which you may judge. You may know the articles as well as the seller; you may know as much about it, every way, as he does. This is ordinarily the case between trader and trader. But between the merchant and the rest of the world, this is usually not the case. And here the ground on which you proceed is, that of confidence in the good faith of the seller. You could make up no satisfactory opinion on the value of the article offered to you, if you did believe that it is what it purports to be, what it appears to be, what the price indicates it to be. If then, there is any secret defect in the article not apparent to you, or if there is any circumstance unknown to you, materially affecting its value, or if the price set upon it is any other than the market price, *there* is fraud. Wherever the contracting parties stand in totally different relations to the matter in hand, the one knowing something, some secret, which the other does not and cannot know, *there* is fraud. The contract is morally vitiated. The obvious conditions of a contract are not complied with. It is well known by one of the parties that the grand condition, that of equivalency, does not exist in the case.

Let us now look back, for a moment, upon the ground which we have passed over in this preliminary discussion. I have, in the first place, attempted to show that no single suggestion or dictate of conscience, or scripture, or of generous feeling, or of the law, is sufficient to solve the moral questions that arise in trade. In the next place, I have said that there is a distinction to be made between principles and rules; the principles of moral conduct being clear and certain; the rules only, the specific actions under these principles, that is to say, being liable to doubt. I thus wished to set one department of this subject above all question. In the third place, I applied myself to the consideration of rules. And here I attempted to show that while, on the one hand, it is expedient that ample scope be given to human ingenuity, sagacity and alertness in business, yet on the other hand, that they are never to transgress the bounds of philanthropy, honesty and justice.

Let us now proceed to examine some of the cases to which these general reasonings apply.

I. The first is the ordinary case of buying and selling, i. e. under ordinary circumstances.

And here, it is expedient and necessary, that men in their dealings with one another should be put to the use of their senses and faculties. There is a discretion and there is a duty proper, respectively, to the seller and to the buyer. Each of them has his part to act, his business to attend to, and neither of them is bound to assume the duty of the other. In ordinary cases there is no difficulty with this maxim, no temptation to dishonesty, no possibility of deception.

The article is open to inspection; its qualities are as obvious to the buyer as to the seller. The buyer is supposed to know his own business, his own occasions; the *buyer* is fairly supposed best to know what the article is worth to him, not the seller; and it is for him to decide, whether he will purchase, and what he will give. The seller cannot be expected to enter into the circumstances of the buyer, and to ascertain by inquiry what he intends to do with the article he purchases; whether he can turn it to good account; or whether he could not buy more advantageously somewhere else; all this belongs to the province of the buyer: it is his business to settle all these questions. And he is not only best able to decide them, but he is as competent to judge of the quality of the goods which are offered him, as the seller, for they are alike open to the inspection of both.

This free action, this competition, we have already

said, is to be restrained in trade as in every thing else, by perfect fairness and honesty. At that point in our preliminary discussion, the theoretical question about the nature of a contract presented itself; in our present inquiry, the natural and practical question is about price. What is the just price of an article? A man has something to sell; he wishes to deal honestly; the question then is, what shall he ask for it? If he can settle this question, all is plain. How shall he settle it? What is it that determines a price to be just? Evidently, not any abstract consideration of value. There can be no such thing as abstract value. The worth of a thing depends on the want of it. Originally, it is true, i. e. in the first rude state of society, men, in exchanging the products of their labour, would naturally estimate the value of each article by the labour required to produce it. But even this estimate, though approaching nearest to it, would not present us with an abstract and absolute value; and it would soon be disturbed by circumstances, effectually and beyond recovery. Labour would not be an accurate measure of value, because one man's labour, through its energy and ingenuity, would be worth far more than another man's. That primitve rule, too, inaccurate as it is, would soon, I repeat, be disturbed by circumstances. For, suppose that one man had manufactured axes, and another, shoes; circumstances would inevitably arise that would give one or another of these articles, a factitious value. In the winter season when protection was needed for the person, and in the summer which was favourable to the felling of timber, the value of those articles must be constantly fluctuating; it would be factitious; it could not be determined by the amount of labour. And as we depart farther from those primitive exchanges, we find circumstances, numerous, complicated and very artificial, which affect value. The wants, fancies and fashions of society; the state of crops and markets, and of trade all over the world; the variations of the seasons; the success or failure of fisheries; improvements in machinery; discoveries in art; and the regulations of governments; all these things and many more, conspire alternately to fix and disturb from day to day, that ever fluctuating thing called price. It is not any one man's judgment or conscience that can ascertain the value of any thing, but millions of individual judgments go to make up the decision. It is in vain to say that such and such things are worth little or nothing; that they are unnecessary or useless, or that they confer no advantage proportionate to their cost; that is not the question. What will they fetch? is the question. You may, in a fit of generosity, or a scruple of conscience, sell them for less; but the moment they are out of your hands, they will rise to the level of the market; you have lost the difference, and gained nothing for your generous principle. In fine, *the value of a thing is the market price of it.* This is the only intelligible idea of value; and the only reasonable adjustment of price. It is certainly most likely to be reasonable; for a multitude of judgments have been employed upon it, and have settled it. It is the legislative voice of the whole world; and it would be as unjust and inexpedient as it is impossible, to resist it.

The way of honesty, then, in the ordinary course of traffic, seems to be very clear. The terms on which we are to buy and sell, are established for us by a very obvious rule. In a general view, we may say, that conscience has nothing to do with affixing a price. That is determined by a thousand circumstances and a million voices. The trader must *buy* at the market price, and he must sell accordingly. *He* does not determine the price, but the suffrage of a whole city or of twenty cities, determines it. All that conscience has to do with price therefore is, not to go beyond the usage of the market. And for the rest, the rule is, to make no false representation, and to conceal no latent defect.

In this view, the moral course in almost the entire business of trade, seems to be exceedingly plain; and certainly it is most grateful to reflect that it is so. He that runs may read. No man needs to carry with him, in regard to most of the transactions of business, a disturbed or a doubtful conscience.

But still cases will arise from a nicer casuistry. The market price is indeed the rule; but there is monopoly that makes a market price, and there is superior information that takes undue advantage of it. These are the cases that remain to be examined.

II. The next case, then, to be considered in the morals of business, is monopoly. This may arise in two ways; intentionally, from combination on the part of several traders, or a plan on the part of one; and unintentionally, where it falls out in the natural and unforced course of trade. It is from confounding these two cases together, perhaps, that a peculiar prejudice is felt in the community against monopoly. That a man should set himself by dexterous management to get into his possession all the corn in market, in order to extort an enormous price for it, is felt to be oppressive and wrong. But there is often a monopoly, to a greater or less degree, resulting from simple scarcity; and in this case, that enhancement of price which is so odious, is perfectly inevitable. Nay, it may be even beneficial. For high prices lessen consumption, and may prevent famine. But at any rate, high prices in a time of scarcity are inevitable. Even if all the corn, or all the coal were in the hands of one man; and he should sell the half of his stock to the wholesale dealers at a moderate rate, and hold the remainder at the same rate to keep the price down, still, I say, the moment the article left his hands, the law of scarcity would prevail and raise the price. Monopoly, therefore, compels, and of course, justifies an enhanced price. The same principle which applies to every other commodity, applies to that commodity called money. And it is only from the habit of considering money not as a commodity, but as a possession of some peculiar and magical value, that any prejudice can exist against what is called usurious interest; saving and excepting when that interest goes beyond all bounds of reason and humanity. The practice of usury has acquired a bad name from former and still occasional abuses of it. But the principle must still be a just one, that money, in common with everything else, is worth what it will fetch.

This, I know, is denied. It is denied, especially, that money is, or is to be regarded, like other commodities in trade. It is said that money is the creature of government; that the mint, when stamping it with the government impress, stamps it with a peculiar character, and separates it entirely from the general condition of a commodity. It is said, too, that the common representative of money, that the banknote, that credit, in other words, is exposed to such expansion and contraction, and management and conspiracy, that it is peculiarly liable to be used to the injury of the necessitous and unwary.

Let us separate this consideration of credit from our discussion for a moment, and consider the question alone, as it affects the use of money in the form of bullion. And I know of no better way of considering questions of this sort, than to resolve them into their simple forms, by going back to the origin of society, or by taking, for example, a small and isolated community. At least, we come to the theory of the questions by this means, and can then consider what modifications are required by more artificial and complicated interests

Suppose then a community of a hundred families, cut off from the rest of the world, engaged in the various callings of life, accustomed to barter, but not accustomed to the use of money. Suppose, now, that a gold-mine were discovered. The metal is found to be very valuable for various purposes; and, like every thing else, it takes its value in the market; an ounce of it is exchanged for so many bushels of corn or yards of cloth. But the permanent and universal value of this metal, and its being so portable and indestructible, would, ere long, very naturally bring it into use as a circulating medium; the farmer would know that if he sold corn for it, he could buy cloth with it in another part of the district, and would be glad thus to be saved the trouble and expense of transporting the produce of his farm to the distant manufactory. In this exchange, the lumps of gold of course would be weighed, and it would be natural to stamp the weight upon each lump. But another step would follow from all this. As there would be the trouble of constantly weighing this circulating medium, and the danger of mistake and deception, the community would appoint a committee, or depute its government, if it had one, to do this very thing; and the metal would be cast into various quantities, bearing distinct denominations, to answer more fully the purposes of a convenient circulating medium. Here, then, we have a mint, and here we have money. Nobody will deny that it was a commodity when each man dug it from the earth, and exchanged it at his pleasure. But the action of the government confers no peculiar character on it. The government simply weighs the metal, and affixes, as it were, a label to it, i. e., stamps it as coin, to tell what it is worth. It does not create this value, but simply indicates it.

I am sensible that many questions may still be asked, but I have not space here, if I had ability, to enter into them ; and besides, if this is a just theory of the value of the specie currency, it may itself suggest the necessary answers. But the great practical difficulties arise from the use of a paper currency. If the paper were strictly the representative of gold and silver ; if the issue of bank-notes did not exceed the specie actually in vault, and thus were used only for convenience, the same principles would apply as before. All other paper does not represent money but credit ; i. e., it represents the presumed ability of a man to pay what he promises ; not his known and ascertained property. And the question is, may credit be bought and sold in the market like any commodity ?

Let us again attempt to simplify the question. You want money, let us suppose, and you go to a money-lender, and ask for it. He says, " I have not the money, but I shall have it a month hence, and I will give my note, payable at that time." This may answer the purpose with your creditor, and the question now is, what interest shall you pay ? Shall credit take its place in the market like money, or like a commodity ? Shall we say that the government has no business to interfere in this matter, with its usury laws, obliging a man to sell his paper for seven per cent. ? Shall we say that all this ought to be left to regulate itself, and that every man shall be left free to act according to his pleasure ?

I certainly feel some hesitation, from deference for the opinions of some able men who are more studious in these matters than I am, about answering this question in the affirmative. There are relations and bearings of that immense and complicated subject, the monetary system, which I may not understand; and usury, perhaps, is connected with that system in ways that are beyond my comprehension. But looking at the question now, in the light of simple justice, separating all unlawful combination and conspiracy from the case, and all deception and dishonesty, I cannot see why a man has not a right to sell his credit for what another is willing to give for it. If a lawyer has so elevated himself above his brethren, that his opinion is worth not twenty, but five hundred per cent. more than theirs, he takes that advance for his counsel. Why then, shall not a merchant, who by the same laborious means, has acquired a fortune and a high commercial reputation, be allowed a similar advantage?

We say, why should he not dispose of his credit, or in other words, pledge his property at such prices as it will naturally bear? But the trurh is, that he cannot prevent this result, let him do what he will. He may sell his paper at one half per cent a month, but the moment it is out of his hands, it will rise to two or three per cent, if that be its real value. I say nothing now about obedience to the usury laws; I do not touch the point of conscience in that respect; but I believe that the laws themselves are both impolitic and unjust; unjust, because they conflict with the real value of things; and impolitic, because they never were, and never can be executed, and in fact, because they only increase the rates of interest by increasing the risk.

But is there, then, no limit it may be said, to the advantage which one man may take of the necessities of another? To ask this question in regard to the lender of money, is but the same thing as to ask it in regard to the man, in every other relationship of life. The duties of humanity, of philanthropy, of natural affection, can never be abrogated by any circumstances, and the only question is, what line of conduct in the case before us, is conformable to those duties. That question cannot, I think, be brought within the compass of any assignable rules; and must be left for every man, seriously to consider for himself. He is put upon his conscience, in this respect, as he is in every other case in life.

III. But the hardest case to determine, is that on which the question is raised, about the use of superior information. And perhaps this question cannot be better stated than in the celebrated case put by Cicero.* A corn merchant of Alexandria, he says, arrived at Rhodes in a time of great scarcity, with a cargo of grain, and with knowledge that a number of other vessels laden with corn, had already sailed from Alexandria for Rhodes, and which he had passed on the passage—was he bound in conscience to inform the buyers of that fact? Cicero decides that he was. Several modern writers on law dissent from his opinion; as Grotius, Puffendorf, and Pothier himself, though with very careful qualifications.†

It appears to me, that the answer to Cicero's question, must depend on the views which are taken of a contract. If a contract is a mere arbitrary convention, if business is a game, a mere contest of men's wits, if every man has a right to make the best bargain he can, if society really has power to ordain that such shall be the laws of trade, then the decision

* De Officiis, Lib. 3. Sec. 12–17.

† Traité du Contrat de vente, Part. II. ch. 2. Art.3.

will be one way. But if a contract implies in its very nature the obligation of fair dealing and truth-telling, then the decision will be the other way. The supposition is, that the Alexandrine trader concealed a certain fact, for the sake of asking a price which he knew would not have been given, had that fact been public. Now what is implied in asking a price? What does a man say, when he sets a certain price on his merchandise? Does he, or does he not say, that the price he asks is, in his opinion, the fair value of the article? I think he does. If you did not so understand him, you would not trade with him. If you observed a lurking sneer on his lip, such as there must be in his heart, when he knows that he is taking you in, you would have nothing to do with him. The very transaction, called a contract, implies that degree of good faith. If this be true, if it is universally understood that he who asks a price, professes in that very act to ask a just and fair price, and if, moreover, he has a letter in his pocket assuring and satisfying him that it is not the just price; then he is guilty of falsehood. If the Alexandrine trader had asked a price, graduated exactly by his opinion of the probability that other vessels would soon arrive, and of the amount of the supply they would bring, his conduct would have been fair and honest. But if he had concealed facts within his knowledge, for the sake of asking an enormous price, or any price beyond what he knew to be the fair value, he would be guilty of falsehood and dishonesty. And the reason is, I repeat, that the very basis of a contract is mutual advantage; that its very essence lies in a supposed equivalency; that he who sets a price is understood to say as much as this, "I think the article is worth it." And if you allow a man to swerve from this truth and good faith at all, where will you stop? Suppose that the people of Rhodes had been suffering the horrors of famine, and the Alexandrine merchant had taken advantage of their situation to exact from them all their disposable property as the price of life, and had borne off that mass of treasure, all the while knowing that bountiful supplies were at hand; what should we have said? We should have said that his perfidy was equal to his cruelty; that he was both a pirate and a villain. But if a man may be guilty of falsehood in one degree, what principle is to prevent his being guilty of it in another? I know what may be said on the other hand. The master of the Alexandrine ship, it may be said, had outstripped the others, by superior sailing; and this superiority in the management of his ship, may have been the fruit of a whole life of industry and ingenuity. He had also been on the alert, it may be supposed; had watched the course of the markets while others slept, and had been ready with his supply to meet the exigency which all others, even the Rhodians themselves, had been too dull to foresee. Is he not entitled to some premium for all this? Nay, but for the prospect held out of such a reward, the Rhodians might have starved. And yet if he gives the information in question, he loses the premium. No, the merchants of Rhodes say, "we will wait till to-morrow." But again; to-morrow comes; the vessels arrive; the market is glutted; and the Alexandrine trader loses money on his voyage. Will the merchants of Rhodes make it up to him, on account of his generosity in giving them the information? Not at all. "We buy at the market price," they say; "we cannot afford any more; if we give more, we are losers;" and thus the Alexandrine, by neglecting his own interests, and taking care of other people, loses not only his voyage, but his whole fortune perhaps, and becomes a bankrupt; and by becoming a bankrupt, he injures those he is most bound to serve, his confiding friends, and beggared family. All this is a very good reason, to be sure, why the Alexandrine trader should be rewarded for his exertions, but it is not any good reason, nor *can* there *ever* be any good reason why a man should tell a falsehood; why he should make a false impression; why he should deceive his neighbour.

On the whole, there are two important distinctions to be made, which will carry us, I think, as far as any thing can carry us, through the intricacies and difficulties of this whole subject. The one is, the difference between positive knowledge and mere opinion. The other is, between the rights of parties, and the general moral policy of trade.

To take up the latter in the first place: It is said, that if merchants or brokers mutually agree to the utmost severity of competition, if the *understanding* between them is, that they may take every possible advantage of one another; then, as *between themselves*, there is nothing unjust, nothing dishonest, in their acting according to the compact. At the broker's board, as at the gamester's board, they may push this principle to the ruin of one another, and nobody has any right to complain. Not only may they fully avail themselves of superior power or knowledge in the ordinary transaction of business, but they may conspire together to contract with their neighbour to deliver to them a certain amount of a certain kind of stock a month hence, and in the meantime, they may buy up all that stock, and then, having the power in their hands, they may use it to ruin him; and yet, as between themselves, it is a fair business transaction.

They agreed to enter into this kind of contest with one another, and they have acted according to their agreement.

All this is true; and yet I maintain, that there is a general moral policy of trade, so to speak, which should forbid such proceedings. I maintain that they have no moral right to make such a compact. It is a compact to defraud. All moral expediency is against it; as much against it as it is against gambling in any form. It *is* gambling, and nothing else. It must be injurious if not fatal, to all benevolence—to all the purity and generosity of the character. The question really is, whether the board of trade should be brought down to the level of the gaming table.

But this moral policy of trade, in other words, this highest well-being of society, in its business, does not forbid the fair use and advantage of superior sagacity, knowledge, attention, alertness in business. The difficult question is, what is that fair use? and with reference to this I propose the other distinction; the distinction, that is to say, between knowledge and opinion. To illustrate what I mean by an instance: a man holds in his hand a lump of gold which he has taken from his mine; he, however, *supposes* it to be copper, but you *know* it to be gold: if you buy it of him as copper, you are a swindler. But now suppose the quality of the lump to be doubtful—that the question about it, is an open question between you; and suppose that you *have* better grounds for your opinion than he for his; in this case I say, you may honestly buy of him at his valuation.

This is the difference between knowledge and opinion; and although it is not easy to draw the exact line between them, yet I say that the leaning to the exercise of opinion, is the safe and right tendency;

and that the leaning to the use of absolute knowledge, is unsafe, and may go to the length of utter and heinous wrong. Let us now say something, in fine, in defence of the one, and in admonition with regard to the other.

Do we then propose to reduce the wise and the ignorant, the sagacious and the stupid, the attentive and the negligent, the active and the indolent, to the same level? Must the intelligent and the enterprising merchant raise up his dull and careless neighbour, to his own point of view, before we may deal with him? Certainly not. Let a wide field be opened, only provided that the boundaries be truth and honesty. Let the widest field for activity and freedom of action be spread, which these boundaries can enclose.

Indeed a man *must* act in trade upon some opinion. That opinion must be founded on some knowledge. And that knowledge he may properly seek. Nay, and he may use it, to any extent, not implying deception or dishonesty. Nor are the cases frequent, in which commercial operations possess any such definite or extraordinary character, as admits of deception. It does not often happen that any great advantage is, or can be taken of complete and unsuspecting ignorance. Men are wary. They will not make questionable sales, when a packet ship from abroad is in the offing. They are set to guard their own interests, and they do guard them. They must assume some responsibilities in this way; they must take some risks. They are liable to err in opinion, and they must take such chance as human imperfection ordains for them. Business, like every other scene of human life, is a theatre for imperfection, for error, for effort, for opinion, and for their results. I do not see how it can possibly be otherwise, and therefore, I consider it as appointed to be so. Undue advantage may be taken of this state of things by the selfish, grasping, and unconscientious; right principles may be wrested to the accomplishment of wrong ends; a system of commercial morality may be good for the community, and yet may be abused by individuals: all this is true; and yet the doctrine which applies everywhere else must apply here, that abuse fairly argues nothing against use.

Let us see how the case would stand if it were otherwise: let us see what the assumption on the part of the trading community, that no man should ever act in any way on superior information, would amount to. "We may sleep," they would say; "we need not take any pains to inform ourselves of the state of the markets; we need not take a step from our own door. If our neighbour come to trade with us, he must first inform us of everything affecting the price of our goods. He makes himself very busy; and he shall have his labour for his pains; for the rule now is, that indolence is to fare as well as activity, and vigilance is to have no advantage over supineness and sloth." Suppose, then, that the vigilant and active man is up betimes, and goes down upon the wharf, or to the news-room, and becomes apprized of facts that affect the price of his goods; he must not go about selling, till he has stepped into the shop of his indolent neighbour, and perhaps, of half a dozen such, to inform *them* of the state of things; for, although he does not directly trade with them, yet, by underselling or selling for more, in consequence of superior information, he injures them just as much as if he did: i. e., he takes profits out of the hands of the slothful, by acting on his superior knowledge. But now enlarge the sphere of the comparison. There is no real difference in the principle between a man's going down to the wharf, and his going to Europe, for information. And if, by superior activity, by building better ships and better manning them, he is accustomed to get earlier advices of the state of foreign markets, I see not, but as a general principle, a principle advantageous to commerce, and encouraging to human industry and ingenuity, he must be allowed to avail himself of those advices. The law of general expediency must be a law for the conscience. It is expedient that industry and attention should be rewarded, and that negligence and sloth should suffer loss. It is expedient that there should be commerce or barter; nay, it is inevitable. It is expedient, therefore, that all that sagacity, power and information, which are the result of superior talent, energy and ingenuity, should yield certain advantages to their possessor. These advantages he may push beyond the bounds of reason and justice; but we must not, on that account, be deterred from maintaining a principle which is right; a principle which is expedient and necessary for the whole community.

And is not the same principle, in fact, adopted in every department of human pursuit? Two men engage in a certain branch of manufactures. The one, by his attention and ingenuity makes discoveries in his art, and thus gains advantages over his indolent or dull neighbour. Is he obliged to impart to him his superior information? Two young men in the profession of the law, are distinguished, the one for hard study, the other for idleness. They are engaged in the same cause; and the one believes that the other is making a false point in the case. Is he obliged to go over to his brother's office, and explain to him his error; or is it not proper, rather, that both himself and his client should suffer for that error, when the cause comes to be argued in open court?

Thus much with regard to the exercise of opinion; but absolute certainty is a different thing. . And in regard to absolute certainty, how, I would ask, are we to distinguish between knowledge in regard to the real value of an article, from knowledge in regard to the real quality of an article? If I sell merchandise in which there is some secret defect, and do not expose that defect, I am held to be a dishonest man. But what matters it to my conscience, whether the secret defect lies in the article, or in the price? It comes to the same thing with my fellow dealer. If I were to sell moth-eaten cloths at four dollars per yard more than they were worth—the defect being known to me and not to my neighbour—all the world would pro nounce me a knave. But there is another sort of moth, a secret in my own keeping, which may have as effectually eaten out four dollars from every yard of that cloth, as if it had literally cut the thread of the fabric. What difference now can it make to my neighbour, whether advantage is taken of his ignorance in one way or another; in regard to the quality or the price? The only material point is the value, and that is equally affected in either case. This is the only conclusion to which I find myself able, on much reflection, to arrive. Knowledge of prices is as material to the value of merchandise, as knowledge of its qualities. This knowledge, therefore, as it appears to me, should be common to all contracting parties. I cannot think that a trader is to be like a fisher, disguising his hook with bait; or like a slight-of-hand man, cheating men out of their senses and money with a face of gravity; or like an Indian, shooting from behind a bush, himself in no danger. Trade, traffic, contracts, bargains—all these words imply parity, equivalency, common risk, mutual advantage.

And he who can arrange a commercial operation, by which he is *certain* to realize great profits and to inflict great losses, is a taker of merchandise, but can hardly be said to be a trader in it.

I am sensible that this is the nice and difficult point in the whole discussion. But, I put it to the calm reflection and to the consciences of my hearers, whether they would not feel easier in their business, if all use of superior and certain knowledge, were entirely excluded from it. Long as this use has obtained, and warmly as it is sometimes defended, yet I ask, if the moral sentiments of the trading community itself, would not be relieved by giving it up? This, if it be true, is certainly a weighty consideration. I admit, indeed, as I have before done, that no vague sentiment is to settle the question. But when I find that there is even in vague sentiment, something like a hook that holds the mind in suspense, or will not let the mind be satisfied with departure from it, that circumstance deserves, I think, to arrest attention. I will frankly confess, that my own mind has been in this very situation. I did not see at one time, how the case of general information and opinion which it is lawful to use, could be separated from the case of particular knowledge. But I now entertain a different, and a more decided opinion. And the consider a tion, with me, which has changed uneasiness into doubt, and doubt into a new, and as I think, correct judgment, is that which I have last stated; it is the consideration, that is to say, of the *very nature of a contract.* A contract does *not* imply equal powers, equal general information, equal shrewdness in the contracting parties; but it does imply, as it appears to me, equal actual knowledge; an equal participation, that is to say, in whatever can claim the character of *certainty* in the case. My neighbour may think himself superior to me in all other respects, and he may tell me so, and yet I will trade with him; we still stand upon ground that I am willing to consider equal. But let him tell me that he *knows* something touching the manufacture, quality, condition, or relations of the article to be sold, which I do not know, and which affects the value of the article; and I stop upon the threshold; we cannot traffic; there may be a game of hazard which he and I consent to play; but there is an end of all trading. If this be true, then the condition of a regular and lawful contract is, that there be no secrets in it; no secrets, either in the kind or quality of the merchandise, or in the breast, or in the pocket of the dealer. Let them all be swept away; let them be swept out, all secrets from all hiding-places, from all coverts of subterfuge and chicanery; and this, at least, I am certain of, that business would occasion fewer wounds of conscience, to all honourable and virtuous communities.

APPENDIX TO THE FOREGOING DISCOURSE.

Some remarks upon the foregoing discourse, which had reached the author's ear during the weekly interval, before the delivery of the next discourse, led him, in entering upon it, to offer the following observations.

It may be thought, that in my discourse of the last Sunday evening, I have leaned to a view of the principles of trade, which is too indulgent to its questionable practices. I am most anxious to guard against such an inference; and yet I must hesitate to yield exactly to the tone of objection which may possibly be adopted by some of my hearers. The pulpit is not to speak any peculiar language on this subject, because it is the pulpit. The language of truth is what we seek; the language which would be true anywhere. Neither is the pulpit to be looked upon as a post of duty, which is to serve only the purpose of assault, whose business it is to assail any particular class of persons, merchants or others; nor is the church a proper place for men to come to, in order to enjoy the gratification of seeing other men attacked. Nor is it the only business of the moral teacher, to denounce the sins of a violated conscience; it is sometimes quite as important to defend weak consciences. Nothing can be worse for a man than to act upon a principle of which he doubts the correctness. He is then doing wrong, even when the *thing* he does, may be right. His conscience becomes weakened by wounds without cause; it is floating on a sea of doubt, and may be borne far beyond the bounds of rectitude. It is thus, that there arises in a community, a general and pernicious habit of paltering with conscience, of talking about certain principles as very good in theory, but as impracticable in fact, of slurring over the Christian rule with inuendoes, of commending it, indeed, and in a sort; but how? Why, of treacherously commending it, with those ironical praises, and ambiguous hints, and knowing glances of eye, which more effectually than any thing else, break down all principle

On the contrary, let us come out fairly and establish the true doctrine, on independent grounds, with fair reasoning, without any bias against men of business or for them, and then shall we stand upon the stable basis of conscience and principle, and be able to define its boundaries If it be expedient and inevitable, that men should, in business as in every thing else, act to a certain extent, upon their own superior sagacity, power and information, let us plainly say so; and then let us faithfully warn them against going too far. Now, nobody doubts, I presume, that they may go too far; that the man of sagacity may overreach an idiot; that the monopolist and the usurer may abuse his power; and that he who possesses superior information may dishonestly and cruelly use it. And, therefore, it was less necessury to insist upon these points, than it was to discuss the great question, and the only question; viz., whether these advantages may be used at all. If they may not be used at all, then all commerce, in its actual, and I think, inevitable procedures, is a system of knavery. If it is not a system of knavery, then it is important to defend it from that charge. And it is the more important, because, against merchants, from their acquiring greater wealth probably, there are peculiar prejudices in the community. The manufacturer may use his superior information—his particular invention; that is, he may get a patent for it, i. e., a monoply and every other profession may do substantially the same thing, and not a word is said against it. But if the merchant does this, he is called into serious question. And influenced by this general distrust, he calls himself in question too. But unfortunately for him, instead of thinking deeply upon the matter, and settling himself upon some foundation of general principle, he is liable to give himself up to the suggestions of temporary expediency. He is not quite satisfied, perhaps, with what he is doing, and yet, he says, that he must do it, or he cannot get along; a way of reasoning that I hold to be most injurious to his character. Let him then, I say, settle some just principle, and conscientiously act upon it.

They are general principles, I must desire you to observe, which I have attempted to establish. The questions that arise upon the application of these principles are, of course, numerous and complicated. I could not enter into all of them. My inexperience disqualified me. And besides, it was impossible to meet the questions of every man's mind.

I must add, in fine, that in defending the right in trade, the impression upon the popular ear, may naturally enough have been, that I have not sufficiently considered the wrong. The wrong, let me observe here, will properly come under our consideration in another place. What I say now is, that if the principles which I have laid down, have seemed to any one to verge towards an undue license, I must most earnestly protest against his inference. That very license, I say, is the point to which the principle shall not go. And I say more explicitly, that although the vender of any goods is not bound to assist the buyer with his judgment, yet that he is bound to point out any latent defect, and he is bound, by the general trust reposed in him on that point, to sell at the market price; and again, that monopoly, whether of money or other commodities, although it must inevitably raise the prices, although it must be governed in all ordinary cases by the market value, yet when it can control the market price, is bound to use its power with moderation; and finally, that he who acts upon superior information, though he may lawfully do so, shall not press his advantage to the extent of any fraudulent use, or to the infliction of any gross and undeserved injury; that he shall not press it further than is necessary, reasonably to reward vigilance and admonish indolence; that he shall not press it further than the wholesome action of trade, and the true welfare of the whole community requires.

XI.

ON THE MORAL END OF BUSINESS.

THERE IS GOLD AND A MULTITUDE OF RUBIES, BUT THE LIPS OF KNOWLEDGE (*i. e. of rectitude,*) ARE A PRECIOUS JEWEL.—Proverbs xx. 15.

My subject this evening, is the moral end of business. Let me first attempt to define my meaning in the use of this phrase; the moral end of business.

It is not the end for which property should be sought. It is not the moral purpose to be answered by the acquisition, but by the process of acquisition. And again, it is not the end of industry in general—that is a more comprehensive subject; but it is the end of business in particular, of barter, of commerce. "The end of business?" some one may say, "why, the end of business is to obtain property; the end of the process of acquisition is acquisition." If I addressed any person whose mind had not gone behind that ready and obvious answer to ultimate and deeper reasons, I should venture to say, that a revelation is to be made to him, of a more exalted aim in business, of a higher, and at the same time, more perilous scene of action in its pursuits, than he has yet imagined. In other words, I hold that the ultimate end of all business is a moral end. I believe that business—I mean not labour but barter, traffic—would never have existed, if there had been no end but sustenance. The animal races obtain subsistence upon an easier and simpler plan; but for man there is a higher end, and that is moral.

The broad grounds of this position I find in the obvious designs of Providence, and in the evident adaptation to this moral end, of business itself.

There is, then, a design for which all things were made and ordained, going beyond the things themselves. To say that things were made, or that the arrangements and relations of things were ordained, for their own sake, is a proposition without meaning. The world, its structure, productions, laws and events, have no good nor evil in them; none, but as they produce these results, in the experience of living creatures. The end, then, of the inanimate creation, is the welfare of the living, and therefore especially, of the intelligent creation. But the welfare of human beings lies essentially in their moral culture. All is wrong everywhere, if all is not right there. All of design that there is in this lower creation, presses upon that point. The universe is a moral chaos without that design, and it is a moral desolation to every mind in which that design is not accomplished. Life, then, has an ultimate purpose. We are not appointed to pass through this life, barely that we may live. We are not impelled, both by disposition and necessity, to buy and sell, barely that we may do it; nor to get gain, barely that we may get it. There is an end in business beyond supply. There is an object, in the acquisition of wealth, beyond success. There is a final cause of human traffic: and that is virtue.

With this view of the moral end of business, falls in the constant doctrine of all elevated philosophy and true religion. Life, say the expounders of every creed, is a probation. The circumstances in which we are placed; the events, the scenes of our mortal lot; the bright visions that cheer us, the dark clouds that overshadow us; all these are not an idle show, nor do they exist for themselves alone, nor because they must exist by the fiat of some blind chance; but they have a purpose; and that purpose is expressed in the word, probation. Now, if any thing deserves to be considered as a part of that probation, it is business. Life, say the wise, is a school. In this school there are lessons; toil is a lesson; trial is a lesson; and business, too, is a lesson. But the end of a lesson is, that something be learned. And the end of business is, that truth, rectitude, virtue, be learned. This is the ultimate design proposed by Heaven; and it is a design which every wise man, engaged in that calling, will propose to himself. It is no extravagance, therefore, but the simple assertion of a truth, to say to a man so engaged, and to say emphatically, "You have an end to gain beyond success; and that is the moral rectitude of your own mind."

That business is so exquisitely adapted to accomplish that purpose, is another argument with me to prove that such in the intention of its Ordainer, was its design. I can conceive that things might have been ordered otherwise; that human beings might have been formed for industry, and not for traffic. I can conceive man and nature to have been so constituted, that each individual should, by solitary labour, have drawn from the earth his sustenance; and that a vesture softer, richer, and more graceful than is ever wrought in the looms of our manufactories, might have been woven upon his body, by the same invisible hands that have thus clothed the beasts of the desert and the birds of the air, and the lilies of the field; so that Solomon in all his glory was not arrayed like one of them. Then might man have held only the sweet counsel of society with his fellow, and never been called to engage with him in the strife of business.

Then, too, would he have been saved from all the dangers and vices of human traffic. But then, too, would the lofty virtues cultivated in this sphere of life, never have had an existence. For business, I repeat, is admirably adapted to form such virtues. It is apt, I know it is said, to corrupt men; but the truth is, it corrupts only those who are willing to be corrupted. An honest man, a man who sincerely desires to attain to a lofty and unbending uprightness, could scarcely seek a discipline more perfectly fitted to that end, than the discipline of trade. For what is trade? It is the constant adjustment of the claims of different parties, a man's self being one of the parties. This competition of rights and interests might not invade the solitary study, or the separate tasks of the work-shop, or the labors of the silent field, once a day; but it presses upon the merchant and trader continually. Do you say that it presses too hard? Then I reply, must the sense of rectitude be made the stronger to meet the trial. Every plea of this nature is an argument for strenuous moral effort. Shall I be told that the questions which often arise are very perplexing; that the case to be decided comes, oftentimes, not under a definite rule but under a general principle, whose very generality is perilous to the conscience? It is indeed. Here, perhaps, lies the great peril of business; in the generality of the rule. For conscience does not in most cases definitely say, "thou shalt do this thing, and thou shalt do that." It says always, "thou shalt do right," but what that is, is not always clear. And hence it is, that a man may take care to offend against no definite remonstrance of conscience, and that he may be in the common acceptation, an honest man; and yet, that he may be a selfish, exacting and oppressive man; a man who can never recognize the rights and interests of others; who can never see any thing but on the side that is favourable to himself; who drowns the voice of his modest neighbour, with always and loudly saying, "Oh! this is right, and that can't be;" a man, in fine, who, although he seldom, perhaps never offends against any assignable or definite precept of conscience, has swerved altogether from all uprightness and generosity. What then is to be done? A work, I answer, of the most ennobling character. A man must do more than to attain to punctilious honesty in his actions; he must train his whole soul, his judgment, his sentiments, his affections, to uprightness, candour and good will.

In fine, I look upon business as one vast scene of moral action. "The thousand wheels of commerce," with all their swift and complicated revolutions, I regard as an immense moral machinery. Meanness and cunning may lurk amidst it, but it was not designed for that degradation. That must be a noble scene of action, where conscience is felt to be a law. And it is felt to be the law of business; its very violations prove it such. It is the enthroned sovereign of the plan; disobedience, disloyalty, give attestation to it. Nothing is too holy to connect with it. There is a temple in one of the cities of Europe, through which is the very passage to the market-place; and those who pass there, often rest their burthens, to turn aside and kneel at the altar of prayer. So were it meet that all men should enter upon their daily business. The temple of mammon, should be the temple of God. The gates of trade should be as the entrance to the sanctuary of conscience. There is an eye of witnessing and searching scrutiny fixed upon every one of its doings. The presence of that all-seeing One, not confined, as some imagine, to the silent church or the solitary grove—the presence of God, I think it not too solemn to say, is in every counting-room and warehouse of yonder mart, and ought to make it holy ground.

I have thus attempted to show that business has an ultimate, moral end ; one going beyond the accumulation of property.

This may also be shown to be true, not only on the scale of our private affairs, but on the great theatre of history. Commerce has always been an instrument in the hands of Providence, for accomplishing nobler ends than promoting the wealth of nations. It has been the grand civilizer of nations. It has been the active principle in all civilization. Or to speak more accurately, it has presented that condition of things, in which civilization has always rapidly advanced, and without which, it never has. The principles of civilization, properly speaking, are the principles of humanity ; the natural desire of knowledge, liberty and refinement. But commerce seems to have been the germ, the original spring, that has put all other springs in action. Liberty has always followed its steps ; and with liberty, science and religion have gradually advanced and improved ; and never without it. All those kingdoms of central Asia, and of Europe too, which commerce has never penetrated, have been and are, despotisms. With its earliest birth on the Mediterranean shore, freedom was born. Phœnicia, the merchants of whose cities, Tyre and Sidon, were accounted princes ; the Hebrew commonwealth, which carried on a trade through those ports ; the Grecian, Carthaginian and Roman States, were not only the freest, but they were the only free states of antiquity. In the middle ages, commerce broke down in Europe the feudal system, raising up in the

Hanse Towns throughout Germany, Sweden and Norway, a body of men who were able to cope with barons and kings, and to wrest from them, their free charters and rightful privileges. In England, its influence is proverbial; the sheet-anchor it has long been considered, of her unequalled prosperity and intelligence. On our own happy shores, it has a still more unobstructed field, and is destined, I trust, to spread over the whole breadth of our interior domain, wealth, cultivation and refinement.

Its influences upon individual character are the only ones of which we stand in any doubt, and these, it need not be said, are of unequalled importance. The philanthropist, the Christian, the Christian preacher, are all bound to watch these influences with the closest attention, and to do all in their power to guard and elevate them. To this work I am attempting to contribute my humble part; and I conceive, that I have now come to the grand principle of safety and improvement, viz., that trade is essentially a *moral business;* that it has a moral end more important than success; that the attainment of this end is better than the acquisition of weath, and that the failure of it, is worse than any commercial failure; worse than bankruptcy, poverty, ruin.

It is upon this point that I wish especially to insist; but there are one or two topics, that may previously claim some attention.

If, then, business is a moral dispensation, and its highest end is moral, I shall venture to call in question the commonly supposed desirableness of escaping from it; the idea which prevails with so many of making a fortune in a few years, and afterwards of retiring to a state of leisure. If business really is a scene of worthy employment and of high moral action, I do not see why the moderate pursuit of it should not be laid down in the plan of entire active life; and why upon this plan, a man should not determine to give only so much time each day to his avocations, as would be compatible with such a plan; only so much time, in other words, as will be compatible with the daily enjoyment of life, with reading, society, domestic intercourse, and all the duties of philanthropy and devotion. If the merchant does not dislike or despise his employment—and it is when he makes himself the mere slave of business, that he creates the greatest real objections to it—if, I say, he looks upon his employment as lawful and laudable, an appointment of God to accomplish good purposes in this world and better for the next; why should he not, like the physician, the lawyer and clergyman, like the husbandman and artisan, continue in it, through the period of active life; and adjust his views, expectations and engagements to that reasonable plan? But now, instead of this, what do we see around us? Why, men are engaging in business—here, at home, in their own country, in the bosom of their families and amidst their friends—as if they were in a foreign and infectious clime; and must be in haste to make their fortunes, that they may escape with their lives to some place of safety, ease and enjoyment!

And now, what sort of preparation for retirement is this life, absorbed in business? It is precisely that sort of preparation that unfits a man for retirement. Nothing will work well or agreeable in experience, which has not some foundation in previous habits and practice. But for all those things which are to be a man's resources in retirement, his previous life, perhaps, has given him not a moment of time. He has really no rural tastes; for he has scarcely seen the country for years, except on hurried journeys of business; the busy wheels of commerce now, alas! roll through the year, and he is chained to them every month. He has made no acquaintance with the fine arts. He has cultivated no habits of reading; and—what I hold to be just as fatal to the happiness of any life, retired or active—he has cultivated no habits of devotion. Add to all this, that he is thrown upon the dangerous state of luxurious leisure—that prepared, enriched, productive hot-bed of prurient imaginations and teeming passions—without any guards against its moral perils. And what is likely to be the consequence? He will become perhaps an indolent and bloated sensualist, cumbering the beautiful grounds, on which he vegetates rather than lives; or, from the violent change of his habits, you will soon hear, perhaps, that he is dead; or he may live on in weariness and ennui, wishing in his heart, that he were back again, though it were to take his place behind the counter of the humblest shop.

I do not pretend, of course, that I am portraying the case of every man, who is proposing to retire from business. There *are* those, doubtless, whose views of retiring are reasonable and praiseworthy; who do not propose to escape from all employment; who are living religiously and virtuously *in the midst* of their business, and not unwisely intending to make up for the deficiency of those qualities in retirement; who wish to improve and beautify some pleasant rural abode, and thus, and in many other ways, to be useful to the country around them. To such a retirement, I have nothing to object: and I only venture to suggest, as an obvious dictate of good sense, that he who proposes, some day, to retire from business, should in the meantime, cultivate those qualities and habits, which will make him happy in retirement. But this I also say, that I do more than doubt, whether any man who is completely engrossed in business, from morning till night, for twenty or thirty years, can be prepared to enjoy or improve a life of leisure.

Another topic, of which I wish to speak, is the rage for speculation. I wish to speak of it now in a particular view; as interfering, that is to say, with the moral end of business. And here, again, let me observe, that I can have nothing to do with instances, with exceptions. I can only speak of the general tendency of things. And it is not against *speculation simply*, that I have any thing to allege. All business possesses more or less of this character. Every thing is bought on the expectation of selling it for more. But this *rage* for speculation, this eagerness of many for sudden and stupendous accumulation, this spirit of gambling in trade, is a different thing. It proceeds on principles entirely different from the maxims of a regular and pains-taking business. It is not looking to diligence and fidelity for a fair reward, but to change and chance for a fortunate turn. It is drawing away men's minds from the healthful processes of sober industry and attention to business, and leading them to wait in feverish excitement, as at the wheel of a lottery. The proper basis of success, vigilant care and labour, is forsaken for a system of baseless credit. Upon this system men proceed, straining their means and stretching their responsibilities, till in calm times they can scarcely hold on upon their position; and when a sudden jar shakes the commercial world, or a sudden blast sweeps over it, many fall like untimely fruit, from the towering tree of fancied prosperity. Upon this system, many imagine that they are doing well, when they are not doing well. They rush into expenses, which they cannot afford, upon the strength, not of their actual, but of their imaginary or expected means. Young men, who in former days, would have been advised to walk awhile longer, and patiently to tread the upward path, must buy horses and vehicles for their accommodation; and mounted upon the car of fancied independence, they are hurried only to swifter destruction.

This system of rash and adventurous speculation, overlooks all the moral uses and ends of business. To do business and get gain, honestly and conscientiously, is a good thing. It is a useful discipline of the character. I look upon a man who has acquired wealth, in a laudable, conscientious and generous pursuit of business, not only with a respect far beyond what I can feel for his wealth—for which indeed, abstractly, I can feel none at all—but with the distinct feeling that he has acquired something far more valuable than opulence. But for this discipline of the character, for the reasonableness and rectitude of mind which a regular business intercourse may form, speculation furnishes but a narrow field, if any at all; such speculation, I mean, as has lately created a popular phrenzy in this country about the sudden acquisition of property. The game which men were playing was too rapid, and the stake too large, to admit of the calm discriminations of conscience, and the reasonable contemplation of moral ends. Wealth came to be looked upon as the only end. And immediate wealth, was the agitating prize. Men could not wait for the slow and disciplinary methods, by which Providence designed that they should acquire it; but they felt as if it were the order of Providence, that fortunes should fall direct from heaven into their open hands. Rather, should we not say, that multitudes did not look to heaven at all, but to speculation itself, instead, as if it were a god, or some wonder-working magician at least, that was suddenly to endow them with opulence. Acquisition became the story of an Arabian tale; and men's minds were filled with romantic schemes, and visionary hopes, and vain longings, rather than with sobriety, and candour, and moderation, and gratitude, and trust in Heaven.

This insane and insatiable passion for accumulation, ever ready when circumstances favour, to seize upon the public mind, is that "love of money which is the root of all evil," that "covetousness which is idolatry." It springs from an undue, an idolatrous estimate of the value of property. Many are feeling, that nothing—nothing will do for them or for their children, but wealth; not a good character, not well-trained and well exerted faculties, not virtue, not the hope of heaven; nothing but wealth. It is their god, and the god of their families. Their sons are growing up to the same worship of it, and to an equally baneful reliance upon it for the future; they are rushing into expenses which the divided property of their father's house will not enable them to sustain; and they are preparing to be in turn and from necessity, slaves to the same idol. How truly is it written, that "they that *will* be rich, fall into temptation, and a snare, and into many foolish and hurtful lusts, which drown men in destruction and perdition!" There is no need that they should be rich; but they *will* be rich. All the noblest functions of life may be discharged without wealth, all its highest honours obtained, all its purest pleasures enjoyed; yet I repeat it, nothing—nothing will do but wealth. Disappoint a man of this, and he mourns as if the highest end of life were defeated. Strip him of this: and this gone, all is gone. Strip him of this and I shall point to no unheard-of experience, when I say, he had rather die than live!

The grievous mistake, the mournful evil implied in this oversight of the great spiritual end, which should be sought in all earthly pursuits, is the subject to which I wished to draw your attention in the last place. It is not merely in the haste to be rich, accompanied with the intention to retire from business to a state of luxurious and self-indulgent leisure; it is not merely in the rage for speculation, that the evils of overlooking the moral aim of business are seen; but they sink deep into the heart, in the ordinary walks of regular and daily occupation; dethroning the spiritual nature from its proper place, vitiating the affections, and losing some of the noblest opportunities for virtue, that can be lost on earth.

The spiritual nature, I say, is dethroned from its proper place, by this substitution of the immediate end, wealth, for the ultimate end, virtue. Who is this being, that labours for nothing but property; with no thought beyond it; with the feeling that nothing will do without it; with the feeling that there are no ends in life that can satisfy him, if that end is not gained? You will not tell me, that it is a being of my own fancy. You have probably known such; perhaps, some of you are such. I have known men of this way of thinking; and men, too, of sense and of amiable temper. Who then, I ask again, is this being? He is an immortal being; and his views ought to stretch themselves to eternity—ought to seek an ever-expanding good. And this being, so immortal in his nature, so infinite in faculties; to what is he looking? To the sublime mountain range, that spreads along the horizon of this world? To the glorious host of glittering stars, the majestic train of night, the infinite regions of heaven? No; his is no upward gaze, no wide vision of the world; to a speck of earthly dust he is looking. He might lift his eye, a philosophic eye, to the magnificence of the universe, for an object; and upon what is it fixed? Upon the mole-hill beneath his feet! That is his end. Every thing is naught, if that is gone. He is an immortal being, I repeat; he may be enrobed in that vesture of light, of virtue, which never shall decay; and he is to live through such ages, that the time shall come when to his eye all the splendours of fortune, of gilded palace and gorgeous equipage, shall be no more than the spangle that falls from a royal robe; and yet, in that glittering particle of earthly dust, is his soul absorbed and bound up. I am not saying, *now*, that he is willing to lose his soul for that. This he may do. But I only say now, that he sets his soul upon that, and feels it to be an end so dear, that the irretrievable loss of it, the doom of poverty, is death to him; nay, to his sober and deliberate judgment—for I have known such instances—is worse than death itself! And yet he is an immortal being, I repeat; and he is sent into this world on an errand? What errand? What is the great mission on which the Master of life hath sent him here? To get riches? To amass gold coins, and bank notes? To scrape together a little of the dust of this earth; and then to lie down upon it and embrace it, in the indolence of enjoyment, or in the rapture of possession? Is such worldliness possible? Worldliness! Why, it is not worldliness. That should be the quality of being attached to a world; to all that it can give, and not to one thing only that it can give; to fame, to power, to moral power, to influence, to the admiration of the world. Worldliness, methinks, should be something greater than men make it, should stretch itself out to the breadth of the great globe, and not wind itself up like a worm in the web of selfish possession. If I must be worldly, let me have the worldliness of Alexander, and not of Crœsus. And wealth too; I had thought it was a means and not an end; an instrument which a noble human being handles, and not a heap of shining dust in which he buries himself; something that a man could drop from his hand, and still be a man, be all that he ever was, and compass all the noble ends that pertain to a human being. What if you be poor? Are you not still a man—Oh, heaven! and mayest be a spirit, and have a universe of spiritual possessions for your treasure. What if you be poor? You may still walk through the world in freedom and in joy. You may still tread the glorious path of virtue. You may still win the bright prize of immortality. You may still achieve purposes on earth that constitute all the glory of earth; and ends in heaven, that constitute all the glory of heaven! Nay, if such must be the effect of wealth, I would say, let me be poor. I would pray God that I might be poor! Rather, and more wisely ought I, perhaps, to say with Agur, "give me neither poverty nor riches; lest I be full and deny thee, and say, who is the Lord? or lest I be poor, and steal, and take the name of my God in vain."

The many corrupting and soul-destroying vices engendered in the mind by this lamentable oversight of the spiritual aim in business, deserves a separate and solemn consideration.

I believe that you will not accuse me of any disposition to press unreasonable charges against men of business. I cannot possibly let the pulpit throw burthens of responsibility, or warnings of danger on this sphere of life, as if others were not in their measure open to similar admonitions. I come not here to make war upon any particular class. I pray you not to regard this pulpit as holding any relation to you, but that of a faithful and Christian friend, or as having any interest in the world connected with business, but your own true interest. Above all things do I deprecate that worldly and most pernicious habit of hearing and approving very good things in the pulpit, and going away, and calmly doing very bad things in the world, as if the two had no real connection; that habit of listening to the admonitions and rebukes of the pulpit with a sort of demure respect, or with significant glances at your neighbours, and then of going away, commending the doctrine with your lips, to violate it in your lives; as if you said, "well, the pulpit has acted its part, and now we will go and act ours." I act no part here. God forbid! I endeavour to be reasonable and just, in what I say here. I take no liberty to be extravagant in this place, because I cannot be answered. I hold myself solemnly bound to say nothing recklessly and for effect. I occupy here no isolated position. I am continually thinking what my hearers will fairly have to say on their part, and striving fairly to meet it. I speak to you simply as one man may speak to another, as soul may speak to its brother soul; and I solemnly and affectionately say, what I would have you say to me in a change of place; I say that the pursuits of business are perilous to your virtue.

On this subject, I cannot, indeed, speak with the language of experience. But I cannot forget that the voice of all moral instruction, in all ages and in all countries, is a voice of warning. I cannot forget that the voice of Holy Scripture falls in solemn accents upon the perils attending the pursuit of wealth. How solemn, how strong, how pertinent those accents are,

I may not know; but I must not, for that reason withhold them. "Wo unto you who are rich," said the holy word, "for ye have not received your consolation. Wo unto you that are full, for ye shall hunger." Hunger? What hath wealth to do with hunger? And yet there is a hunger. What is it? What can it be but the hungering of the soul; and that is the point which, in this discourse, I press upon your attention. And again it says, "your riches are corrupted; your gold and silver is cankered:" and is it not cankered in the very hearts of those whom wealth has made proud, vain, anxious and jealous, or self-indulgent, sensual, diseased and miserable? "And the rust of them," so proceeds the holy text, "shall be a witness against you, and shall eat your flesh as it were fire." Ah! the rust of riches! not that portion of them which is kept bright in good and holy uses—"and the consuming fire" of the passions which wealth engenders! No rich man—I lay it down as an axiom of all experience—no rich man is safe, who is not a benevolent man. No rich man is safe, but in the imitation of that benevolent God, who is the possessor and dispenser of all the riches of the universe. What else mean the miseries of a selfishly luxurious and fashionable life everywhere? What mean the sighs that come up from the purlieus, and couches, and most secret haunts of all splendid and self-indulgent opulence? Do not tell me that other men are sufferers too. Say not that the poor, and destitute and forlorn, are miserable also. Ah! just heaven! thou hast in thy mysterious wisdom, appointed to them a lot hard, full hard to bear. Poor houseless wretches! who "eat the bitter bread of penury, and drink the baleful cup of misery;" the winter's wind blows keenly through your "looped and windowed raggedness;"

your children wander about unshod, unclothed and untended; I wonder not that ye sigh. But why should those who are surrounded with everything that heart can wish, or imagination conceive; the very crumbs that fall from whose table of prosperity might feed hundreds; why should they sigh amidst their profusion and splendour? *They have broken the bond that should connect power with usefulness, and opulence with mercy.* That is the reason. They have taken up their treasures, and wandered away into a forbidden world of their own, far from the sympathies of suffering humanity; and the heavy night-dews are descending upon their splendid revels; and the all-gladdening light of heavenly beneficence is exchanged for the sickly glare of selfish enjoyment; and happiness, the blessed angel that hovers over generous deeds and heroic virtues, has fled away from that world of false gaiety and fashionable exclusion.

I have, perhaps, wandered, a moment from the point before me, the peril of business; though as business is usually aiming at wealth, I may be considered rather as having only pressed that point to some of its ultimate bearings.

But the peril of business specifically considered; and I ask, if there is not good ground for the admonitions on this point, of every moral and holy teacher of every age? What means, if there is not, that eternal disingenuity of trade, that is ever putting on fair appearances and false pretences; of "the buyer that says, it is naught, it is naught, but when he is gone his way, then boasteth;" of the seller, who is always exhibiting the best samples, not fair but false samples, of what he has to sell; of the seller, I say, who, to use the language of another, "if he is tying up a bundle of quills, will place several in the centre, of not half the value of the rest, and thus sends forth a hundred liars, with a fair outside, to proclaim as many falsehoods to the world?" These practices, alas! have fallen into the regular course of the business of many. All men expect them; and therefore, you may say, that nobody is deceived. But deception is intended: else why are these things done? What if nobody is deceived? The seller himself is corrupted. He may stand acquitted of dishonesty in the moral code of worldly traffic; no man may charge him with dishonesty; and yet to himself he is a dishonest man. Did I say that nobody is deceived! Nay, but somebody is deceived. This man, the seller, is grossly, wofully deceived. He thinks to make a little profit by his contrivances; and he is selling, by penny-worths', the very integrity of his soul. Yes the pettiest shop where these things are done, may be to the spiritual vision, a place of more than tragic interest. It is the stage on which the great action of life is performed. There stands a man, who in the sharp collisions of daily traffic might have polished his mind to the bright and beautiful image of truth, who might have put on the noble brow of candour and cherished the very soul of uprightness. I have known such a man. I have looked into his humble shop. I have seen the mean and soiled articles with which he is dealing. And yet the process of things going on there, was as beautiful, as if it had been done in heaven! But now, what is this man, the man who always turns up to you the better side of everything he sells, the man of unceasing contrivances and expedients, his life long, to make things appear better than they are? Be he the greatest merchant or the poorest huckster, he is a mean, a knavish—and were I not awed by the thoughts of his great and solemn nature, I should say

—a contemptible creature; whom nobody that knows him can love, whom nobody can trust, whom nobody can reverence. Not one thing in the dusty repository of things, great or small, which he deals with, is so vile as he. What *is* this *thing* then, which is done, or may be done in the house of traffic? I tell you, though you may have thought not so of it; I tell you that *there*, even *there*, a soul may be lost; that that very structure, built for the gain of earth, may be the gate of hell! Say not that this fearful appellation should be applied to worse places than that. A man may as certainly corrupt all the integrity and virtue of his soul in a warehouse or a shop, as in a gambling-house or house of darker infamy.

False to himself, then, may a man become, while he is walking through the perilous courses of traffic; false also to his *neighbour*. I cannot dwell much upon this topic; but I will put one question; not for reproach, but for your sober consideration. Must it not render a man extremely liable to be selfish, that he is engaged in pursuits whose immediate and palpable end, is his own interest? I wish to draw your attention to this peculiarity of trade. I do not say, that the motives which originally induce a man to enter into the sphere of life, may not be as benevolent as those of any other man; but this is the point which I wish to have considered; that while the learned professions have knowledge for their immediate object, and the artist and the artisan have the perfection of their work as the thing that directly engages their attention, the merchant and trader have for their immediate object, profit. Does not this circumstance greatly expose a man to be selfish? Full well I know that many are not so; that many resist and overcome this influence; but I think that it *is* to be resisted.

And a wise man, who more deeply dreads the taint of inward selfishness than of outward dishonour, will take care to set up counter influences. And to this end, he should beware how he clenches his hand and closes his heart against the calls of suffering, the dictates of public spirit, and the claims of beneficence. To listen to them is, perhaps, his very salvation!

But the vitiating process of business may not stop with selfishness; it is to be contemplated in still another and higher light. For how possible is it, that a man while engaged in exchanging and diffusing the bounties of heaven, while all countries and climes are pouring their blessings at his feet, while he lawfully deals with not one instrument, in mind or matter, but it was formed and fitted to his use by a beneficent hand; how possible it is that he may forget and forsake the Being who has given him all things! How possible is it, that under the very accumulation of his blessings may be buried all his gratitude and piety; that he may be too busy to pray, too full to be thankful, too much engrossed with the gifts to think of the Giver! The humblest giver expects some thanks; he would think it a lack of ordinary human feeling in any one, to snatch at his bounties, without casting a look on the bestower; he would gaze in astonishment at such heedless ingratitude and rapacity, and almost doubt whether the creatures he helped could be human. Are they any more human; do they any more deserve the name of men, when the object of such perverse and senseless ingratitude is the Infinite Benefactor? Would we know what aspect it bears before his eye? Once, and more than once, hath that Infinite Benefactor spoken. I listen, and tremble as I listen, to that lofty adjuration, with which the sublime prophet hath set forth *His* contemplation of the ingratitude of his creatures. "Hear, O heavens, and give ear, O earth! for the Lord hath spoken; I have nourished and brought up children, and they have rebelled against me. The ox knoweth his owner, and the ass his master's crib; but Israel doth not know; my people do not consider." Sad and grievous error even in the eye of reason! Great default even to nature's religion? But if thou art a Christian man, what law shall acquit thee, if that heavy charge lies at thy door; at the door of thy warehouse; at the door of thy dwelling! Beware, lest thou forget God in his mercies! the Giver in his gifts! lest the light be gone from thy prosperity, and prayer from thy heart, and the love of thy neighbour from the labours of thy calling, and the hope of heaven from the abundance of thine earthly estate!

But not with words of warning, ever painful to use, and not always profitable, would I now dismiss you from the house of God. I would not close this discourse, in which I may seem to have pressed heavily on the evils to which business exposes those who are engaged in it, without holding up distinctly to view the great moral aim on which it is my main purpose to insist, and attempting to show its excellence.

There is such a nobleness of character in the right course, that it is to that point I would last direct your attention. The aspirings of youth, the ambition of manhood, could receive no loftier moral direction than may be found in the sphere of business. The school of trade, with all its dangers, may be made one of the noblest schools of virtue in the world; and it is of some importance to say it: because those who regard it as a sphere only of selfish interests and sordid calculations, are certain to win no lofty moral prizes in that school. There can be nothing more fatal to ele vation of character in any sphere, whether it be oi business or society, than to speak habitually of that sphere as given over to low aims and pursuits. If business is constantly spoken of as contracting the mind and corrupting the heart; if the pursuit of property is universally satirized as selfish and grasping; too many who engage in it will think of nothing but of adopting the character and the course so pointed out. Many causes have contributed, without doubt, to establish that disparaging estimate of business; the spirit of feudal aristocracies, the pride of learning, the tone of literature, and the faults of business itself.

I say, therefore, that there is no being in the world for whom I feel a higher moral respect and admiration, than for the upright man of business; no, not for the philanthropist, the missionary, or the martyr. I feel that I could more easily be a martyr, than a man of that lofty moral uprightness. And let me say yet more distinctly, that it is not for the generous man, that I feel this kind of respect; that seems to me a lower quality, a mere impulse, compared with the lofty virtue I speak of. It is not for the man who distributes extensive charities, who bestows magnificent donations. That may be all very well; I speak not to disparage it; I wish there were more of it; and yet it may all consist with a want of the true, lofty, unbending uprightness. That is not the man then, of whom I speak; but it is he whc stands, amidst all the swaying interests and perilous exigencies of trade, firm, calm, disinterested and upright. It is the man, who can see another man's interests, just as clearly as his own. It is the man whose mind, his own advantage does not blind nor cloud for an instant; who could sit a judge, upon a question between himself and his neighbour, just as safely, as the purest magistrate upon the bench of justice. Ah! how much richer than ermine, how far nobler than the train of magisterial authority, how more awful than the guarded bench of majesty, is that simple, magnanimous and majestic truth. Yes, it is the man who is true; true to himself, to his neighbour and to his God; true to the right —true to his conscience; and who feels, that the slightest suggestion of that conscience, is more to him than the chance of acquiring a hundred estates.

Do I not speak to some such one now? Stands there not here, some man of such glorious virtue, of such fidelity to truth and to God? Good friend! I call upon you to hold fast to that integrity, as the dearest treasure of existence. Though storms of commercial distress sweep over you, and the wreck of all worldly hopes threaten you, hold on to that as the plank that shall bear your soul unhurt to its haven. Remember that which thy Saviour hath spoken— "what shall it profit a man, if he gain the whole world, and lose his own soul?" Remember that there is a worse bankruptcy than that which is recorded in an earthly court; the bankruptcy that is recorded in heaven; bankruptcy in thy soul; all poor, and broken down, and desolate there; all shame and sorrow and mourning, instead of that glorious integrity, which should have shone like an angel's presence, in the darkest prison that ever spread its shadow over human calamity. Heaven and earth may pass away, but the word of Christ, the word of thy truth; let it pass from thee never!

XII.

ON THE USES OF LABOUR, AND THE PASSION FOR A FORTUNE.

FOR EVEN WHEN WE WERE WITH YOU, THIS WE COMMANDED YOU, THAT IF ANY MAN WOULD NOT WORK, NEITHER SHOULD HE EAT.—2 Thessalonians, iii. 10.

I WISH to invite your attention this evening to the uses of labour, and the passion for a fortune. The topics, it is obvious, are closely connected. The latter, indeed, is my main subject; but as preliminary to it, I wish to set forth, as I regard it, the great law of human industry. It is worthy, I think, of being considered, and religiously considered, as the chief law of all human improvement and happiness. And if there be any attempt to escape from this law, or if there be any tendency of the public mind, at any time, to the same point, the eye of the moral observer should be instantly drawn to that point, as one most vital to the public welfare. That there has been such a tendency of the public mind in this country, that it has been most signally manifest within a few years past, and that although it has found in cities the principal field of its manifestation, it has spread itself over the country too; that multitudes have become suddenly possessed with a new idea, the idea of making a fortune in a brief time, and then of retiring to a state of ease and independence—this is the main fact on which I shall insist, and of which I shall endeavour to point out the dangerous consequences.

But let me first call your attention to the law which has thus, as I contend, in spirit at least, been broken. What then is the law? It is, that industry—working, either with the hand or with the mind—the application of the powers to some task, to the achievement of some result, lies at the foundation of all human improvement.

Every step of our progress from infancy to manhood, is proof of this. The process of education, rightly considered, is nothing else but wakening the powers to activity. It is through their own activity alone, that they are cultivated. It is not by the mere imposition of tasks, or requisition of lessons. The very purpose of the tasks and lessons is to awaken and direct that activity. Knowledge itself cannot be gained, but upon this condition, and if it could be gained, would be useless without it.

The state into which the human being is introduced, is from the first step of it to the last, designed to answer the purpose of such an education. Nature's education, in other words, answers in this respect, to the just idea of man's. Each sense, in succession, is elicited by surrounding objects, and it is only by repeated trials and efforts, that it is brought to perfection. In like manner, does the scene of life appeal to every intellectual and every moral power. Life is a severe discipline, and demands every energy of human nature to meet it. Nature is a rigorous taskmaster; and its language to the human race is, "if a man will not work, neither shall he eat." We are not sent into the world like animals, to crop the spontaneous herbage of the field, and then to lie down in indolent repose: but we are sent to dig the soil and plough the sea; to do the business of cities and the work of manufactories. The raw material only is given us; and by the processes of cookery and the fabrications of art, it is to be wrought to our purpose. The human frame itself is a most exquisite piece of mechanism, and it is designed in every part for work. The strength of the arm, the dexterity of the hand, and the delicacy of the finger, are all fitted for the accomplisment of this purpose.

All this is evidently, not a matter of chance, but the result of design. The world is the great and appointed school of industry. In an artificial state of society, I know, mankind are divided into the idle and the labouring classes; but such, I maintain, was not the design of providence. On the contrary, it was meant that all men, in one way or another, should work. If any human being could be completely released from this law of providence, if he should never be obliged so much as to stretch out his hand for anything, if everything came to him at a bare wish, if there were a slave appointed to minister to every sense, and the powers of nature were made, in like manner, to obey every thought, he would be a mere mass of inertness, uselessness and misery.

Yes, such is man's task, and such is the world he is placed in. The world of matter is shapeless and void to all man's purposes, till he lays upon it the creative hand of labour. And so also is the world of mind. It is as true in mind as it is in matter, that the materials only are given us. Absolute truth ready made, no more presents itself to us in one department, than finished models of mechanism ready made, do in the other. Original principles there doubtless are in both; but the result—philosophy, that is to say, in the one case is as far to seek, as art and mechanism are in the other.

Such, I repeat, is the world, and such is man. The

earth he stands upon and the air he breathes are, so far as his improvement is concerned, but elements to be wrought by him to certain purposes. If he stood on earth passively and unconscious, imbibing the dew and sap, and spreading his arms to the light and air, he would be but a tree. If he grew up capable neither of purpose nor of improvement, with no guidance but instinct, and no powers but those of digestion and locomotion, he would be but an animal. But he is more than this; he is a man; he is made to improve; he is made, therefore, to think, to act, to *work*. Labour is his great function, his peculiar distinction, his privilege. *Can* he not think so? Can he not see, that from being an animal to eat and drink and sleep, to become a worker; to put forth the hand of ingenuity, and to pour his own thought into the moulds of nature, fashioning them into forms of grace and fabrics of convenience, and converting them to purposes of improvement and happiness; can he not see, I repeat, that this is the greatest possible step in privilege? Labour, I say, is man's great function. The earth and the atmosphere are his laboratory. With spade and plough, with mining-shafts and furnaces and forges, with fire and steam; amidst the noise and whirl of swift and bright machinery, and abroad in the silent fields, beneath the roofing sky, man was made to be ever working, ever experimenting. And while he, and all his dwellings of care and toil, are borne onward with the circling skies, and the shows of heaven are around him, and their infinite depths image and invite his thought, still in all the worlds of philosophy, in the universe of intellect, man must be a worker. He is nothing, he can be nothing, he can achieve nothing, fulfil nothing, without working. Not only can he gain no lofty improvement without this; but without it, he can gain no tolerable happiness. So that he who gives himself up to utter indolence, finds it too hard for him; and is obliged in self-defence, unless he be an idiot, to *do* something. The miserable victims of idleness and ennui, driven at last from their chosen resort, are compelled to work, to do something; yes, to employ their wretched and worthless lives in—"*killing time.*" They must hunt down the hours as their prey. Yes, time, that mere abstraction, that sinks light as the air upon the eye-lids of the busy and the weary, to the idle is an enemy, clothed with gigantic armour; and they must kill it, or themselves die. They cannot *live* in mere idleness; and all the difference between them and others is, that they employ their activity to no useful end. They find, indeed, that the hardest work in the world, is, to do nothing!

This reference to the class of mere idlers as it is called, leads me to offer one specification in laying down this law concerning industry. Suppose a man, then, to possess an immense, a boundless fortune, and that he holds himself discharged, in consequence, from all the ordinary cares and labours of life. Now, I maintain, that in order to be either an improving, worthy or happy man, he must do one of two things. He must either devote himself to the accomplishment of some public objects; or he must devote some hours of every day to his own intellectual cultivation. In any case, he must be, to a certain extent, a laborious man. The thought of his heart may be far different from this. He may think it his special privilege, as a man of fortune, to be exempt from all care and effort. To lounge on soft couches, to walk in pleasant gardens, to ride out for exercise, and to come home for feasting; this may be his plan. But it will never do. It never did yet answer for any human being, and it never will. God has made a law against it, which no human power ever could annul, nor human ingenuity evade. That law is, that upon labour, either of the body or of the mind, all essential well-being shall depend. And if this law be not complied with, I verily believe that wealth is only a curse, and luxury only a more slippery road to destruction. The poor idler, I verily believe, is safer than the rich idler: and I doubt, whether he is not happier. I doubt whether the most miserable vagrancy, that sleeps in barns and sheds, and feeds upon the fragments of other men's tables, and leaves its tattered garments upon every hedge, is *so* miserable, as surfeited opulence, sighing in palaces, sunk in the lethargy of indolence, loaded with plethory, groaning with weariness which no wholesome fatigue ever comes to relieve. The vagrant is at least, obliged to *walk* from place to place, and thus far has the advantage over his fellow idler who can ride. Yes, he walks abroad in the fair morning; no soft couch detains him, he walks abroad among the fresh fields, by the sunny hedges, and along the silent lanes, singing his idle song as he goes; a creature poor and wretched enough, no doubt; but I am tempted to say, if I must be idle, give me that lot, rather than to sit in the cheerless shadow of palace roofs, or to toss on downy beds of sluggish stupor or racking pain.

I have thus endeavoured to state one of the cardinal and inflexible laws of all human improvement and happiness. I have already premised, that my purpose in doing so, was to speak of the spirit of gain, of the eagerness for fortune, as characteristics of modern business, which tend to the dishonour and violation of the law of labour.

In proceeding to do this, let me more generally observe, in the first place, that there has always been a public opinion in the world, derogatory to labour. The necessity of exertion, though it is the very law under which God has placed mankind for their improvement and virtue, has always been regarded as a kind of degradation, has always been felt as a kind of reproach. With the exception of a few great geniuses, none so great as those who do nothing. Freedom from the necessity of exertion is looked upon as a privileged condition; it is encircled with admiring eyes; it absolutely gathers dignity and honour about it. One might think that a man would make some apologies for it, to the toiling world. Not at all; he is proud of it. It is for the busy man to make apologies. "He hopes you will excuse him; he *must* work, or he *must* attend to his business." You would think he was about to do some mean action. You would think he was about to do something of which he is ashamed. And he *is* ashamed of it!

The time has hardly gone by, when even literary labour, labour of the mind, the noblest of all labour, has suffered under this disparaging estimate. Authorship has always been held to be the proper subject for the patronage of wealth and rank. Some of the most distinguished authors, have lived in obscurity, compared with the rich and fashionable around them, and have only forced their way into posthumous celebrity. The rewards of intellectual toil have usually been stinted to the provision of a bare, humble subsistence. Not seldom has the reward been scarcely a remove from starvation. But when we descend to manual labour, the comparison is still more striking. The labouring classes, *operatives* as they are significantly called in these days, are generally regarded but as a useful machinery to produce and manufacture comforts and luxuries for those that can buy them. And the labouring classes are so regarded, mainly, not because they are less informed and cultivated, though that may be true, but *because* they are the labouring classes. Let any one of them be suddenly endowed with a fortune, let him be made independent of labour, and without any change of character, he immediately, in the general estimation, takes his place among what are called the upper classes. In those countries where the favouritism extended to the aristocracy, has made many of its members the vainest, most frivolous and useless of beings, it must be apparent, that many persons among the business classes are altogether their superiors in mind, in refinement, in all the noblest qualities; and yet does the bare circumstance of pecuniary independence carry it over everything. They walk abroad in lordly pride, and the children of toil on every side, do homage to them. Let such an one enter any one of the villages of England, or of this country; let him live there, with nothing to do and doing nothing, the year round; and those who labour in the field and the workshop, will look upon him, in bare virtue of his ability to be idle, as altogether their superior. Yes, those who have wrought well in the great school of providence, who have toiled faithfully at their tasks and learned them, will pay this mental deference to the truant, to the idler, to him who learns nothing and does nothing; ay, and because he does nothing. Nay, in that holy church, whose ministry is the strongest bond to philanthropic exertion, the clergy, the very ministry of him who went about doing good and had not where to lay his head, sinks, in the estimation of the whole world to the lowest point of depression, the moment it is called "a working clergy." That very epithet, *working*, seems, in spite of every counteracting consideration, to be a stigma upon everything to which it can be applied.

But besides this general opinion, there is a specific opinion or way of thinking, to which I have already referred, as opposed to our principle, and to which I wish now to invite your more particular attention. This opinion, or way of thinking, I must endeavour to describe with some care, as it constitutes the basis of fact, from which the moral reflections of the remainder of this discourse will arise.

It will be admitted, then, in the general, I think, that modern business—*modern*, I mean, as compared with that of a hundred or even fifty years ago—has assumed a new character; that it has departed from the staidness, regularity, and moderation of former days. The times when the business of the father descended to the son, and was expected to pass down as an heir-loom in the family; when the risks were small and the gains were moderate, or if ample, still comparatively sure, seem to have given way to the intense desire and the hazardous pursuit, of immediate and immense accumulation. It is not necessary to the statement I am making, that I should enter into the causes of this change. They are, doubtless, to be found in the unusual opportunities for gain, in the extraordinary extension of credits, and I think also, in the rapid expansion of the principle of liberty; that is to say, in the intellectual activity, personal ambition, and unfettered enterprise, which that principle has introduced into society. But whatever be the causes of the change, it will not be denied, I presume, that there has sprung up in connection with it, a new view of acquisition; or rather, to state more exactly what I mean, that a view of acquisition, which, in former times, was confined to a few minds, has now taken possession of almost the entire business community, and constitutes, therefore, beyond all former example, one of the great moral features of the age. I cannot, perhaps, briefly describe this view better than by denominating it, a *passion for making a fortune*, and for making it speedily. I do not, of course, mean to say that this *passion* has not existed before. The love of money has always been a desire so strong, that it has needed for its restraint, all the checks and admonitions of reason and religion. There have always been those who have set their affections and expectations on a fortune, as something indispensable to their happiness. There have also appeared, from time to time, seasons of rash and raging speculation, as in the case of the South Sea and Mississippi stocks in England and France; disturbing, however, but occasionally the regular progress of business. But the case with us, now, is different. We have, at length, become conversant with times, in which these seasons of excess and hazard in business, are succeeding one another periodically, and with but brief intervals. The pursuit of property, and that in no moderate amount, has acquired at once an unprecedented activity and universality. The views, with which multitudes now are entering into business, are not of gaining a subsistence they disdain the thought; not barely of pursuing a proper and useful calling—that is far beneath their ambition; but of acquiring a fortune, of acquiring ease and independence. In accordance with this view, is the common notion of retiring from business. It is true, that we do not see much of this retiring, but we hear much about it. The passion exists, though the course of business is so rash as constantly to disappoint, or so eager as finally to overcome it.

In saying that a great change is passing over the business character of the world, and that it is in some respects dangerous, I do not intend to say that it is altogether bad, or even that there is necessarily more evil than good in it. I hold it to be an advantage to the world, that restrictions, like those of the guilds of Germany and the Borough laws in England, are thrown off; and that a greater number of competitors can enter the lists, and run the race for the comforts and luxuries of life. The prizes, too, will be smaller as the competitors are more numerous; and *that*, I hold, will be an advantage. I believe, also, that the system of doing business on credit, in a young and enterprising country, is, within proper bounds, useful; and that our own, owes a part of its unexampled growth and prosperity to this cause. I only say, what I think all will admit, that from these causes, there are tendencies in the business of the country which are dangerous.

But to return to my statement; I undertake to say, not only in general, that there are wrong practical tendencies, but that there is a way of thinking about business which is wrong. Your practical advisers may tell you that there has been over-trading, that this is the great evil, and that it must be avoided in future. I do not say, for I do not know, whether this has been the great evil or not; but this I say, that it probably will not be avoided in future, if it has been the evil. And why not? Because there is an evil beneath the evil alleged, and that is an excessive desire for property, an eagerness for fortune. In other words, there is a wrong way of thinking, which lies like a canker at the root of all wholesome moderation. The very idea that a property is to be acquired in the course of ten or twenty years, which shall suffice for the rest o' life; that by some prosperous traffic or grand specula tion, all the labour of life is to be accomplished in a brief portion of it; that by dexterous management, a large part of the term of human existence is to be exonerated from the laws of industry and self-denial; all this way of thinking, I contend, is founded in a mistake of the true nature and design of business, and ot the conditions of human well-being.

I do not say, still to discriminate, that it is wrong to desire wealth, and even, with a favourable and safe opportunity, to seek the rapid accumulation of it. A man may have noble ends to accomplish by such accumulation. He may design to relieve his destitute friends or kindred. He may desire to foster good institutions, and to help good objects. Or he may wish to retire to some other sphere of usefulness and exertion, which shall be more congenial to his taste and affections. But it is a different feeling, it is the desire of accumulation for the sake of securing a life of ease and gratification, for the sake of escaping from exertion and self-denial; this is the wrong way of thinking which I would point out, and which I maintain to be common. I do not say that it is universal among the seekers of wealth. I do not say that *all* who propose to retire from business, propose to retire to a life of complete indolence or indulgence; but I say that many do; and I am inclined to say, that all propose to themselves an independence, and an exemption from the necessity of exertion, which are not likely to be good for them; and, moreover, that they wed themselves to these ideas of independence and exemption, to a degree, that is altogether irrational, unchristian, and inconsistent with the highest and noblest views of life. That a man should desire so to provide for himself, as in case of sickness or disability, not to be a burthen upon his friends or the public, or in case of his death, that his family should not be thus dependent, is most reasonable, proper and wise. But that a man should wear out half of his life in an almost slavish devotion to business; that he should neglect his health, comfort and mind, and waste his very heart, with anxiety, and all to build a castle of indolence in some fairy land; this, I hold to be unwise and wrong. I am saying nothing now of particular emergencies into which a man may rightly or wrongly have brought himself; I speak only of the general principle.

And the principle, I say, in the first place, is unwise, wrong, injurious and dangerous, with reference to business itself. It is easy to see that the different views of business, implied in the foregoing remarks, will impart to the whole process a different character. If a man enters upon it as the occupation of his life; if he looks upon it as a useful and honourable course; if he is interested in its moral uses, and what we demand of every high-minded profession, if he thinks more of its uses than of its fruits, more of a high and honourable character than of any amount of gains; and if, in fine, he is willing to conform to that ordinance of Heaven which has appointed industry, action, effort, to be the spring of improvement, then of course, he will calmly and patiently address himself to his task, and fulfil it with wisdom and moderation. But if business is a mere expedient to gain a fortune, a race run for a prize, a game played for a great stake; then it as naturally follows that there will be eagerness and absorption, hurry and anxiety; it will be a race for the swift, and a game for the dexterous, and a battle for the strong; life will be turned into a scene of hazard and strife, and its fortunes will often hang upon the cast of a die.

I must add that the danger of all this is greatly in creased by a circumstance already alluded to; I mean the rapid expansion of the principle of political freedom. Perhaps, the first natural development of that principle was to be looked for in the pursuit of property. Property is the most obvious form of individual power, the most immediate and palpable ministration to human ambition. It was natural, when the weights and burthens of old restrictions were taken off, that men should first rush into the career of accumulation. I say restrictions; but there have been restraints *upon the mind*, which are, perhaps, yet more worthy of notice. The mass of mankind, in former ages, have ever felt that the high and splendid prizes of life were not for them. They have consented to poverty, or to mediocrity at the utmost, as their inevitable lot. But a new arena is now spread for them, and they are looking to the high places of society as within their reach. The impulse imparted to private ambition by this possibility, has not, I think, been fully considered, and it cannot, perhaps, be fully calculated. And it should also be brought into the account, that our imperfect civilization has not yet gone beyond the point of awarding a leading, and perhaps, paramount consideration in society to mere wealth. Conceive, then, what must be the effect, upon a man in humble and straitened circumstances, of the idea that it is possible for him to rise to this distinction. The thoughts of his youth, perhaps, have been lowly and unaspiring; they have belonged to that place which has been assigned him in the old *regime* of society. But in the rapid progress of that equalizing system which is spreading itself over the world, and amidst the unprecedented facilities of modern business, a new idea is suddenly presented to him. As he travels along the dusty road of toil, visions of a palace—of splendour, and equipage and state, rise before him; his may be the most enviable and distinguished lot in the country; he who is now a slave of the counting-room or counter, of the work-bench or the cartman's stand, may yet be one, to whom the highest in the land shall bow in homage. Conceive, I say, the effect of this new idea upon an individual, and upon a community. It must give an unprecedented and dangerous impulse to society. It must lead to extraordinary efforts and measures for acquisition. It will have the most natural effect upon the extension of traffic and the employment of credit. It may be expected, that in such circumstances, men will borrow and bargain as they have never done before; that the lessons of the old prudence will be laid aside; that the old plodding and pains-taking course will not do for the excited and stimulated spirit of such an age.

This eagerness for acquiring fortunes, tends equally to defeat the ultimate, the providential design of business. That design, I have said, is to train men by action, by labour and care, by the due exertion of their faculties, to mental and moral accomplishment. It is necessary to this end, that business should be conducted with regularity, patience and calmness; that the mind should not be diverted from a fair application of its powers, by any exaggerated or fanciful estimate of the results. Especially, if that contemplation of results involves the idea of *escaping* from all care and occupation, must it constantly hinder the fulfilment of the providential design. The very spirit of business *then*, the spirit of resistance to that design,

But even if it were not, yet it is evident, that neither the mental nor moral faculties of a human being have any fair chance, amidst agitations and anxieties, amidst dazzling hopes and disheartening fears. Certainly, it must be admitted, that a time of excessive absorption in business, is anything but a period of improvement. How many in such seasons have sunk in character and in all the aims of life, have lost their habits of reading and reflection, their habits of meditation and prayer!

Business, in its ultimate, its providential design is a school. Neglected, forgotten, perhaps ridiculed, as this consideration may be, it is the great and solemn truth. Man is placed in this school, as a learner of lessons for eternity. What he shall learn, not what he shall get, is of chief, of eternal import to him. As to property, it is certain, to use the language of an Apostle, "that as we brought nothing into this world, we can carry nothing out of it." But there is one thing which we shall carry out of it, and that is, the *character* which we have formed in the very pursuits, by which property has been acquired.

In the next place, this passion for rapid accumulation, thus pushed to eagerness and vehemence, and liable to be urged to rashness and recklessness, leads to another evil, which to any rational apprehension of things, cannot be accounted small; and that is the evil of sacrificing in business, the end to the means.

"Live while you live," is a maxim which has a good sense as well as a bad one. But the man who is sacrificing all the proper ends of life, for something to be enjoyed twenty years hence, can scarcely be said to live *while* he lives. He is *not* living *now* in any satisfactory way, he confesses; he is going to live by and by; that is, when and where he does not live, and never may live; nay, where it is probable, he never will live. For not one man in thirty, of those who intend to retire from business, ever does retire And yet, how many suffer this dream about retiring, to cheat them out of the substantial ends of acquisition—comfort, improvement, happiness, as they go on.

How then stands the account? In seeking property, a man has certain ends in view. Does he gain them? The lowest of them, comfort; does he gain that? No, he will tell you, he has little enough of comfort. That is to come. Having forsaken the path of regular and moderate and sure acquisition in which his fathers walked, he has plunged into an ocean of credit, spread the sails of adventurous speculation, is tossed upon the giddy and uncertain waves of a fluctuating currency, and liable, any day, to be wrecked by the storms that are sweeping over the world of business. The means, the *means*, of ease, of comfort, of luxury, he must have; and yet the things themselves, ease, comfort, and the true enjoyment of luxury, are the very things which he constantly fails to reach. He is ever saying, that he must *get out* of this turmoil of business, and yet he never does get out of it. The very eagerness of the pursuit, not only deprives him of all ease and comfort as he goes on, but it tends constantly to push the whole system of business to that excess, which brings about certain reaction and disappointment. Were it not better for him to live while he lives, to enjoy life as it passes? Were it not better for him to live richer and die poorer? Were it not best of all for him to banish from his mind, that erring dream of future indolence and indulgence; and to address himself to the business of life, as the school of his earthly education; to settle it with himself now, that independence if he gains it, is *not* to give him exemption from employment; that in order to be a happy man, he must always, with the mind or with the body, or with both, be a labourer; and, in fine, that the reasonable exertion of his powers, bodily and mental, is not to be regarded as mere drudgery, but as a good discipline, a wise ordination, a training in this primary school of our being for nobler endeavours, and spheres of higher activity hereafter? For never surely is activity to cease; and he who proposes to resign half his life tc indolent enjoyment, can scarcely be preparing for the boundless range and the intenser life that is to come.

But there are higher ends of acquisition than mere comfort. For I suppose, that few seekers of wealth can be found, who do not propose mental culture, and a beneficent use of property, as among their objects. And with a fulfilment of these purposes, a *moderate* pursuit is pefectly compatible. But how is it, when that pursuit becomes an eager and absorbing strife for fortune? What is the language of fact and experience? Amidst such engrossing pursuits, is there any time for reading? Are any literary habits, or any habits of mental culture, formed? I suppose these questions carry with them their own answer. But the over-busy man, though he is neglecting his mind now, means to repair that error by and by. *That* is the greatest mistake of all! He will not find the habits he wants, all prepared and ready for him, like that pleasant mansion of repose to which he is looking. He will find habits there, indeed; but they will be the habits he has been cultivating for twenty years; not those he has been neglecting. The truth he will then find to be, that he does not love to read or study, that he never did love it, and that he probably never will love it.

I do not say that reading is the only means of mental cultivation. Business itself *may* invigorate, enlarge and elevate the mind. But then it must be, because large views are taken of it; because the mind travels beyond the counter and the desk, and studies the geography, politics and social tendencies of the world; investigates the laws of trade, and the philosophy of mechanism, and speculates upon the morals and ends of all business. Nay, and the trader and the craftsman, if he would duly cultivate his mind, must, like the lawyer, physician and clergyman, travel beyond the province of his own profession, and bring the contributions of every region of thought, to build himself up in the strength and manhood of his intellectual nature.

And therefore, I say, with double force of asseveration, that he who has pursued business in such a way as to have neglected all just mental culture, has sacrificed the end to the means. He has gained money, and lost knowledge; he has gained splendour, and lost accomplishment; gained tinsel, and lost gold; gained an estate, and lost an empire; gained the world, and lost his soul!

And thus it is with all the ends of accumulation. The beneficent use, the moral elevation, which every high-minded man will propose to himself, are sacrificed in the eagerness of the pursuit. A man may give, and give liberally; but this may be a very different thing from *using* property beneficently and wisely. I confess, that on this account, I look with exceeding distrust upon all our city charities; because men have no time to look into the cases and questions that are presented to them; because they give recklessly, without system or concert. I believe that immense streams of charity are annually flowing around us, which tend only to deepen the channels of poverty and misery. He who gives money, to save time, cannot be acting wisely for others; and he who does good *only* by agents and almoners, cannot be acting wisely for himself. And yet, this is the course to which excessive devotion to gain must lead. The man has no time to think for himself; and, therefore, custom must be his law, or his clergyman, perhaps, is his conscience. He is an excellent disciple in the school of implicit submission. He attends a sound divine; he gives bountifully to the missions or to the alms-houses; he suffers himself to be assessed, perhaps, in the one-tenth of his income; and there end with him, all the use and responsibilities of wealth. His mind is engrossed with acquisition to that extent, that he has no proper regard to the ends of acquisition. Nay more, he comes, perhaps, to that pass in fatuity, that he substitutes altogether the means for the end, and embraces his possessions with the insane grasp of the miser.

On the whole, and in fine, this passion for a fortune diverts man from his true dignity, his true function; which lies in exertion, in labour.

I can conceive of reasons, why I might lawfully, and even earnestly desire a fortune. If I could fill some fair palace, itself a work of art, with the productions of lofty genius; if I could be the friend and helper of humble worth; if I could mark it out, where failing health or adverse fortune pressed it hard, and soften or stay the bitter hours that are hastening it to madness or to the grave; if I could stand between the oppressor and his pre , and bid the fetter and the dungeon give up its victim; if I could build up great institutions of learning and academies of art; if I could open fountains of knowledge for the people, and conduct its streams in the right channels: if I could do better for the poor than to bestow alms upon them—even to think of them, and devise plans for their elevation in knowledge and virtue, instead of forever opening the old reservoirs and resources for their improvidence; if, in fine, wealth could be to me, the handmaid of exertion, facilitating effort and giving success to endeavor, then might I lawfully, and yet warily and modestly, desire it. But if wealth is to do nothing for me but to minister ease and indulgence, and to place my children in the same bad school; I fearlessly say, though it be in face of the world's dread laugh, that I do not see why I should desire it, and that I do not desire it!

Are my reasons asked for this strange decision? Another, in part, shall give them for me. "Two men," says a quaint writer, "two men I honour, and no third. First, the toil-worn craftsman, that with earth-made implement laboriously conquers the earth, and makes her man's. Venerable to me is the hard hand; crooked, coarse; wherein, notwithstanding, lies a cunning virtue, indefeasibly royal, as of the sceptre of this planet. Venerable, too, is the rugged face, all weather-tanned, besoiled, with its rude intelligence; for it is the face of a man, living man-like. Oh, but the more venerable for thy rudeness, and even because I must pity as well as love thee! Hardly-entreated brother! For us was thy back so bent, for us were thy straight limbs and fingers so deformed. Thou wert our conscript, on whom the lot fell, and fighting our battles, wert so marred. For in thee, too, lay a God-created form, but it was not to be unfolded; encrusted must it stand with the thick adhesions and defacement of labour; and thy body, like thy soul, was not to know freedom. Yet toil on, toil on; thou art in thy duty, be out of it who may; thou toilest for the altogether indispensable, for daily bread.

"A second man I honour, and still more highly; him who is seen toiling for the spiritually indispensable; not daily bread, but the bread of life. Is not he, too, in his duty; endeavouring towards inward harmony; revealing this, by act or by word, through all his outward endeavours, be they high or low? Highest of all, when his outward and his inward endeavour are one; when we can name him artist; not earthly craftsman only, but inspired thinker, that with heaven-made implement conquers heaven for us! If the poor and humble toil that we have food, must not the high and glorious toil for him, in return, that he have light and guidance, freedom, immortality?—these two, in all their degrees, I honour; all else is chaff and dust, which let the wind blow whither it listeth.

"Unspeakably touching is it, however, when I find both dignities united; and he, that must toil outwardly for the lowest of man's wants, is also toiling inwardly for the highest. Sublimer in this world know I nothing, than a peasant saint, could such now, anywhere be met with. Such a one will take thee back to Nazareth itself; thou wilt see the splendour of heaven spring forth from the humblest depths of earth, like a light shining in great darkness."*

And who, I ask, is that *third* man, that challenges our respect? Say, that the world were made to be the couch of his repose, and the heavens to curtain it. Grant, that the revolving earth were his rolling chariot, and all earth's magnificence were the drapery that hung around his gorgeous rest; yet could not that august voluptuary—let alone the puny idler of our city streets—win from a wise man one sentiment of respect.

* Thomas Carlyle.

What is there glorious in the world, that is not the product of labour, either of the body or of the mind? What is history but its record? What are the treasures of genius and art, but its work? What are cultivated fields, but its toil? The busy marts, the rising cities, the enriched empires of the world; what are they, but the great treasure-houses of labour? The pyramids of Egypt, the castles and towers and temples of Europe, the buried cities of Mexico; what are they but tracks, all round the world, of the mighty footsteps of labour? Antiquity had not been without it. Without it, there were no memory of the past; without it, there were no hope for the future.

Let then, labour, the world's great ordinance, take its proper place in the world. Let idleness too, have the meed that it deserves. Honour, I say, be paid whereever it is due. Honour, if you please, to unchallenged indolence; for that which all the world admires, hath, no doubt, some ground for it; honour, then, to undisturbed, unchallenged indolence; for it reposes on treasures that labour some time gained and gathered. It is the effigy of a man, upon a splendid mausoleum; somebody built that mausoleum; somebody put that dead image there. Honour to him that does nothing, and yet does not starve; he hath his significance still; he is a standing proof that *somebody* has worked.

Nay, rather let us say, honour to the worker; to the toiler; to him who produces, and not alone consumes; to him who puts forth his hand to add to the treasure-heap of human comforts, and not alone to take away! Honour to him who goes forth amidst the struggling elements to fight his battle, and shrinks not, with cowardly effeminacy, behind pillows of ease! Honour to the strong muscle and the manly nerve, and the resolute and brave heart! Honour to the sweaty brow and the toiling brain! Honour to the great and beautiful offices of humanity; to manhood's toil and woman's task; to parental industry, to maternal watching and weariness; to teaching wisdom and patient learning; to the brow of care that presides over the state, and to many-handed labour that toils in the work-shops and fields, beneath its sacred and guardian sway!

XIII.

ON THE MORAL LIMITS OF ACCUMULATION

GIVE ME NEITHER POVERTY NOR RICHES; LEST I BE FULL AND DENY THEE, AND SAY, WHO IS THE LORD? OR LEST I BE POOR, AND STEAL, AND TAKE THE NAME OF MY GOD IN VAIN.—Proverbs, xxx. 8, 9.

IN my last discourse, I considered some of the evil consequences of the passion for accumulation; in the present, I propose to point out some of the moral limits to be set to that passion. In other words, the limits to accumulation, the wholesome restraints upon the passion for it, which are prescribed by feelings of general philanthropy and justice, by the laws of morality, and by a sober consideration of the natural effects of wealth upon ourselves, our children and the world; these are the topics of our present meditation.

I cannot help feeling here the difficulties under which the pulpit labours, in the discussion of the points now before us. Some, indeed, will think them unsuitable to the pulpit, as not being sufficiently religious. Others seem to be disposed to limit the pulpit to the utterance of general and unquestionable truths. To these views I cannot assent. The points which I am discussing are, in the highest degree, moral; they are practically religious; they belong to the morality and religion of daily life. And then again, as to what the preacher shall say, I do not think that he is to be confined to truisms, or to self-evident truths, or to truths in which all shall agree. We come here to deliberate on great questions of morality and duty; to consider what is true, what is right. In doing this, the preacher may bring forward views in which some of his hearers cannot agree with him; how, indeed, should it be otherwise. But he does not pretend to utter infallible sentences. He may be wrong. But he is none the less bound to utter what he does believe, and thinks to be worthy of attention. This office I attempt to discharge among you. And I ask you not to take ill, at my hands, that which you would not so take, if I uttered it by your fire-sides. And if I am wrong, on some such occasion, perhaps you will set me right.

Let me proceed, then, frankly to lay before you some reflections that have impressed my own mind, in regard to the limitations which good feeling, justice and wisdom ought, perhaps, to set to the pursuit of wealth.

1. In the first place, then, I doubt whether this immense accumulation in a few hands, while the rest of the world is comparatively poor, does not imply an unequal, an unfair distribution of the rewards of industry. I may be wrong on this point, and if I were considered as speaking with any authority from the pulpit, I should not make the suggestion. Yet speaking as I do, with no assumption, but with the modesty of doubt, I shall venture to submit this point to your consideration.

It would seem to be an evident principle of humanity and justice, that property and the means of comfort should bear some proportion to men's industry. Now we know that they do not. I am not denying that, in general, the hard-working man labours less with the mind; and that he is often kept poor, either by improvidence and wastefulness, or because he has less energy and sagacity than others bring into the business of life. I do not advocate any absurd system of agrarian levelling. I believe that wealth was designed to accumulate in certain hands, to a certain extent; because, I perceive, that this naturally results from the superior talents and efforts of certain individuals. But I cannot help thinking, that the disproportion is greater than it ought to be.

In order to bring this question home to your apprehension, let me ask you to suppose that some years ago, any one of you had come to this city with a beloved brother to prepare for a life of business. Let me suppose that you had been placed with a merchant, and he with a cartman; both, lawful, useful necessary callings in society; somebody must discharge each of these offices. Now you know that the results would likely enough be, that you would be rich, or at least possessed of an easy property, and that he would be poor; or at any rate, that you would have a fair chance of acquiring a fortune from your industry, and that he would have no such chance from his industry. Now let me further suppose, that you did not treat him as *some* men treat their poor relations; passing them by and striving to forget them—almost wishing they did not exist; but that you continued on terms of kind and intimate intercourse with him; that you constantly interchanged visits with him, and could compare the splendour of your dwelling with the poverty of his; I ask you if you would not feel, if you could help feeling, that society had dealt unjustly with you and with him in this matter? But I say that every man is your brother; and that what you would thus feel for your brother, you are bound to feel for every man!

I know that it is said in regard to accumulation in general, that capital has its claims; but I cannot help thinking that they are overrated, in comparison with the claims of human nerves and sinews. Suppose that of a thousand men engaged in a great manufacturing establishment, ten possess the capital and oversee the establishment, and the nine hundred and ninety do the work. Can it be right, that the ten should grow to immense wealth, and that the nine hundred and ninety should be for ever poor? I admit, that something is to be allowed for the risk taken by the capitalist. I have heard it pleaded, indeed, that he is extremely liable to fail, and often does so; while the poor, heaven help them! never fail. But it seems to me, that this consideration is not quite fairly pleaded. It is said, that there is a risk. But does not the capitalist, to a certain extent, make the risk? Is not his risk, often in proportion to the urgency with which he pushes the business of accumulation, and to that neglect and infidelity of his agents and workmen, which must spring from their having so slight a common interest with him in his undertakings? The risks will be smaller when the pursuit of property is more restrained and reasonable; and when the rewards of industry are more equal and just. But I hear it said again, that "the poor are wasteful; and that to increase their wages, is only to increase their vices." Let me tell you, that poverty is the parent of improvidence and desperation. Those who have been brought up in that school may very probably, for a while, abuse their increased means. But in the long run, it cannot be so. Nay, by the very terms of your proposition, the abuse will cease with the desperation of poverty. Give the poor some hope; give them some means; give them something to lean upon; give them some interest in the order and welfare of society; and they will become less wasteful, less reckless and vicious.

Indeed, is it not obvious, can any one with his eyes open deny, that the extremes of condition in the world, the extremes of wealth and poverty, furnish us with the extremes of vice and dissipation? And does not this fact settle and prove, beyond all question, that it is desirable that accumulation should be restrained within some bounds, on the one hand, and on the other, that indigence should be lessened? What is the state of the operatives in the manufacturing districts of England? Only worse, than that of the idlers in that kingdom, who are living and rioting upon overgrown fortunes. Let the conditions of men approach the same inequality in this or any other country, and we shall witness the same results. The tendency of things among us, I rejoice to believe, is not to that result; but it is, no doubt, the constant tendency of private ambition.

I am sensible, my friends, that I have made a large demand on your candour, in laying this question before you. It is paying the highest compliment I could pay to your fairness of mind. I only ask that you will treat my argument with equal generosity.

II. But I proceed to another point. In order to the rapid accumulation of property, in all ordinary cases, a great expansion of credit is necessary. A man cannot grow suddenly rich by the labour of his hands, and he must therefore use the property or the promises of others, in order to compass this end. Now. there is a question which I have never seen stated in the books of moral philosophy, which I have not heard discussed in the pulpit, and yet it is a point which deserves a place in the code of commercial morality; and that is, how far it is right for a man to use credit; that is, to extend his business, beyond his actual capital? I am sensible that it is extremely difficult, if it is not indeed impossible, to lay down any exact rule on this subject; and yet it seems to me none the less worthy of consideration. Certainly, it must be admitted, that there is a point somewhere, beyond which it is not prudent, and, therefore, not right, to go. Certainly, it can not be right, as it appears to me, for a man to use all the credit he can get. It could not be right, for instance, that upon a capital of ten thousand, a man should do a business of ten millions. No man ought to trust his powers to such an indefinable extent. No man's creditors, were he to fail, could be satisfied with his having accepted trusts from others in the shape of credits, which common prudence shall pronounce to be rash and hazardous. There is a common prudence, if there is no exact rule about this matter; and the borrower is most especially bound to observe it; and certainly, every honest man, being a borrower, would observe it, if he did but sufficiently think of it. The want of this thought is the very reason why I bring forward the subject.

With regard to the rule, I have it as the deliberate opinion of one of the greatest bankers in Europe, that a man should not extend his business to more than three times his capital, and if it be a large business, to not more than twice his capital. I do not say that this is the rule, though I have the greatest respect for the judgment that laid it down. I do not say that it is the rule, because I am advised on the other hand, by very competent judges, that the rule must vary exceedingly with the different kinds of business which a man may pursue.

I do not undertake, then, to lay down any particular rule, but I urge the claims of general prudence. I wish to call attention to this point. I am persuaded that it is for want of reflection and not from want of principle, that many have adventured out upon an ocean of credit, where they have not only suffered shipwreck themselves, but carried down many a goodly vessel with them. The borrower, I hold, is specially and solemnly bound to be prudent. He is bound to be more prudent in the use of other men's property, than of his own. A man should be more cautious in taking credit, than in using capital. But I fear that the very reverse of this is commonly the fact. I fear that most men are more reckless when they use the means which credit gives them, than they would be in using their own absolute and fixed property. In small matters, we know that immediate payment is a check to expenditure. Why is it, but for this, that every petty dealer is anxious to open a credit with your family? He knows that your expenditures will be freer, your purchases larger, and that a more considerable amount will be made up at the end of the year, because you buy on credit. But to look at the subject in a wider view; I know that some men do plunge more recklessly into the great game of business, because the game is played with credit; with counters, and not with coins. I have heard it observed, and I confess, that it was with a coolness and nonchalance that amazed me, that a man may as well take a good strong hold of business while he is about it, since he has nothing to lose by it. The sentiment is monstrous. It ought to shake the very foundations of every warehouse where it is uttered. There ought to be a sacred caution in the use of credit. And although I cannot pretend to define the precise law of its extension, yet this I will say, that never till I see a man adventuring his own property more freely than he adventures that which he borrows of his neighbour, can I think he is right. Let this great, and undeniably just moral principle be established; and I am persuaded that we shall at once see a wholesome restraint laid upon the use of credit.

There is one further point to which I wish to invite your attention; and that is the practice, in cases of bankruptcy, of giving preference to certain creditors, who have made loans on that condition. Now, I maintain, that no man ought to offer credit, and that no man ought to accept it, on that condition. The practice is abolished in England; and I know that *there* it is regarded as bringing a stain upon the commercial morality of this country.

I do not mean to charge with personal dereliction any person who has, in time past, taken advantage of this rule. It has been the rule of the country, and has passed unquestioned. And so long as it has been the rule, and money has been borrowed and lent on that principle, and it was considered right so to do, it was perhaps right, as between man and man, that cases of insolvency should be settled on that principle. But as a theoretical principle of general application, I hold, that it is utterly wrong. Our laws indeed disallow it, and public opinion ought not, for another hour, to sustain it.

The principle is dishonest. It is treachery to the body of a man's creditors. He appeared before them with a certain amount of means; and upon the strength of those means, they were willing to give him credit. Those means were the implied condition, the very basis of the loan; without them they would not have made it. They saw that he had a large stock of goods; that he was doing a large business, and they thought there was no danger. They depended, in fact, upon that visible property, in case of difficulties. But difficulty arises, failure comes; and then they find that much or all of that property is preoccupied and wrested from their hands, by certain confidential pledges. If they had known this, they would have stood aloof; and therefore, I say, that there is essential deception in the case.

Again, lending on such a principle loses all its generosity, and borrowing is liable to lose all the prudence and virtue that properly belong to it. If a man lends to his young friend or relative, on the sole strength of affection and confidence towards him, it is a transaction which bestows a grace upon mercantile life. But if he lends as a preference creditor, he takes no risk, and shows no confidence. For he knows, that the borrower upon the strength of *his* loan, can easily get property enough into his hands, to make *him* perfectly secure. And let it be observed, that in proportion as the acquisition of confidence is less necessary; in proportion, that is to say, as virtue and ability are less necessary to set up a man in business, are they less likely to be cultivated: and so far as this principle goes, therefore, it tends to sap and undermine the whole business character of a country. Nay, it is easy to see, that under the cloak of these confidential transactions, the entire business between the borrower and lender may be the grossest and most iniquitous gambling. I do not say that this is common. But I say that the principle ought not to be tolerated, which is capable of such abuses.

This principle, I think, moreover, is the very keystone of the arch, that supports many an overgrown fabric of credit. And this observation has a two-fold earing. Much of the credit that is obtained, could not exist without this principle. That is one thing; but furthermore, I hold that all the exertion of credit which depends on this principle, ought not to exist at all. It ought not, because the principle is dishonest and treacherous. And it would not, because the first credit which often puts a man in the possession of visible means, is not given on the strength of confidence in him, but on the strength of the secret pledge; and then the after credits are based on those visible means. Let every man that borrows tell, as he ought to do, the amount of his confidential obligations, and many would find their credit seriously curtailed. And to that extent, most assuredly, it ought to be curtailed.

I have thus spoken of the spirit of gain as liable—not as *always being*, but as liable to be, in conflict with the great principles of social and commercial justice. I might add, that the manner in which the gains of business are sometimes clung to, amidst the wreck of fortunes, is a powerful and striking illustration of the same moral danger. He who regards no limits of justice in acquiring property, will break all bonds of justice to keep it.

And here I must carefully and widely distinguish. I give all honour to the spirit which many among us have shown in such circumstances; to the manly fortitude and disinterestedness of men, who have comparatively cared nothing for themselves, but who have been almost crushed to the earth by what they have suffered for their friends; to the heroic cheerfulness and soothing tenderness of woman in such an hour, ready to part with every luxury, and holding the very pearl of her life, in the unsullied integrity of her husband. I know full well, that that lofty integrity is the only rule ever thought of by many, in the painful adjustment of their broken fortunes. And I know, and the public knows, that if they retain a portion of their splendour for a season, it is reluctantly, and because it cannot, in the present circumstances, be profitably disposed of; and that they retain it in strict trust for their creditors. But, there are bankrupts of a different character, as you well know. I do not know that any such are in this presence; but if there were a congregation of such before me, I should speak no otherwise than I shall now speak. I say, that there are men of a different character; men who intend permanently to keep back a part of the price they have sworn to pay; and I tell you, that God's altar, at which I minister, shall hear no word from me, conconcerning them, but a word of denunciation. It is dishonesty, and it ought to be infamy. It is robbery, though it live in splendour, and ride in state; robbery, I say, as truly as if, instead of inhabiting a palace, it were consigned to the dungeons of Sing-Sing. And take care, my brethren, as ye shall stand at the judgment-bar of conscience and of God, that ye fall not at all beneath this temptation. The times are times of sore and dreadful peril to the virtue of the country. They are times in which it is necessary, even for honest men, to gird up the loins of their minds, and to be sober and watchful; ay, watchful over themselves. Remember, all such, I adjure you, that the dearest fortune you can carry into the world, will not compensate you for the least iota of your integrity surrendered and given up. Oh! sweeter in the lowliest dwelling to which you may descend, shall be the thought that you have kept your integrity immaculate, than all the concentrated essence of luxury to your taste, all its combined softness to your couch, all its gathered splendour to your state. Ay, prouder shall you be in the humblest seat, than if, with ill-kept gains, you sat upon the throne of a kingdom.

III. I come now to consider, in the last place, the limitations to be set to the desire of wealth, by a sober consideration of its too probable effects upon ourselves, upon our children, and upon the world at large. And here, let me ask two preliminary questions.

Can that be so necesrary to human well-being, as many consider wealth to be, which necessarily falls to the lot but of a few? Can that be the very feast and wine of life, when but a few thousands of the human race, are allowed to partake of it? If it were so, surely God's providence were less kind and liberal, than we are bound to think it. God has not made a world of rich men, but rather a world of poor men: or of men, at least, who must toil for a subsistence. That then must be the good condition for man; nay, the best condition; and we see, indeed, that it is the grand sphere of human improvement.

In the next place, can that be so important to human welfare, which, if it were possessed by all, would be the most fatal injury possible? And here I must desire, that every person whose pursuit of property, this question may affect, will extend his thoughts beyond himself. He may say that it would be a good thing if *he* could acquire wealth; and perhaps it would. He may say that he does not see that riches would do *him* any harm; and perhaps, they would not. He may have views that ennoble the pursuit of fortune. But the question is; would it be well and safe, for four-fifths of the business community around him, to become opulent? He must remember that his neighbours have sought as well as he, and in a proportion, too, not far distant from what I have stated. They have sought, and had as good a right to succeed, as he had. Would it be well that so general an expectation of fortune, should be gratified? Would it be well for society; well for the world? Only carry the supposition a little further; only suppose the whole world to acquire wealth; only suppose it were possible that the present generation could lay up a complete provision for the next, as some men desire to do for their children; and you destroy the world at a single blow. All industry would cease with the necessity for it; all improvement would stop with the demand for exertion; the dissipation of fortunes, whose mischiefs are now counterveiled by the healthful tone of society, would then breed universal disease, and break out into universal license; and the world would sink into the grave of its own loathsome vices.

But let us look more closely, for a moment, at the general effect of wealth upon individuals and upon nations.

I am obliged, then, to regard with considerable distrust, the influence of wealth upon individuals. I know that it is a mere instrument, which may be converted to good or to bad ends. I know that it is often used for good ends. But I more than doubt whether the chances lean that way. Independence and luxury are not likely to be good for any man. Leisure and luxury are almost always bad for every man. I know that there are noble exceptions. But I have *seen* so much of the evil effect of wealth upon the mind—making it proud, haughty and impatient, robbing it of its simplicity, modesty and humility, bereaving it of its large and gentle and considerate humanity; and I have *heard* such testimonies, such astonishing testimonies to the same effect, from those whose professional business it is to settle and adjust the affairs of large estates, that I more and more distrust its boasted advantages. I deny the validity of that boast. In truth, I am sick of the world's admiration of wealth. Almost all the noblest things that have been achieved in the world, have been achieved by poor men, poor scholars and professional men; poor artisans and artists; poor philosophers, and poets, and men of genius.

It does appear to me, that there is a certain staidness and sobriety, a certain moderation and restraint, a certain pressure of circumstances, that is good for man. His body was not made for luxuries; it sickens, sinks, and dies under them. His mind was not made for indulgence. It grows weak, effeminate, and dwarfish, under that condition. It is good for us to bear the yoke; and it is especially good to bear the yoke in our youth. I am persuaded that many children are injured by too much attention, too much care; by too many servants at home; too many lessons at school; too many indulgences in society. They are not left sufficiently to exert their own powers, to invent their own amusements, to make their own way. They are often inefficient and unhappy, they lack ingenuity and energy, because they are taken out of the school of providence; and placed in one which our own foolish fondness and pride have built for them. Wealth, without a law of entail to help it, has always lacked the energy even to *keep* its own treasures. They drop from its imbecile hand. What an extraordinary revolution in domestic life is that, which, in this respect, is presented to us all over the world! A man, trained in the school of industry and frugality, acquires a large estate. His children, possibly, keep it. But the third generation almost inevitably goes down the rolling wheel of fortune, and *there* learns the energy necessary to rise again. And yet we are, almost *all* of us, anxious to put our children, or to ensure that our grand-children shall be put, on this road to indulgence, luxury, vice, degradation, and ruin!

This excessive desire and admiration for wealth, is

one of the worst traits in our modern civilization. We are, if I may say so, in an unfortunate dilemma in this matter. Our political civilization has opened the way for multitudes to wealth, and created an insatiable desire for it; but our mental civilization has not gone far enough, to make a right use of it. If wealth were employed in promoting mental culture at home, and works of philanthropy abroad; if it were multiplying studios of art, and building up institutions of learning around us; if it were every way raising the intellectual and moral character of the world, there could scarcely be too much of it. But if the utmost aim, effort, and ambition of wealth, be to procure rich furniture, and provide costly entertainments, I am inclined to say, that there could scarcely be too little of it. "It employs the poor," do I hear it said? Better that it were *divided* with the poor. Willing enough am I, that it should be in few hands, if they will use it nobly—with temperate self-restraint and wise philanthropy. But on no other condition, will I admit that it is a good, either for its possessors or for any body else. I do not deny that it may lawfully be, to a certain extent, the minister of elegancies and luxuries, and the handmaid of hospitality and physical enjoyment; but this I say, that just in such proportion as its tendencies, divested of all higher aims and tastes, are running that way, are they running to evil and to peril.

That peril, moreover, does not attach to individuals and families alone; but it stands, a fearful beacon, in the experience of cities and empires. The lessons of past times, on this subject, are emphatic and solemn. I undertake to say, that the history of wealth has always been a history of corruption and downfall. The people never existed that could stand the trial.

Boundless profusion—alas! for humanity—is too

little likely to spread for any people, the theatre of manly energy, rigid self-denial, and lofty virtue. Where is the bone and sinew and strength of a country? Where do you expect to find its loftiest talents and virtues? Where, its martyrs to patriotism or religion? Where are the men to meet the days of peril and disaster? Do you look for them among the children of ease and indulgence and luxury?

All history answers. In the great march of the races of men over the earth, we have always seen opulence and luxury sinking before poverty and toil and hardy nurture. It is the very law that has presided over the great processions of empire. Sidon and Tyre, whose merchants possessed the wealth of princes; Babylon and Palmyra, the seats of Asiatic luxury; Rome, laden with the spoils of a world, overwhelmed by her own vices more than by the hosts of her enemies—all these, and many more, are examples of the destructive tendencies of immense and unnatural accumulation. No lesson in history is so clear, so impressive, as this.

I trust, indeed, that our modern, our *Christian* cities and kingdoms are to be saved from such disastrous issues. I trust that, by the appropriation of wealth, less to purposes of private gratification, and more to purposes of Christian philanthropy and public spirit, we are to be saved. But this is the very point on which I insist. Men must become more generous and benevolent, not more selfish and effeminate, as they become more rich, or the history of modern wealth will follow in the sad train of all past examples; and the story of American prosperity and of English opulence, will be told as a moral, in empires beyond the Rocky Mountains, or in the newly-discovered continents of the Asiatic Seas!

MISCELLANEOUS AND OCCASIONAL.

XIV.

AN ORATION DELIVERED AT CAMBRIDGE, BEFORE THE SOCIETY OF PHI BETA KAPPA, AUGUST, 1830.

MR. PRESIDENT AND GENTLEMEN,

THIS Society was formed for the promotion, though chiefly by an indirect influence, of a sound and healthful literature. And the use of this anniversary festival,—for I think it has a use, beyond the pleasure that it brings with it,—is to strengthen the bonds of literary duty and friendship; to rekindle the fires which, separate and solitary, are apt to die away; to revive that zeal for study, which is too liable to fail, or to falter at least, in its struggle with professional cares. From the midst of those cares, from the labours of the pulpit, from the toils of the bar, from the watchings of the sick room, from the weariness of the teacher's form, our tribes have come up to pay the annual offering, and keep the yearly jubilee.

What are the principles which, on our return to those fields, will ensure us the most successful cultivation of them? What is the true science, the *rationale*, if I may say so, of thorough improvement and refinement? What are the true means of spreading at once wealth and beauty over the paths of literary labour?

From the wide range of discussion which this question opens to us, I shall select two views, two principles of intellectual culture—(this is my general subject)—the one practical, the other theoretical; both of which derive urgent claims to attention, as I think, from the character of the literature that is prevalent at the present day, and from the state of our little republic of letters. My practical principle is, that the loftiest attainments of the mind in every sphere of its exertion, are immediately—much as the original tendency or temperament may vary—are *immediately* the fruit of nothing but the deepest study; that, for instance, the great poet and the great artist, as well as the profound metaphysician or astronomer, is by nothing more distinguished than by his thorough and patient application; that natural genius, as it is called, appears in nothing else, and is nothing else, but the power of application; that there is *no* great excellence without great labour; that the inspirations of the muse are as truly studies, as the lucubrations of philosophy. In other words, it is the deepest soil that yields not only the richest fruits, but the fairest flowers; it is the most solid body which is not only the most useful, but which admits of the highest polish and brilliancy; it is the strongest pinion, which not only can carry the greatest burden, but which soars to the loftiest flight.

That the most intense study is necessary to the loftiest attainments in every department, whether of philosophy or poetry, of science or imagination, of reality or fiction, of judgment or taste, would perhaps be best made to appear, by showing the strict and close connexion there is between them; and that there is such a connexion is indeed my theoretical principle. To some suggestions on these subjects, as all that the present occasion permits,—to some suggestions, I must say, rather than discussions, let me now invite your attention.

My position then, in theory, is, that between these various qualities of mind and departments of literature, of which I have just spoken, there is no incongruity, none of the commonly supposed warfare, but perfect harmony. These extremes, as they are usually considered, do actually meet and mingle in every perfect mind and in every perfect literature. In fact, the most distinguishing trait in all the greatest minds of the world, the preëminent seal of genius upon all its noblest works, has been this union of opposite qualities; of sense and sprightliness, of philosophy and fancy, of acuteness and invention.

The maxim that "extremes meet," has, indeed, been commonly received, and too often exemplified in a very different sense. The too constant imperfection of our own experiments in the science of the mind, has nearly overthrown what in theory is the only perfect rule. It is true, that metaphysical speculation, for instance, when it goes to what is called an extreme; when it goes beyond fact, beyond the range of simple induction, runs into transcendental mysticism, and is at war with plain good sense, and tends to chill the fervour of fancy and feeling. The hoary wisdom of learning, too, sometimes verges very nearly upon childish pedantry; the extreme of acuteness sinks, in some instances, into a trifling and petty accuracy about details; and extreme good sense—alas! it is sometimes dull and unmeaning as nonsense. And there is nothing, indeed, that is more sure to become vapid and tedious, than the incessant, even though it be for a time the successful, endeavour to be brilliant and sprightly; as the agreeable trifling of our foreign Monthlys has, at some periods of their history, strikingly demonstrated. Even Cervantes, is often, to my mind, but a sorry jester, in the overstrained effort at perpetual wit; an effort, whose occasional failure, indeed argues no want of power, since it is as impossible to succeed in it, as it would be to make the lightning, which falls in transient flashes from the cloud, the permanent medium of vision.

But what follows from these instances in the history of the human mind? Does it follow, that, compatible with the nature of these qualities, there can be too much of true wisdom, acuteness, sense, sprightliness, or wit? Never. The truth is, that these things become other things when they go too far—when, in the bad sense, they go to extremes. The maxim, in this sense, like all false paradoxes, keeps its meaning only to the ear, and breaks it to the judgment.

It may be said, indeed, with sufficient accuracy, perhaps, for common parlance, and when speaking of common men, that such an one is a man of strong sense, but has not a particle of imagination; that another dwells in a world of fiction and knows nothing of reality, is a poet and knows nothing of human nature; and some harmless people may harmlessly imagine that the grand mark of intellectual distinction is maudlin sentiment and visionary nonsense; but in the severe and high cultivation of the mind it is necessary to set up a different principle. It is necessary to maintain that, in their perfection, the noblest qualities of the mind meet and modify each other. They may go to their utmost extent, they may go to their extremes, yet if they do meet, if they do control each other, if they mingle in perfect harmony, their union presents us, at once, with the strongest and the most beautiful forms of intellectual power. So that the severest sense is not barely compatible but consonant with the richest fancy; so that genuine logic is no enemy to genuine poetry; so that perfect wisdom is identical with perfect beauty.

For the correctness of the principle which I maintain, I appeal now, for a moment, to the philosophy of the mind. The questions to be asked here are very simple, but they are very decisive. What *is* the mind? Is it not one intelligence? And is it not the same intelligence and no other, that is employed in every intellectual effort, and in every department of literature? Is not that intelligence, I still ask, whether it builds up a science or an art, deals with theory or practice, constructs a problem or a poem, one and the same thing? Is not the aliment by which the mind is to grow, truth,—simple, single, harmonious, divinely accordant truth? And is not the right order in which its faculties are to rise to their highest excellence, that of perfect proportion? And must not all disproportion among its powers indicate an imperfect and crude development? Furthermore, is there any clashing among the natural powers of the mind? Is there to be found, in fact, on an accurate analysis, any of the commonly supposed incongruity between reason and fancy, between the judgment and the imagination? What is reason? It is usually defined to be the power of comparing our ideas, and of discriminating their resemblances and differences. What is the imagination? It is the power of calling up at will, and assembling congruous ideas, so as to form harmonious pictures. These powers, then, do not exist in a state of war, but of perfect alliance with each other. They are mutually necessary to each other's strength and perfection. Fancy without judgment is extravagance and folly. Judgment without fancy is unproductive drudgery. It may be correct as far as it goes; but without any of that power called fancy, without any new or extensive combinations of thought, without any capability of stirring from the field of observation immediately before it, the judgment does not go far. In the habit that still prevails of regarding the mind as if it were divided into distinct departments, thought and feeling are constantly distinguished as if they were opposite powers. But what is feeling? It is an emotion arising from the perception of some object; arising, that is, from, or rather with, some thought. Feeling, then, so far from being opposed to thinking; is oftentimes but a more vivid and intense thinking; and Pythagoras, when he demonstrated the Forty-seventh proposition, and offered his hecatomb in thanksgiving for that discovery, no doubt *felt* as strongly as Homer, when he described the wrath of Achilles, or the tears of Andromache. Different minds possess indeed different capacities, both of thought and feeling: but with this qualification, and speaking as I now do, not of animal sensations, but of intellectual states of mind, I say that the strong feeling is the strong thought.

These views, simple as they may seem, form the best argument, perhaps, against the commonly supposed incongruity of the different efforts and productions of the mind, and therefore I have been willing to bring them forward at the risk of wearying my audience with scholastic statements. The actual results in literature seem to me to correspond with these acknowledged elements of our philosophy. Supposing a certain amount of talent, an amount sufficient to stand in the trial for literary distinction; and then I say, that the reason of failure is always to be found in the want, either of the due proportion, or of the due exertion, of the faculties of the mind. The whole history of literature bears me out in this position. How many poems, for instance, charged and overcharged with imagination, have fallen into worse than the hated and fatal mediocrity, for the want of a sound judgment! How many treatises, on the contrary, laden and weighed down with good sense, and much learning too, have sunk to oblivion, because there was no kindling warmth of imagination to buoy them up and bear them on to after ages! And in the few works that have secured the consenting homage of all countries and of all times, what a singular union has there been of the severest sense with the most brilliant fancy! The very idea, that these are warring principles, shows, that in general they have not been well and rightly developed. No doubt the imagination may be cultivated and perhaps strengthened at the expense of the judgment, but then it is not well cultivated. And we see the judgment, in certain instances, acquiring vigor at the expense of the imagination. It is said to be so, at times, in the pursuits of the law, and of the mathematics. But, then, I shall venture to aver that, for the whole man, the judgment is not well cultivated. If such cultivation is a sacrifice, on the part of the individual, to the advancement of the particular science he studies, that is the most that can be said of it. But even then, it is not a necessary sacrifice, as there are many illustrious instances to show. And so far from believing that any of these principles are bestowed, as natural endowments, to the exclusion of others, I undertake to say, that wherever there is a powerful imagination, there, with proper culture, might be a powerful judgment, and the contrary; and that wherever there is strong feeling, there might be strong thinking. There it *is*, for the moment. The strong feeling implies a vivid perception of its object. And the perception that is vivid for a moment, may, by sufficient care, become habitually keen, discriminating, strong, and comprehensive. In truth, it is not the fanatic, in religion or in literature, that feels the most strongly. The true feeling, as well as the true judgment, is deep, calm, sustained, and thus powerful.

If all this is true, we are prepared to judge what connexion there is between profound philosophy and poetry, between judgment and taste, between profound thought and a fine imagination. This connexion, did the time permit, is capable of other illustrations from the philosophy of the mind. For it might be shown, that those departments of literature, which have now been named, are not only co-ordinate and harmonious, but that each imparts a distinct and signal power over the other. It might be shown, and indeed it must be obvious, that he who understands the philosophy of the mind is, for that reason, better prepared to address the mind ; that he who understands the philosophy of poetry, of its subjects, of its machinery, its figures, its appropriate thoughts and feelings, will possess advantages in that knowledge ; that his taste, too, will be better, who has studied its principles ; that his fiction will be better, who is most familiar with reality. It is true, that a man, without these aids, may blunder into the right path ; or he may be carried into it by the strong impulse of genius ; by a philosophy, in fact, which he has not analyzed. For the guidance here is not instinct : that is heaven's guidance and is always safe. While the whole history of criticism shows, that genius even of the noblest order has always been committing the most deplorable errors for the want of knowledge.

If, Gentlemen, I am stating new doctrines, I may be

permitted, at least to desire that they be not misunderstood. I do not deny, that in different individuals the various faculties of the mind exist in great disproportion to each other; that in some the imagination is stronger than the judgment, and that in others, the reverse is manifest; but I do deny the *necessity* of any such disproportion, and maintain, that the greatest failures of realy lofty talent have arisen from this very incongruity. I do not deny, that different writers, and more especially in the present state of intellectual cultivation, are particularly qualified for different departments of literary labour; but I maintain, that to the perfection of each of these departments all the faculties must harmoniously contribute: that poetry as truly requires judgment as imagination; and that philosophy as truly requires imagination as judgment. I scarcely need except, indeed, the Mathematics; product of pure reason as it is commonly thought to be. It would have failed of many of its interesting applications; it would have stopped short of its boundless range amidst the pathways of heaven, but for the prompting and guidance of imagination. I say, therefore, that for rearing up the intellectual man, for raising the noblest forms of intellectual production, every faculty of the soul must do its part; and not only so, but that every power must labour; that fancy is a working faculty as truly as reason.

This indeed is the practical principle which I have already stated, and which I shall now undertake to defend. The denial of it has commonly appeared in the form which my language has just implied; in the exemption, that is to say, of certain powers, such as fancy, taste, genius, &c., from the necessity of study. No popular error in literature, I conceive, is deeper or more injurious than this. To counteract this; to show the universal necessity of study, of a thorough and patient application of mind, in every department of literature: to bring all the intellectual faculties under the one grand condition of *improving by exercise*, I have thought it not irrelevant to insist, briefly as I have, on the congruity which exists among them all. Let me not, however, be understood to say, for I do not and shall not say, that study, formal study, can compensate for all defects of original genius, or that there are no differences of natural endowment, for they certainly are great; but this I maintain, that, let the original power be what it may, without strong and fixed application, formal or informal, seen or unseen, with books or without them, that power can produce nothing that will live, or is worthy to live. Indeed, I might say, that without such study there is neither fruit nor evidence of high natural endowment. I will only further premise, that in my remarks on the value and importance of study, I shall solicit your indulgence to a pretty free range of topics, and that I shall occupy the passing hour, not so much with an abstract discussion of the principle I contend for, as with strictures on some of those circumstances of our intellectual condition, and some of those opinions in the literary world, which are unfriendly to severe and thorough mental culture and application.

From that fair proportion of the mind, of which I have spoken, from the severe old models of united strength and grace, and, more than all, from the study necessary to the imitation of them, I apprehend, it is the tendency of much of our modern literature, as well as of many maxims among us, to depart. And the peculiar situation of scholars in this country, or of those who should be scholars, is lending its aid to the same result. I venture to say of those who should be scholars; for the truth is, that we are, so many of us, men of business and men of action rather than of study, and there is as yet so little division of intellectual labour among us, that superficial acquisitions, and vague pursuits, and negligent habits of mind, are our greatest dangers.

But I must undertake more particularly to point out some of the causes that are leading to this result; that are leading many, certainly, to a neglect of hard study, and to a disproportioned and defective culture of the mind. As one of these causes, I was speaking of the general tendencies of our modern literature.

It is often said, that the present age is characterized by a strong thirst for excitement. Is it a craving for excitement, or is it that somewhat less respectable characteristic, a craving for entertainment, that marks the age? There is no occasion, however, to set them up as rival passions; being, as they doubtless are, but different degrees of the same passion. They are not stronger, probably, than they have always been, among nations of the European stock; than they were amidst "the fierce democracy" of Greece, the stern Roman delight in gladiatorial shows, or amidst the chivalry of the middle ages. But the observation, which is of importance, is this, that while the world is becoming more civilized, more intellectual, and more addicted to peaceful pursuits, both of these passions, the thirst for excitement and the thirst for entertainment, are making demands upon literature, such as they have never made at any former period. The spread of education is bringing forward a host of readers; the art of printing is providing them with books; and the gradual disuse of public sports and spectacles, the decline of fêtes and tournaments, the departure from the public eye of the "pomp and circumstance of glorious war," are carrying home the want of entertainment to millions of peaceful fire-sides.

This state of things is creating a new era in literature. Books, to an extent before unprecedented, are becoming luxuries; and these luxuries are having the usual effect when substituted in the place of substantial food; they are making men effeminate; they are making effeminate scholars. It is true, that many of the great productions of antiquity were designed for the people; but few of them for their entertainment; and none, that I remember, for the idle or weary hours of domestic relaxation. They were designed for the people; but still for the assembled people, for the eager throng of the forum, of the Centuries, of the Olympic games, or of the theatre; and the theatre too, it is to be remembered, was a school of far severer morals and more pointed satire, than our own. In one form or another, the great public was ever before the eyes of the ancient popular writers. What they wrote for the people at all, was designed for popular, not for private use. And, inspired as their productions were by this stirring sense of general interests, and by the anticipated and immediate verdict, upon their claims, of great assemblies, they are of a character not to enervate, but to arouse and strengthen the mind of the reader. Literature, in modern times, is domesticated. It is converted, indeed, to a most important use; but it is passing too, by the ordinary process of refinement, from use to luxury.

The immediate effects of that great change, which the spread of education and the development of new social wants are creating, of that change which has substituted a reading for a hearing public, and the lounger at the fire-side for the agitated asembly; the immediate effects, I say, are sufficiently obvious.

The remote consequences may not be so obvious, but they are no less certain.

The first effect is to lower the style of literary composition, and to render the standard more vague and uncertain. The style is to be read. It may, therefore, be negligent and irregular at less hazard. The sentence that is not clear, on the first reading, may be read again; and if, as is not uncommon, it requires a third reading, the author is not present to receive the salutary tokens of the displeasure or vexation he causes. The standard, too, becomes vague from the extension and variety of the audience to be addressed. There is no *one public*, of grave Romans or acute Athenians,where an author's rivals were ready to note him, and the common people were critics; but his style takes its chance for praise or censure among all the reading families of an empire. Hence, if it is not, in fact, more difficult to tell what good English is, than to decide the same point in the ancient languages, it is at any rate more difficult to check the aberrations of literary pretension and vanity.

The next effect of the change which has taken place in the intellectual and social condition of the world is the prodigious multiplication of books of entertainment, for the people. We are deluged with works of this class; and the passing tide bears us, every day, not only new productions, but new forms of literary production. It would be a very serious task to master even the literature of the Annuals. Meanwhile periodical publications crowd upon us, keeping pace with every division of time but hours and minutes, (for even the newspapers grow learned,) filling all the spaces not occupied by larger trifles, and covering, with grievous and pertinacious disorder and disarray, the tables that, fifty years ago, were pressed only by goodly quartos, or reverend folios. Seriously; it is impossible to keep up with the literature of the day, without losing sight of things far more important. Professional duties *must* be attended to; and these discharged, the contest lies, with many, between sound learning and trifling entertainment.

And here is found the worst effect of all, of the state of modern literature; more remote, as I have said, but not less certain. For it is not to be doubted, that many fail in that contest; that many, who might and should be sound scholars, become mere men of taste, and of very superficial taste, too, for the want of severe study and of thorough and philosophical habits of mind. If I do not very much mistake the literary signs of the times, this is not a matter of mere groundless apprehension. It is not only true, that the mighty folios of former days have gone out of fashion, but I venture to think, that books and essays of the most moderate dimensions, that require profound attention, stand less chance in the competition with lighter works, than they once did.

It shall be allowed that there have been great temptations. The muse of fiction, it is true, has laid aside some of her enchantments and sorceries; but she has clothed herself in the sober livery of history, and no one fears her; she has clothed herself with immortal genius and beauty, and no one can resist her. She has become no less powerful, and far more wise. It is this that has carried the works of the mighty Magician, and with them a multitude of humbler friends, into universal society. For that master-spirit has proved himself a magician, in a wider sense than that of having enchanted his individual readers; he has given a bias to the whole reading of the age. The novel-reading of former days was, comparatively, a lady's luxury; it is now the business of men; it is one of the great employments of society; it is invading the department of the scholar's labours. The novel is no longer "a book of the boudoir," but it is a book of the study. That long and lengthening series of volumes in our libraries, marked Waverly, though it may be high up in the pile, threatens insecurity to the whole fabric.

This influence of the literature of the day to beguile us from deep study and profound thought, is not left to operate by itself; but we have sundry clever and convenient maxims to help it on. The prevailing ideas of originality of thought, of imagination, of poetry, of eloquence, of fine writing, and of study itself lean, as I think, to this injurious result.

I say, in the first place, of study itself—of the very business of mental culture. And speaking on this point and going to the primary deficiency, I venture to question, whether the very ideas of intellectual improvement, even among thinking men, do not fall farther short of the thoroughness and consistency of a real system and science than any other ideas that prevail among us. I put it to the scholars who hear me, with all deference, how far they have settled within themselves, the plan, so to speak, of what they will be, or will attempt—nay, whether, in fact, the indistinct conceptions which are commonly entertained are not as wavering and fluctuating, as they are ill defined. The idea of a perfect man, upon which Cicero so often and eloquently discourses, under the name of the orator, seems scarcely to have any place among our modern speculations. He was to be not a philosopher only, not a mathematician, nor a student of history, nor an amateur in the arts, nor a poet, nor a good man, (yea, and a pious man,) only; but he was to be all of them in one; and so trained in all his faculties, that when he put forth their united effort, that effort should be expressed by nothing but the Demosthenic word, action—concentrated, intense, all-powerful action!

It may be said that the extent of modern science, and the multiplicity of its details, absolutely require a division of intellectual labour, inconsistent with Cicero's description of a perfect man. I am not about to enter upon the discussion of a topic so extensive. But this at least may be said, that there are living instances of all that extent and variety of attainment which his description requires; instances, too, in which all this, instead of distracting or diverting the mind, contributes in fact to its pre-eminence in some one department; and this, from all professional men, at least, is the true division of intellectual labour.

But not to dwell upon this point, concerning which perhaps it does not become me to pronounce; it may be questioned, whether the most thorough and powerful principles are yet fairly, and prominently enough, introduced into our systems for improving the mind. I say nothing of studying sixteen hours a day; sixteen hours a day! for fifty years, and then finding a fresh and vigorous old age: an achievement to be looked for in the moon—or in Germany! I say nothing of the vaunted practical spirit of the age, whose wisdom seems to consist in overlooking all necessary means, all previous training, to spring to the end. I say nothing of the imperfect courses of education with which many of our youth are obliged to be content, or to which at least they are obliged to confine themselves. But what are the grand impulses and projects offered to those who have the best opportunities? We are labouring hard at the mind;

and the main lever—I should not complain if it were only an auxiliary power—but the main lever with which we are striving to raise it up is ambition, and ambition, too, for immediate display and distinction. This is the grand principle in almost all our schools. We are working with this convenient and ready, but comparatively gross and clumsy instrument, rather than inspiring the soul with those principles and bringing forth from within it that development by which it will rise, irresistibly rise of itself. With the Greek and Roman systems of moral teaching, ambition was the only principle, perhaps, that could be relied on. But with our systems, with the simple and sublime precepts of Christianity, with the solemn revelation of a future life, that pours contempt upon all human pride, the selfish love of distinction, in all noble minds, is deprived of more than half its vigour; and when the whole weight is leaned upon it, it is found to be a reed, that is constantly wavering and swaying beneath us.

Observe, also, how cautiously religion, the strongest impulse in the human soul, is excluded from the paths of our literature; how little our literary men have been taught to draw from that deepest fountain of human nature; how little our scholars, those minds that should bear the brightest impress of the Divinity—how little they have felt themselves, as scholars, to have anything to do with religion. Observe how staid and precise an air it has worn, when it has entered one of our literary Reviews; not Puritanism was ever more precise; it has been a scholastic dignitary, or a fine gentleman, decent, decorous, superficial, cold. Thus, too, has it passed through almost the entire range of our classic English literature. Even of Addison, Soame Jenyns has somewhere said, with too much justice, that he seemed to regard the Supreme Being with an awe, as vague and indefinite as that with which a child gazes upon the mighty elephant. Even our great Moralist, as it has been said, when Mr. Boswell urged upon him some of the deeper and more anxious questionings of the human heart on the subject of religion, had nothing to say, but, "My dear Sir, keep your mind free from cant." We may not say, perhaps, that our literature is singularly irreligious; but it certainly is, taken as a body, singularly deficient in the depth and power that belong to that sentiment.

I cannot altogether join in a similar charge, which is now somewhat familiarly brought against our intellectual philosophy. I should be glad, at least, to *understand* Kant and Coleridge, before I can agree to it. I should be glad to understand that some of their language has any meaning, or any that answers to the mystical depths of their phraseology. And, indeed, so much of simple and of glorious truth do I find in the transcendental school, that it would be far easier to be reconciled to its doctrines, than to the absurd language in which their advocates have seen fit to clothe them.

But, after all, what chance there is for a thorough philosophy, in the tendencies of our English literature at the present day, is a doubtful point. The good old times, when men sat down amidst comparatively few books to think for themselves, seem to be giving place to days of multifarious and monstrous reading. I look in vain in England for patient thinkers like Bacon, and Locke, and Tucker and Reid; and I know not precisely where we are to look among ourselves, for men like Edwards and his school of metaphysical divines.

Indeed, in almost every department, there is too

little of that patient and thorough cultivation, which measures years in its plan, before it proposes to come to its finished result. It is a striking remark of Dégérando, that "the extraordinary most generally have sacrificed some condition essential to future progress." It is worth the consideration of eminent men, how far their distinction may be procured at this sacrifice, or may be liable to bring about this result in the progress of their future being; how far the cultivation of some powers may have been carried on, to the neglect of others, or of their whole intellectual and moral nature. Be this as it may, and it is not necessary as I have undertaken to show,—it is certain that in the youthful student, a diseased and superficial ambition, eager for display, anxious to be known, panting for distinction rather than for excellence, seeking for manifestation rather than for development, urging itself,—not urged from within,—but urging itself on, with a premature and feverish excitement; that such an ambition, I say, *is* making fatal sacrifices of future merit, and distinction also, to present notoriety. It is painful to see the disposition of so large a portion of the early and promising talent among us, to rely upon its present attainments or its hasty efforts, to rely upon the ready coin which it bears about with it, rather than patiently to cultivate the deep mine within; and were it not for the salutary admonition afforded us, it would be yet more painful to behold its brief, spendthrift career, and final poverty.

In short, the very first article, in a sound literary creed, is but half believed among us; and this scepticism vitiates all our faith. We believe in genius, and eloquence, and poetry; we believe in glorious thoughts, and intellectual inspirations, and visions of beauty; but we do not believe in—STUDY; and we do but half believe in *truth.* "Truth!" says the sceptic sage, "it is a very dangerous thing."—"Truth!" says the small, practical philosopher, "what is truth good for, if it will not give us a warmer hearth, or a more plentiful board?" In short, utility, we are told, is taking such a lead in the affairs of mankind, that the world must grow intellectually dull, tame, and spiritless; it is getting to be too cultivated for poetry, too comfortable for eloquence, too busy for literature, and too sharp-sighted for faith. All its nobler productions, it is said, must decline amidst this grand modern improvement; and the world must henceforth be governed, not by mind, but by machinery; it is no longer to seek for truth,—painful toil! but for comfort. Whatever will promote this,—sciences or arts, governments or manufactories, railways or books, no matter what, that tends to this result, is to engross the future attention of mankind.

"We run, alas! after truth," said Voltaire, long ago, "ah! believe me, error has its value." That is the real and infidel text, from which all this fine doctrine is derived; for the old French philosophy was as infidel with regard to what is human, as with regard to what is divine. And even Mr. Burke may be quoted for the observation, that "the pleasures of the imagination are much higher than any which are derived from a rectitude of the judgment," as if the two qualities were inconsistent with each other. And we have the proverbial authority of Dr. Johnson for the declaration, (I do not undertake to give his words,) that all eloquence is founded on extravagance. And a lady, who has risen to the dignity of being the author of forty volumes, has, not long since, told us, that, for her own sex at least, intuition is better than reasoning. And our poets have ever been singing of the charm and rapture of youthful fancy; leaving it to be inferred, that riper years and sounder judgment must chill and quench its fervors, instead of guiding them upward to an increasing, steady, noon-tide strength and splendour. And our philosophers have decided, that the favoured age of poetry is the *youth* of the world; as if the poems of Homer *could* have been the production of a rude and undisciplined mind.

But let us collect some of these maxims, that have long, with undefined shape and uncertain tendency, been floating about in the world, and put them in some form, and place them directly before us. Let us examine some of those qualities and efforts of mind which are commonly thought to be, less than any others, the fruit of patient study. The instances, which every one's reflection will at once present us with; are such as poetry, eloquence, the walks of fiction, and especially such as originality of mind, and native genius. These forms and features of literary talent, I shall have occasion to touch in but a single point; and although it were easy, no doubt, to make each of them, even on this point, the subject of extensive discussion, it will not be necessary, perhaps, to my argument; it must, at any rate, on this occasion be dispensed with.

What, then, is poetry? The common answer would be, that it is some peculiar gift, some intellectual effluence, distinct, not merely in form, not merely in rhythm, but essentially and in its very nature distinct from all prose writings. Its numbers are mystic numbers; its themes are far above us, and away from us, in the clouds, or in the hues of the distant landscape; it is at war with the realities of life, and it is especially afraid of logic. It is using no extravagant language, it is committing no vulgar mistake to say, that poetry is regarded as a kind of "peculiar trade and mystery," nay, in a sense beyond that of this technical language, as a real and absolute mystery. In one of the most distinguished journals of the day, we find a writer complaining after this sort; "Poetry," says he, "the workings of genius itself, which, in all times, and with one or another meaning, has been called inspiration, and held to be mysterious and inscrutable, is no longer without its scientific exposition."* And why, let us ask, why should it be without its exposition?—ay, and if there were any such thing as a science of criticism among us (for the truth is, there is a great deal less of it than there was in the days of Addison and Johnson), I would say it is *scientific* exposition? What *is* poetry? What is this mysterious thing, but one form in which human nature expresses itself? What is it but embodying, what is it but "showing up," in all its moods, from the lowliest to the loftiest, the same deep and impassioned, but universal mind, which is alike and equally the theme of philosophy? What does poetry tell us, but that which was already in our own hearts? What are all its intermingled lights and shadows; what are its gorgeous clouds of imagery, and the hues of its distant landscapes; what are its bright and blessed visions, and its dark pictures, of sorrow and passion, but the varied reflection of the beautiful and holy, and yet overshadowed, and marred, and afflicted nature within us? And how then is poetry any more inscrutable than our own hearts are inscrutable! To whom or to what, let us ask again, does poetry address itself? To what, in its heroic ballads, in its epic song, in its humbler verse, in its strains of love, or pity, or indignation,—to what does it speak, but to human nature, but to the common mind of all the world? And its noblest productions, its Iliads, its

* Edinburgh Review.

Hamlets and Lears, the whole world has understood,—the rude and the refined, the anchorite and the throng of men. There *is* poetry in real life, and in the humblest life. There *is* "unwritten poetry"; there is poetry in prose; there is poetry in all living hearts.

Let him be the true poet who shall find it, sympathize with it, and bring it to light. He that does so must deeply study human nature. He that does so, must, whether he knows it or not, be a philosopher. Much there is, no doubt, of technical language, much about quiddities and entities, that he may not know. But he must know, and that by deep study and observation, how feelings and passions rise in the human breast, what are those which coexist, what repel each other, what naturally spring one from another; he must know what within is moved, and how it is put in action, by all this moving world around us; what chords are struck, not only by the rough touches of fortune, but what are swept by invisible influences; he must know all the wants, and sufferings, and joys of this inward being, what are its darkest struggles, its sublimest tendencies, its most soothing hopes, and most blessed affections; and all this is divine philosophy. He must wait almost in prayer at the oracle within; he must write the very language of his own soul; he must write no rash response from the shrines of idolized models; but asking, questioning, listening to the voice within as he writes; and then will the deepest philosophy take the form of the noblest inspiration.

And what more does the eloquent man, let us ask again—what more does he, than express that which, in greater or less power, is within us all? He creates nothing. He is but an interpreter of what God has created within us. He only gives it language. In the old Puritan phrase, as true in philosophy as in religion, he is "but an instrument." He but unlocks the sources of feeling, and it flows of itself. And the key which is to open for him a way to the hearts of others, is a profound study, a deep knowledge, an exquisite sense of what is in his own heart.

And what is fiction?—for I find that I must not dwell upon these instances,—what is fiction, but assembling in various combinations the traits of real life? Nor do all the efforts of imagination ever go beyond the simple reality. Nor can all the tales of imaginary distress or joy ever equal what takes place in the dwellings of human affection. The tones of rapturous or agonized human sympathy, tenderness, love, pity, the gentle voices of kindness that echo from the familiar hearth-stone, the accents in which a mother speaks to her sick and suffering child, surpass all that fancy can imagine, or the stage exhibit. And no fictitious heroism is more noble than that which swells many a heart, in the secret and solitary strife of virtue. And all the sentimental descriptions in the world are but cold rhapsody, in comparison with what is actually witnessed and felt in the daily communion of heart with heart.

The argument which, in pursuance of my design, I might draw from these observations, is evident. By laying the foundation of poetry, eloquence, and fiction in human nature, I say, that they are brought within the range of the strictest philosophy, and that they demand the most thorough and philosophical study.

While I thus refer again to the argument I am pursuing, I will advert, in passing, to the common objection. It is said, that study often has the effect to chill the sensibility and enthusiasm necessary to success in these lofty arts, or that it leads to those fine discriminations of thought, which take proportionably from its strong and bold outline and coloring. The answer is, that the study which produces this effect is not of the right kind, that it is not healthful to the mind, nor in the highest degree thorough, sound, and discriminating in itself, that it certainly is not properly adapted to its end, that, with reference to its end, it certainly is not philosophical. No doubt there are instances in which the poetic fire is chilled by metaphysical abstraction. There are those who have become less eloquent writers for being more refined thinkers, and others who have become less eloquent speakers in the study to improve. But in every such instance, I contend, that the study is not sound, and wise, and well applied. I cannot admit, that the mystical and misty speculations of Mr. Coleridge, with however much of noble thought and deep penetration, they discover, are any exception to the remark. I cannot admit, that he is any the better philosopher for being the worse, if he *is* the worse, poet. The essayist, Foster, is a remarkable example of an eloquent writer sinking, as he has done, in his later productions, under the weight of tedious and perplexed sentences, from too much refinement of thought. His brain has spun the matter of his late discussion so thick and fine with qualifications, that his own manly sense is scarcely able to break through them; and his reader is wearied with pursuing out, first one line of qualification and then another, till he loses the main thread of the discourse.* But, then, I maintain that the same acuteness, which led him to perceive the innumerable discriminations into which thought branches out, should have led him in popular discourse, to cut off those smaller limbs which detract alike from the strength, beauty, and

*As in the Essays on Popular Ignorance.

distinctness of the picture. What we have to require of such writers is, not that they should think less, but they should think more. We demand an effort beyond that of philosophizing,—the effort of communication; an effort which is declared by Dr. Brown to be the very end of "a judicious logic." And in order to the success of this effort, we demand the study, the strong and vivid perception, that emblazons its main thought, on every page, with a brightness that extinguishes every inferior light.

The case of those writers, and it is not rare, who, from the time of their first successful production, fall ever after into a lower and poorer style, will not be thought to offer any objection. The deterioration arises percisely from want of study, from self-confidence and carelessness, from poverty of thought in many cases, and in some, from the vanity, in the writers, of supposing, that it was the charm of their peculiarities, and not the claim of their general merits, that had attracted the public notice.

The same general remarks apply to the labours for improvement of the public speaker. There is one common observation on this subject, however, which is often made with great confidence, and as a triumphant argument against study, to which I shall not reply as an objection, because I entirely controvert its truth. It is said that some of our most eloquent speakers are native orators, and have never studied their productions at all, with reference to delivery. This I deny; for one of the most important departments of rhetorical study is left out of this statement. I mean what rhetoricians call the "silent study" of a piece,—in which the celebrated Siddons is said so much to have exercised herself,—and which, however unconsciously, I am as certain that eloquent speakers have used, as I am that the painter has studied the picture on his canvass.

But to refer to the common rhetorical exercises; I maintain, that study fails here, if at all, from the want of thoroughness, patience, or good sense,—fails especially because it is not study enough. The orator is thinking too much of his art perhaps, is thinking of principles and rules and criticisms, at the very moment when he attempts to exchange his art for action. But what is the inference? Not that philosophy and practice prevent success; not that they are useless; but that he does not know how to use them; that he has not used them enough. He is not familiar with them. He is encumbered by that which might aid him. He is intimidated, in fact, by the *armour* which he has not learned to wield. He is like the raw recruit, who is all the while thinking what terrible weapons he is using, and what fearful passes he makes. We would have the soldier certainly taught the art of fence; but if he were constantly thinking of its rules and principles, if his head were filled with his books and his practice, as he went into the battle, he would of course fight timidly and awkwardly; his philosophy, so to call it,—his superficial accomplishment, that is to say,—would be a bad thing for him. But, then, again, the inference would be, not that the art of fence is a bad thing, but that he is badly or imperfectly instructed in it.

There is a great deal of real study, of real philosophy, in fact, without the name, and without even the consciousness of it. And I undertake to say, as to mere style, that, in the composition of a single paragraph of a high order and of any great beauty, though the writer may be insensible of it, there is as keen and careful a selection and discrimination of thoughts, as exact a proportion of one thing to another, as decisive and determinate a rejection of every thought that would interfere with the whole effect, as there is judgment or taste in the construction of a fine building, or in the delineation of a splendid picture. The process, the art, the writer may not be perceived, or even thought of, by the reader. So neither in the full impression of architectural or pictorial beauty, do we think of the artist. Yet, in either case, the judgment and the taste are there, and have laboured hard at their finished work.

And although the talent employed may possess the almost mystic charm which is usually expressed by the phrase, original talent, yet it is only the more true that it must labour for its distinction. What is true originality of thought but that thorough and painful elaboration of ideas, which gives them the peculiar cast and character of the mind they pass through? The original mind is but the crucible in which old and well known materials are transmuted into new forms; and it is not a flash or a gleam that gives the result, but the trial of fire! The scripture declaration applies here more truly than anywhere else, since it applies to the permanent intellectual nature of man, that "there is nothing new under the sun." Even the vaunted modern systems of metaphysical philosophy, if we may believe Professor Cousin, are but reproductions of the old: and the world, after its long sleep in the night of the Middle Ages, is but just coming up with Plato and Aristotle. To make new and superior fabrics out of common materials, must be a work of labour. Singularity, eccentricity, may be the natural and mushroom products of a shallow and barren soil, but originality is a plant of another and different growth. The man who thinks for himself, who thinks differently from other men, and pays their opinions the respect to compare them with his own, who strikes out new paths of reflection and investigates them—the original thinker, in other words, deserving the name, must think deeply and patiently. He is bound to do this, beyond all men, and if he is faithful to his own mind he will do it. It may be doubted indeed, whether much that passes for originality is not some novel and really indefensible modification of thought, which the author of it labours hard and ingeniously to clothe in such forms as not to shock the general judgment. But even this, the lowest and most doubtful form of original thought, is any thing, it is apparent, but the result of hasty impulses and suggestions.

As the most illustrious example of true originality, of the almost mysterious development of great native powers, Shakspeare is constantly quoted. He is called the child of nature. His works pass with us for a sort of inspiration. Our ignorance of this wonderful being, of whom nearly all that can be said is in the words of a critic, that "after having written his thirty-eight plays, he went carelessly down to the country, and lived out his days, apparently unconscious of having done any thing at all extraordinary;"—this mystery, which shrouds the circumstances of his life, helps to spread over his immortal productions an air, not of effort, but of enchantment. Into that deep and silent world of thoughts and passions, the mind of Shakspeare, well shadowed forth by the outward silence of history, few men have sent any searching analysis; few can. There is enough, indeed, of verbal annotation and small criticism upon his works in his native tongue. And German critics have written of him, in language of unbounded admiration, often bordering on rhapsody, and yet of much deeper sympathy with him too; but the philosophy of Shakspeare's genius is yet to be studied.* Yet who can doubt that that world of his secret thoughts was a world of labour? Who can doubt that to him who lingered in some humble employment about the theatre, the great globe itself was a stage, and that all men passed before him as actors; that he saw them as they passed as none other had seen them; saw through every disguise, the mean man and the mighty, the dark, the fierce, the passionate, the meek, the lovely, the sorrowful, the rejoicing—sympathized with all, studied all, revolved in his own bosom all human thought, feeling, passion, desire, till they came forth the living beings of his own mind, and destined to live in the admiration and delight of men for ever.

As a further and final example of the point I have laboured to establish, let me refer to that undefined and much misapprehended quality, called genius.

The favourite idea of a genius among us, is of one who never studies, or who studies, nobody can tell when—at midnight, or at odd times and intervals—and now and then strikes out, *at a heat*, as the phrase is, some wonderful production. This is a character that has figured largely in the history of our literature, in the person of our Fieldings, our Savages, and our Steeles—"loose fellows about town," or loungers in the country, who slept in ale-houses and wrote in bar-rooms, who took up the pen as a magician's wand to supply their wants, and when the pressure of necessity was relieved, resorted again to their carousals. Your real genius is an idle, irregular, vagabond sort of per-

* It is scarcely necessary to except from this remark the Lectures of A. W. Schlegel; though of all the writers on Shakspeare, he would be most justly designated, perhaps, as the man to execute this noble task.

sonage, who muses in the fields or dreams by the fireside; whose strong impulses—that is the cant of it—must needs hurry him into wild irregularities or foolish eccentricity; who abhors order, and can bear no restraint, and eschews all labour: such an one, for instance, as Newton, or Milton! What! they must have been irregular, else they were no geniuses.

"The young man," it is often said, "has genius enough, if he would only study." Now the truth is, as I shall take the liberty to state it, that genius will study, it is that in the mind which does study; that is the very nature of it. I care not to say that it will always use books. All study is not reading, any more than all reading is study. By study I mean—but let one of the noblest geniuses and hardest students of any age define it for me: "Studium," says Cicero, "est animi assidua et vehemens ad aliquam rem applicata magnâ cum voluntate occupatio, ut philosophiæ, poëticæ, geometriæ, literarum."* Such study, such intense mental action, and nothing else, is genius. And so far as there is any native predisposition about this enviable character of mind, it is a predisposition to that action. That is the only test of the original bias; and he who does not come to that point, though he may have shrewdness, and readiness, and parts, never had a genius. No need to waste regrets upon him, as that he never could be induced to give his attention or study to anything; he never had that which he is supposed to have lost. For attention it is, though other qualities belong to this transcendent power,—attention it is, that is the very soul of genius: not the fixed eye, not the poring over a book, but the fixed thought. It is, in fact, an action of the mind which is steadily concentrated upon one idea, or one series of

* De Inventione, Lib. I. c. 25.

ideas,—which collects in one point the rays of the soul till they search, penetrate, and fire the whole train of its thoughts. And while the fire burns within, the outward man may indeed be cold, indifferent, negligent,—absent in appearance; he may be an idler, or a wanderer, apparently without aim or intent: but still the fire burns within. And what though "it bursts forth," at length, as has been said, "like volcanic fires, with spontaneous, original, native force?" It only shows the intenser action of the elements beneath. What though it breaks like lightning from the cloud? The electric fire had been collecting in the firmament through many a silent, calm, and clear day. What though the might of genius appears in one decisive blow, struck in some moment of high debate, or at the crisis of a nation's peril? That mighty energy, though it may have heaved in the breast of a Demosthenes, was once a feeble infant's thought. A mother's eye watched over its dawning. A father's care guarded its early growth. It soon trod with youthful step the halls of learning, and found other fathers to wake and to watch for it,—even as it finds them here. It went on: but silence was upon its path, and the deep strugglings of the inward soul marked its progress, and the cherishing powers of nature silently ministered to it. The elements around breathed upon it and "touched it to finer issues." The golden ray of heaven fell upon it, and ripened its expanding faculties. The slow revolutions of years slowly added to its collected treasures and energies; till in its hour of glory, it stood forth embodied in the form of living, commanding, irresistible eloquence! The world wonders at the manifestation, and says, "Strange, strange that it should come thus unsought, unpremeditated, unprepared!" But the truth is, there is no more a miracle in it, than there is in the towering of the pre-eminent forest tree, or in the flowing of the mighty and irresistible river, or in the wealth and the waving of the boundless harvest.

Fathers and Guardians of our youthful learning!—behold it here—the germ of all that glorious power, in the strong, generous and manly spirits of the rising youth around you; and say, if you would relinquish an office, so honoured, and so to be rewarded, for the sceptre of any other dominion. Youthful aspirants after intellectual eminence!—forget, forget, I entreat you; banish, banish forever, the weak and senseless idea, that anything will serve your purpose, but study; intense, unwearied, absorbing study; "animi assidua et vehemens occupatio."

I recall one who more than thirty years since trod these hallowed paths of learning, whose life of literary enterprise and labour shows that he had taken that word for his motto. The leisure of his early manhood was devoted to works that have done honour to our youthful literature, and his zeal for letters found a place for similar studies, even amidst the labours of a responsible, and honorable, and well-discharged commission abroad, from the government of his country. I need not say that I allude to the accomplished and lamented Tudor. The distinguished place which he held in our republic of letters, as well as in this association, would justly require of us an apology, not for speaking of him, but for being, on this occasion, silent. As my acquaintance with his character was not personal, I can speak only of those literary projects and productions which certainly entitle him to a respectful and grateful commemoration among us. To die in a foreign land, to die amidst strangers, to die on the eve of a long-desired return to his country, is mournful. But to have performed honourable and honoured services for his country; to have left the impress of his mind on its permanent literature; to have left memorials of himself, too, in the still ripening fruits of his intelligent enterprises; to have portrayed, with a discriminating hand, "the living manners as they rise," and well and worthily to have celebrated the glorious dead, and at last, himself to have gone down to the grave amidst the regrets of all who knew him; these are testimonials to literary usefulness and honour, which any man among us might covet, when his own labours also shall come to their end.

How soon they may be brought to it, and how suddenly, Divine Providence has very lately given us a most affecting and solemn intimation. I know that the minds of many who hear me will turn, without hesitation, and not without strong emotion, to our late, distinguished, most honoured,—and I give the full force to that word, when I add,—to our beloved Chief Justice!* Speaking as I do in the presence of those who have been his associates and companions through many favoured years, I feel that they will not ask of one, who has not enjoyed that happiness, to pronounce his eulogy. Nor needs it to be spoken here; for his praise is in all the borders of this Commonwealth, and it is permanently recorded on one of the highest pages in the history of its jurisprudence. And yet there is one—apology, shall I call it?—for the admiration and homage of all who knew him. For of no man could it be more properly said, that his distinction, his honour, his worth were the property of us all; for they shone upon all; they made friends of all; they cheered every one, whether high or low, whether old or young, whom

*Chief Justice Parker died on the 25th of July, 1830.

he took by the hand with a simplicity and kindness as honourable to him even as his eminent talents and distinguished learning. Noble and excellent man! now, alas! added to the number of the lamented and venerated! be the path that thou hast trod—the path of labour, of toil, of study, of virtue, of piety,—be it our own path to usefulness and honour!

In the presence of such contemplations, I need not be reminded that further discussion would be improper. Suffice the argument which is supported by such examples; examples more powerful than any words of mine to illustrate and enforce our duty as scholars. Suffice the inducements, when every year's assembling here, with sad commemoration of the departed, solemnly teaches us, that life is short, is shortening; while the field of knowledge spreads before us in bright and boundless prospect. "That which I know," were the dying words of the illustrious La Place,—"That which I know is limited; that which I do not know, is infinite!"

XV.

THE ARTS OF INDUSTRY; WITH THEIR MORAL AND INTELLECTUAL INFLUENCE UPON SOCIETY.*

MR. PRESIDENT, AND GENTLEMEN OF THE INSTITUTE:

WE have come together this evening, to celebrate the great and noble arts of industry. I say, the great and noble arts of industry. I cannot say, the humble arts, in deference to popular phraseology; the splendid spectacle of your Annual Fair, would rebuke me if I did so. I confess that it has given me new ideas of what industry can do—of what mind can do with matter. As I have stood in your magnificent hall of exhibition, visions of oriental magnificence—descriptions from the gorgeous page of Milton, have been in my thoughts. And yet, "the wealth of Ormus or the Ind," "barbaric pearls and gold," could offer nothing so gratifying to the eye of patriotism, as that splendid assemblage of the products of mechanic art. To one who had not witnessed that spectacle, this might seem extravagant. But I am sure that I should not do justice to the feelings of those who have seen it, without speaking of it as I do. And when we remember that it is but two centuries, since the rude savage wandered across this wooded island—all his weapons, tools and instruments together, but a tomahawk, a scalping knife, and a hunter's bow—we might imagine that the Genius of Civilization had stretched out its wand,

* An Address delivered before the members of the American Institute, in the City of New York, October, 1837.

and conjured up this fairy scene, to celebrate its triumph.

How characteristic is this spectacle, gentlemen, of the times in which we live! In other days, it would have been the tournament, or the feasting hall, hung round with helmets and swords, and the grim and shaggy trophies of the chase. And, indeed, if we had fixed our eye first upon the upper end of that hall, we might have imagined that we were witnessing only the same thing, in higher perfection—only more gorgeous caparisons and trappings of the war-horse, more polished weapons, and more fatal instruments of death. But, as we look around us, we see other tokens; the products of the peaceful loom and planing tool, carving and tapestry, works of equal utility and beauty in iron, and marble, and glass, and shining metals; comforts for home, and conveniences for travel; and books, in bindings splendid enough to seduce the eye from those attractive and ponderous ledgers—in which there is to be so much more profitable writing. We see, too, that the busy and delicate hand of woman has been there. Meanwhile, music, far other than that of the war-song, flings its notes over the gay scene, and all around us breathes of peace and prosperity. It is a characteristic and striking exhibition of the arts that conduce to human improvement; and it is to some reflections bearing upon this point, that I wish, on the present occasion, to invite the attention of this assembly.

The distinguished Gentlemen who have preceded me in the delivery of this annual discourse, and whose eminence has made the office as difficult as the appointment of the American Institute has made it honourable, have been very naturally led, by their public stations and duties, to consider the political questions which are connected with the arts of industry. Those questions are, doubtless, important; and they have probably been settled to your satisfaction. I suppose no doubt is entertained in this assembly, whether American industry ought, in some degree, to be protected. But whether American industry, or any other industry, is honoured as it ought to be: whether, in fact, it is usually sensible of its own dignity, and of its many and important relations to the public welfare, may not be so clear. This is the direction, therefore, that I would give to your thoughts on the present occasion; and, not to wander over too large a field, my principal design will be to consider the connection between the arts of industry, and especially the mechanic arts, and the *intellectual* and *moral* improvement of society.

This topic is very naturally presented by the occasion that has brought us together. For this annual Fair is not held merely for the sake of a splendid and idle display. It is so splendid, indeed, that it appears to me worthy of being made for its own sake. The delighted and satisfied visitor can hardly ask for any object beyond the pleasure of seeing it. But this is not the only object. Nor is its only end to gratify private ambition, or to advance private interests; lawful and proper for them, as it is, indeed, thus to present themselves to the public attention. But the occasion points to something beyond; it points directly to the ultimate and great design of your association; which is, not only to benefit yourselves, but to benefit your country; not merely to develop and foster the arts of life, but to develop, and foster, and exalt the life of society—that life of society, which depends for its highest welfare upon an intellectual and moral cul ture.

All improvement avails but little, that does not result in this culture of the mind and heart. All that is done in the world, without this end, is but weary toil without reward; a splendid apparatus, without result. Separated from this, none but an idiot could enjoy the spectacle. For, to what purpose is it, that all the comforts and elegancies of life are spread around us; to what purpose is it, that the products of the forest and the mine, and all the powers of earth, air, fire and water, are brought into subservience to the human will; to what purpose is it, that the earth is better tilled, and the ocean is more successfully navigated, and more splendid cities are rising all round its spreading shores, if man, in the presence of all this profusion and magnificence is only growing more ignorant, slavish, effeminate and corrupt? Too rapid is the march of improvement, too swift are our travelling cars, though ambitious of a greater speed, if they are bearing us on this. Too high already is the structure of mechanic art, if, like the lofty pyramid, it is only to overshadow a dwarfed and degraded people. And sad and thankless were the task, if all that the most accomplished industry of human hands can do, is to build but a more splendid couch for the premature disease, decay and death of society.

And such, in fact, you know is said, by some, to be the inevitable tendency of the arts of civilization. The inventions and devices of art are sometimes regarded as only disturbing the order of society, in their progress; and in their consummation, as only precipitating it to a speedier downfall. Sentimental sighings over barbarous ages, (miscalled, golden ages,) now past and gone, and practical resistance to new inventions in machinery, have alike given testimony to this absurd way of thinking.

I can scarcely admit, indeed, that it deserves a serious refutation; and I do not so much propose an argument in favour of the mechanic arts, as an illustration of their natural tendency and immense power to improve society.

And the first and lowest illustration of this nature is found in the influence which the products of art exert, through that mental law, called the law of association.

The things that are about us impart a hue and shape to our minds. They are our teachers, the models of our thought. It is scarcely conceivable, that the minds of men in general should have been turned to admiration and touched to rapture, if they had not been surrounded, in the works of nature, with a world of beauty. The fair and tranquil scene around us, steals insensibly into the heart, and becomes within us, an image and a life. I know, indeed, that the mind imparts a character to the scene around it; but it also receives a character in turn. And so powerful and so necessary is this influence in the infancy of man and of nations, that a world bereft of beauty, fragrance and music, and of all graceful forms—all rude and shaggy as our mountain-tops—must have been a world of beings far worse than barbarians.

That which is true of the habitation that God has builded for us, is true of those which we build for ourselves. A man who lives like the Bedouin Arab and the wild Tartar, in a barn, and among the cattle that he tends or drives, is likely to have as much of the brute as the man in him. The first step of improvement for such a people, would be improvement in the arts of living. Nay, filth and slovenliness almost inevitably dwell in mud-walled and unfloored cottages; and it is scarcely too much to say, that filth and slovenliness are enemies to good morals. "Cleanliness," says John Wesley, "is next to godliness." We are all in some sense actors, and we naturally suit our action to the scene in which we move. We have often heard that Diogenes lived in a tub; but it has not been as often considered, perhaps, that his rude manners and speech were such as befitted his residence; that, if we were to give an account of his proverbial rudeness, we should say, not that Diogenes made the tub, but that the tub made Diogenes.

He, then, who is building commodious dwellings, or filling them with splendid furniture, is making no mean contribution to the grace and accomplishment of human life. He is often creating a school, in fact, for vulgar wealth, in which it cannot resist improvements; he is often the master, as he is the superior, of the idle and flattered inheritor of fortune. And it may well be a grateful consideration to him who is toiling at his work-bench, that he is toiling for the improvement of society. It is a noble stimulus to the perfection of his work; to the production of more perfect conveniences, more graceful forms, more exquisite instruments for the mind's culture. He who designs and erects a noble structure, speaks to passing multitudes, who seldom perhaps read a book, and helps to refine and humanize the ages that shall come after him. Even he who makes a musical instrument, is laying up, in those hidden chambers of melody, the sweet influences that shall amuse, and soften, and refine many a domestic circle through life.

The first point, then, which I present to your consideration, is, that by the very law of mental association, we are improved by the improvements that are around us. It is true that every law may be broken, and this is doubtless sometimes broken by the pride of display. But still, when I look upon the most gorgeous scene which the most vulgar passion for display has spread around it, it is not without some complacency in the thought, that that scene may help in turn to elevate the mind of its possessor. He who inhabits a palace may really be inferior to him who built, or to him who adorns it; but it would be strange if he should not catch something from that school of taste in which he is placed. Wealth is indeed the friend of mechanic art; but the favour is often well and fully returned; opulence is often as much indebted to art, as art is to opulence. At any rate, it is something that the sense of our own dignity is affected by the objects that surround us; as well it may be by the glorious mansion which the Infinite Architect has provided for us. When Nero had caused to be built his magnificent palace on the Palatine Hill, called his "golden house," which was of such extent that it had a single piazza of three rows of columns, more than half a mile long—a single room 148 feet long and 98 broad; which covered acres enough for a moderately sized farm; and was in fact a little city by itself, of quadrangles, towers, pillars, statues, baths and fountains; he is reported by Suetonius to have said, that he had now a house fit for a MAN to live in. There was something of nobility, if there was more of pride, in that saying. And if he had remembered, that while the man Nero dwelt in the golden house, the men, Severus and Celerus, who built it, ay, and every hod-carrier, dwelt in that habitation, whose foundation is earth, whose pillars the mountains, and whose dome, the spreading heavens—yes, if he had rightly remembered this, his pride had been less, and his true nobility greater.

But the next observation I have to offer, is on the

effects of mechanic art, in promoting the comfort and relieving the toils of mankind.

The advantage in this respect, I know, has been held to be more than questionable. The operatives who have been from time to time, flung out of employment by the successive inventions of mechanic art, have said that their toils were indeed relieved to their injury, and that their comforts were not increased, but much lessened. And this reasoning has not been confined to the operatives. William Lea, the inventor of the stocking-frame, made a pair of stockings by the frame, we are told, in the presence of King James the First; but his invention, though approved, was discountenanced, upon the plea, that it would deprive the poor,

> "the knitters in the sun,
> And the free maids who weave their thread with bones,"

of their subsistence. And after having met with similar disappointments in France, William Lea died in Paris of a broken heart. The inventor of the first cotton-spinning machine, in 1733, himself destroyed it. under the generous apprehension that it might deprive the poor of bread. And such, indeed, may be the temporary effect of improved machinery in certain instances; but the conclusion, as one of general and permanent application, is altogether a mistake. For it is found that with the easier and cheaper production of any article, a more general use obtains, a quicker and wider demand is created, and the field of labour, instead of being straitened, is indefinitely extended. The invention of Arkwright, labour-saving as it is, has given employment to millions. We may always be sure that the expanding desire, i. e. the market demand of society, will keep in advance of the supply. If it falls behind for a moment in any case, it will soon come up, and will always win the race. For it is the race of mind with matter, the contest of ever boundless desire, with ever boundless supply. The swiftest car will flag in that contest. The drivers of coaches are apt, at first, to look with jealousy upon a rail-road. But they soon find that the stream of travel which flows upon it, sends off branches for them to occupy, greater than the original stream. The Vetturini of Italy usually travel at the tedious rate of about thirty miles a day; and they demand the monopoly of public conveyances. When, a few years ago, an attempt was made to run an English coach from Florence to Leghorn, the coachman and guard were murdered on the way, by a banditti, composed probably of these fierce and ignorant Vetturini. Had this improvement been admitted, they would have found by this time, that their business had increased fourfold.

But I have said enough on this point; and I return to the proposition, that the mechanic arts improve society by increasing its comforts and lessening its toils.

Comfort, to a certain extent, is undoubtedly favourable to social improvement; and toil, beyond a certain extent, is as clearly unfavourable. I make this statement in these guarded terms, because the comforts of civilized life may be carried to a vicious and enervating indulgence; and because labour, when not excessive, so far from being an evil, is a blessing to the world. If a man can make a machine to work for him, it is not best indeed for him to stand idle; nor is he likely to stand idle. He will probably turn his hand to something else. He will set himself to relieve some want; to remove some annoyance; to smooth some roughness in his path, or to extract some thorn of vexation; and thus to make his way easier and happier. A certain state of ease and comfort is good for our moral nature. Courage and frugality may be virtues of savage life, but good nature, gentleness, generosity and patience, have but a poor chance amidst its rough and desolate fortunes. It is not good for a man to live like a bear, or an otter. It is scarce likely to improve his temper, for him to wear hair cloth, or to freeze in winter, or to breathe in his house the smoke that ought to have gone up the chimney; or when he travels, to have his carriage broken down on rough roads: or when he rests, to sleep, as the old chronicles say was common in England three centuries ago, "with a good round log under his head for a bolster."*

Let us be permitted to dwell a moment on one or two of the points now referred to; for I suppose that details are not improper on such an occasion as this; and that the suggestions even of the unskilful, if they aim at improvement in the arts of civilized life, will meet with indulgence. We do not sleep, it is true, with a good round log for a pillow. Our pillows are as soft as feathers and down can make them. To them, I have nothing to object. But our beds, I am tempted to say, are either too soft or too hard. Neither feathers, nor hair, is so good a material for this purpose as wool. The French bed, which usually consists of two thin mattresses of wool, upon a foot deep of hay or straw, is four times as cheap as ours, and twice as comfortable. On the subject of warming our houses, also, permit me to say a word. It is scarcely too much to aver, that one half of the fuel burnt in this country is literally thrown away; the heat passing as it does into the dead wall of the chimney. The air chamber, which should take its place, is but little known in the country, and is seldom used, I believe, even in this city. Then, again, with regard to the

* Hollingshead.

use of anthracite coal, great difficulty is experienced from the want of a little knowledge. Many who have tried it, complain of its effect in drying the air, destroying furniture, and even injuring health. They say, that in mild and moist weather it burns too freely, and in cold and dry weather, it goes out entirely; and that in the warm days of the autumn and spring, they cannot regulate it at all. For this last difficulty, let me observe in passing, there is a very simple remedy. A bank of fine coal of proper thickness, spread over a grate-full of already ignited coarse coal, will make a fire that will burn moderately forty-eight hours without being touched. But the chief remedy for all the inconveniences before mentioned, is the evaporation of water. Within the mason work of every grate that is set for this kind of coal, and of course, entirely out of sight, and about an inch—you will pardon me for being particular, for I have made experiments—*about* an inch, a *little* less, from the soapstone at the side of the grate, should be set a copper-fastened or earthen evaporator, with a pipe leading out to the side of the breast-work of the chimney. This vessel will evaporate about two quarts of water in a day, which will give a sufficiently humid and entirely healthful atmosphere; and will cause the coal to burn with undiminished intensity, the coldest and driest day in winter. One word more, if you please, in connection with fuel; and that is, upon smoky chimneys—that plague and vexation to almost half the houses in the country. It is sufficiently extraordinary that it should be so, when the fact which I am about to state is unquestionable. And this fact is, that a Franklin stove, set in the fire-place of one of these smoky chimneys, is usually found to correct the error committed in their construction. And if this fact, when it is considered will not lead to the true principle of chimney-building, the artisan must be more stupid than the brick and mortar that he works in.

In making these suggestions, I have scarcely strayed from the topic on which I am engaged. For, I can hardly think that the *mind* is fairly dealt with,—I can hardly think that virtue, good nature, ay, that patience itself, has any fair chance, when the body is dried like a potsherd, or the eyes are bleared and vexed with smoke, or rheumatisms, aches and pains, as bad as those of the cave of Prospero, are ever coming in, through the half open door, upon an apartment, almost as much exposed to the searching air without, as the mountain itself.

But I have also spoken under this head of the relief from toil, which is, and is yet more to be, effected by the progress of the mechanic arts. It may, however, be recollected, and therefore objected against this topic, that I have already said, that labour-saving machines have ultimately had the effect, thus far, to increase labour, or at least to employ a greater number of hands. It is necessary, then, to discriminate. *What* toil is relieved? I answer, it is the hardest, the most uninteresting toil—the drudgery of toil, that is relieved. To speak more definitely, it is that part of labour which is employed as power. The wheel now is turned, and the saw is pushed, and even the planing tool is propelled, by steam. The consequence is, that labour is becoming more a business of dexterity and less of strength; and toil is constantly rising to the dignity of an art. Man is learning that there is power enough in nature; and that his high office is to acquire the skill necessary to direct it. It is a further advantage to the mind, that the power which man thus brings to aid him, is certain; and he is no longer obliged to *wait* for the wind to blow, or the stream to rise. He is not doomed, I say, to *waiting*—that most tedious method of passing time, that utter loss of time, that only utter loss of time; for it is the only condition in which a man can neither do anything, nor think anything—that loss, in fact, of patience itself. I have sometimes been tempted to wish that there were some machinery, moral or physical, that would bring men punctually to committee meetings, to lec tures, ay, and to church itself!

But further; will not the time come when the improvements in machinery will yet more signally relieve mankind; when not only their strength, but their attention in a greater degree, may be spared from the care of gaining a subsistence; when, in other words, they will give less labour to mere manual tasks, and have more time for reading and thinking. Without some intelligence, without some thought, labour is an intolerable drudgery. Man was not made to be a mere beast of burthen. The elements of toil are dark and heavy, and forever they must be, till they are mixed up with intellectual and moral light. It is, in this view, that I look with pity upon much of the toil that is in the world. I do not pity, there is no occasion to pity, the intelligent labourer; "the peasant saint, if such a one were anywhere to be met with, now a days." I can scarcely conceive of any position more desirable, than that of the man who goes to his field or his workshop, with a moderate task to discharge, and a mind to think as well as a hand to work; who looks upon the elements he deals with as the teachers of wisdom and the ministers of piety; who studies and understands the philosophy of his mechanism and manufacture, his soil and flower-garden; and lives in his family to teach it the like wisdom. Labour, alas! too often wants such high and cheering ministration, and such holy ends. Its brow is too vacant and heavy. I know that there are exceptions; but to my eye oftentimes its brow is too heavy; its lips are too silent; its steps too weary. In every dark mass of worldly materials before it, there is some truth, some principle; but the eye of labour too seldom kindles at that truth, that principle. Man may not sink towards the condition of the animal, and find it well for him. Let him go to what task, to what conflict he will, and leave the immortal principles of his nature behind him, and he will find himself deprived, not only of his shield, but of the very fire of courage. So it is on the very steppes of Russia; so it is even in the valley of the Rhine, and on the plains of Italy. To my eye, there is no courage, no cheering there; but faces, bowed down in sad and bitter earnest to the daily task. May it be otherwise with us! May invention relieve labour, and intellect be mixed with toil, till it become that high dispensation which God designed it to be, for the improvement and blessing of the world!

But I find myself entering upon a topic which I intended to make a distinct one. For the arts of industry not only indirectly tend to improve society by increasing its comforts and relieving its toils, but they have a *direct* bearing upon the same end.

For in the first place, they elicit and employ the mind of society. I have already said, indeed, that it is most desirable and needful that more thought, more insight into principles, should be mixed up with the employments of the mass of the people. But still it is not to be forgotten, that labour, and especially cultivated labour, does and must exercise and task the intellect. It would be the mistake only of the most arrant book-worm, to suppose that the mind never labours, but over the written page or the abstract proposition. The merchant, the manufacturer, the mechanic, is oftener a harder thinker than the student. The machinist and the engineer are employed in some of the finest schools of intellect. Books, so far as they relate to these several employments, are only designed to make those engaged in them more accomplished and intellectual *labourers.* There are tasks, indeed, rising but little above the toils of the tread-mill, for which no such consideration can be pleaded; and I cannot help hoping, that some method will be found to relieve the labours of the hod. That which Herodotus tells us, of the workmen who built the pyramids, is not strange; that they held the memory of the royal projectors of those unsightly mountains of stone and mortar, upon the bare construction of one of which—not the working in quarries, that upon the bare construction of the largest of which, 100,000 men were employed for twenty years—that in Egypt, I say, they held the memory of these mighty tyrants in perpetual execration.

In the next place, industry is the great school of human virtue. It is not enough to say, that this dispensation is necessary to keep men out of evil and mischief. It is not enough to say that the industrious are always the most virtuous classes. But it is to be observed that human industry is placed in peculiar circumstances, especially fitted and designed to elicit and try the virtues of human beings. The animal, following his instincts, finds a certain facility in his path. Human industry, on the contrary, is always a conflict with difficulties. The animal organs are precisely fitted to their respective tasks, and are already sufficient to all the purposes of animal industry. But man has to adjust his powers to an infinite variety of exertions; ten thousand delicate manipulations and feats of dexterity are required of him; his eye is to be trained to precision, and his mind to taste; new instruments, too, are constantly to be invented to overcome the difficulties in his way. This, then, is the theatre of energy and patience; yes, and I add, of moral wisdom and self-restraint. The animal may gorge himself, and can then lie down and sleep off his surfeit; and he takes no harm from midnight dew, or the open and chill canopy that is spread over him. But man cannot endure such indulgence or exposure. If he gives himself up to sensual excess, his powers at once begin to fail him. His eye loses its clearness, his hand its dexterity, his finger its nicety of touch; and he becomes a lame, deficient and dishonoured workman.

Nor is this all. How many natural ties are there between even the humblest scene of labour, and the noblest affections of humanity! In this view the employment of mere muscular strength is ennobled. There is a central point in every man's life, around which all his toils and cares revolve. It is that spot which is consecrated by the names of wife, and children, and home. A secret, an almost imperceptible influence from that spot, which is like no other upon earth, steals into the breast of the virtuous labouring man, and strengthens every weary step of his toil. Every blow that is struck in the workshop and the field, finds an echo in that holy shrine of his affections. If he who fights to protect his home, rises to the point of heroic virtue; no less may he who labours, his life long, to provide for that home. Peace be within those domestic walls, and prosperity beneath those humble roofs! But should it ever be otherwise; should the time ever come when the invader's step approaches to touch those sacred thresholds, I see in the labours that are taken for them, that wounds will be taken for them too; I see in every honest workman around me, a hero.

So material do I deem this point—the true nobility of labour, I mean—that I would dwell upon it a moment longer, and in a larger view. Why, then, in the great scale of things, is labour ordained for us? Easily, had it so pleased the great Ordainer, might it have been dispensed with. The world itself might have been a mighty machinery for the production of all that man wants. The motion of the globe upon its axis might have been the power, to move that world of machinery. Ten thousand wheels within wheels might have been at work; ten thousand processes, more curious and complicated than man can devise, might have been going forward without man's aid; houses might have risen like an exhalation,

> "with the sound
> Of dulcet symphonies and voices sweet,
> Built like a temple;"

gorgeous furniture might have been placed in them, and soft couches and luxurious banquets spread, by hands unseen; and man, clothed with fabrics of nature's weaving, richer than imperial purple, might have been sent to disport himself in these Elysian palaces. "Fair scene!" I imagine you are saying; "fortunate for us, had it been the scene ordained for human life!" But where then, tell me, had been human energy, perseverance, patience, virtue, heroism? Cut off with one blow from the world; and mankind had sunk to a crowd, nay, far beneath a crowd of Asiatic voluptuaries. No, it had not been fortunate. Better that the earth be given to man as a dark mass, whereon to labour. Better that rude and unsightly materials be provided in the ore-bed and the forest, for him to fashion into splendour and beauty. Better, I say, not because of that splendour and beauty, but because the act creating them is better than the things themselves; because exertion is nobler than enjoyment; because the labourer is greater and more worthy of honour than the idler. I call upon those whom I address, to stand up for that nobility of labour. It is heaven's great ordinance for human improvement. Let not that great ordinance be broken down. What do I say? It *is* broken down; and it *has been* broken down for ages. Let it then be built up again; here if anywhere, on these shores of a new world, of a new civilization. But how, I may be asked, is it broken down? Do not men toil, it may be said? They do indeed toil, but they too generally do it because they must. Many submit to it as, in some sort, a degrading necessity; and they desire nothing so much on earth, as escape from it. They fulfil the great law of labour in the letter, but break it in spirit; fulfil it with the muscle, but break it with the mind. To *some* field of labour, mental or manual, every idler should hasten, as a chosen and coveted theatre of improvement. But so is he not impelled to do, under the teachings of our imperfect civilization. On the contrary, he sits down, folds his hands, and blesses himself in his idleness. This way of thinking is the heritage of the absurd and unjust feudal system; under which serfs laboured, and gentlemen spent their lives in fighting and feasting. It is time that this opprobrium of toil were done away. Ashamed to toil, art thou? Ashamed of thy dingy work-shop and dusty labour-field; of thy hard hand, scarred with service more honourable than that of war; of thy soiled and weather-stained garments, on which mother nature has stamped midst sun and rain, midst fire and steam, her own heraldic honours? Ashamed of these tokens and titles, and envious of the flaunting robes of imbecile idleness and vanity? It is treason to nature; it is impiety to heaven; it is breaking heaven's great ordinance. TOIL, I repeat—TOIL, either of the brain, of the heart, or of the hand, is the only true manhood, the only true nobility!

But I am not willing to leave this subject, of which I have spoken thus generally—the *direct* tendency, i. e. of labour to improve society—without some brief suggestions of a more specific bearing.

The effect of our political institutions on society, makes it necessary that we should extend a special and fostering care to our domestic industry; to the industry, I mean, of families, on their own property. In many of the families, especially of farmers, in the country, there is a want of employment for the female members of them; and many a man have I seen sinking beneath that dearly cherished but unproductive portion of his domestic charge. The state and feeling of equality among our people, makes him unwilling to employ his daughters, or to consent to their employment, in services out of his own family. He should therefore find something for them to do within it. And on this account, as well as for other reasons, all manufactures capable of being made purely domestic, as of woolen cloths, stockings, &c., and especially the culture of the mulberry and the making of silk, are entitled to the strongest commendation and patronage. No community, as a mass, can thrive, which does not employ all its members; no body of families can flourish, where one, two, or three persons in each family are unproductive; a sufficient proof that God never made the world for idleness. Thus, I think, you will find that the grazing and dairy making townships in the country are the most prosperous; and the grain-growing townships, where women have less employment, far less so. I do not deny that there are other reasons for this difference, but I think this is one. And I have observed, too, that the people from the hill-pastures are constantly coming down and buying up the pleasant-looking valleys that lie spread out beneath them. You have seen, perhaps, the experiment of putting coloured particles into boiling water, to show how the water ascends on the outside of the vessel and descends in the centre, towards the bottom. In some tracts of country, I have observed the hill and valley-process to be almost as regular as that.

Let me now advert to an entirely different subject; that is to say, the supply of our cities with pure water. The introduction of New-River into London, gives every family in that vast metropolis 200 gallons per day, for two pence. What a means of comfort and cleanliness this must be, need not be said. But this is not all. I have heard scientific persons, medical men in London, speaking of the almost unprecedented improvement of their city in health, ascribe more of it to the introduction of New-River, than to all other causes put together. It is, in fact, a rushing stream, bearing away all the filth from the innumerable sewers connected with it. It may be no better than the suggestion of fancy and inexperience, but I cannot help wishing that the Croton River, when it is brought here may be made—after supplying the citizens with water, and twenty generous fountains besides—to pass down in a grand sewer under Broadway, and by branches under the principal cross-streets of the city to either river. Even then we should not have done what Rome did to supply herself with water, and to build her *Cloaca maxima* and other drains. And as to the feasibility of the project, a hint may be derived from the fact, that the stock in the New-River Company, (London,) which originally cost one hundred pounds, is now worth fifteen hundred.

One topic more under this head, and I shall have approached the point of relieving your patience; and that is, the direct tendency of the arts to improve society, by increasing its intercourse.

A journey, to an observing man, is as the opening of a volume; ay, and with something better too, than plates and illustrations. He reads men and manners, and events, and circumstances, and improvements. His knowledge is increased, his prejudices are abated, his charities are kindled, his ties to his countrymen and his kind are strengthened. In countries where there is little travel, one is struck with the broad and separating marks of provincialism at every step. Men cultivate the earth as their fathers did, build like their fathers, live like their fathers, and die like their fathers. The wheels of social improvement stand still. One little circle, indeed, of social being, acts upon those perpetual dwellers at home, who sometimes live and die without ever seeing a neighbouring city; but the great engine of society, its mighty impulse, they do not feel.

Our steamboats and rail-roads are tending constantly to make us a more homogeneous, sympathizing, and humane people. A visit to one's distant friends, everybody knows, is a very pleasant thing; but are its uses in the great family of society, often considered? Intercourse, in such circumstances, is usually an interchange of all the thoughts, views and improvements that prevail in different parts of the country. "Their talk is of oxen," if you please, or it is of soils and grains, or it is of manufacture and trade, or it is of books and philosophies; but it is all good—good for somebody at least—good in the main for every body. Thus, our steamboats are like floating saloons, and our rail-roads like the air-pipes of a mighty whispering gallery; and men are conversing with one another, and communicating and blending their daily thoughts, throughout the whole length and breadth of the land. These means of communication are thus constantly interchanging, not only different views, but the advantages of different kinds of residence. They are imparting rural tastes to the citizen, and city polish to the countryman. I cannot help thinking, that in time, they will produce a decided effect upon city residence; relieving us, somewhat, of our crowded and overgrown population; sending out many from these pent-up abodes in town, to the green and pleasant dwelling places of the country.

The progress of communication during the last twenty years, leaves us almost nothing to wish, and yet entitles us to expect everything. Many of you remember what a passage up the Hudson was, twenty years ago. You remember the uncertain packet, lingering for a wind at the wharf, till patience was almost exhausted; and then, at length, pursuing its zig-zag course, now wavering in the breeze, now halting in the calm, like a crazy traveller, doubtful of his way, or whether to proceed at all. And now, when you set your foot on the deck of one of our steamboats, you feel as if the pawings of some reined courser were beneath you, impatient to start from the goal; anon, it seems to you as if the strength and stride of a giant were bearing you onward; till, at length, when the evening shadow falls, and hides its rougher features from your sight, you might imagine it the queenly genius of the noble river, as it moves on between the silent shores, and flings its spangled robe upon the waters.

There is one further and final suggestion, which, at the risk of its being thought professional, I would not altogether omit in this survey of the moral tendencies of mechanic art. It leads the mind to the infinite wisdom of nature, to the infinite wisdom of its Author.

The materials, for instance, on which art is to work, —how wonderfully are they adapted to one another, and to the natural powers of the workman! The steel is adapted to the wood it cuts; the water to the wheel it moves, and to the ship it bears; the plough to the soil it turns. Weight is adjusted to power. If the hammer weighed a hundred pounds, vainly would the hand strive to wield it. If the earth were covered with a forest of iron, man would labour in vain to cut it down and build it into houses.

If an intelligent manufacturer or mechanic would carefully note down in a book all the instances of adaptation that presented themselves to his attention, he would in time have a large volume; and it would be a volume of philosophy; a volume of indisputable facts in defence of a Providence. I could not help remarking lately, when I saw a furnace upon the stream of the valley, and the cartman bringing down ore from the mountains, how inconvenient it would have been if this order of nature had been reversed; if the ore-bed had been in the valley, and the stream had been so constituted as to rise, and to make its channel upon the tops of the ridges. Nay, more; treasures are slowly prepared and carefully laid up in the great store-houses of nature, against the time when man shall want them. When the wood is cut off from the plains and the hills, and fuel begins to fail, and man looks about him with alarm at the prospect, lo! beneath his feet are found, in mines of bitumen and mountains of anthracite, the long hidden treasures of Providence—the treasure-houses of that care and kindness, which at every new step of human improvement, instead of appearing to be superseded, seem doubly entitled to the name of *Providence.*

Nature, too, is itself a world of mechanism; and it invites mechanic art at every step to admire that intelligent, and if I may say so, that congenial wisdom which is displayed in it. The human body is a structure of art, fearfully and wonderfully made. The human arm and hand is a tool, an instrument; and what an instrument!—composed of twenty or thirty solid, separate parts, besides the cartilages, ligaments and nerves, that give it its wonderful security, strength and tact. What indefeasible cunning lies in that right hand; nay, what latent cunning—every new year of mechanic discovery developing it more and more—what latent cunning sleeps in the sinews and nerves of that folded palm! And then that curious rotary motion of the fore-arm; what efforts of mechanic art have there been to imitate that skill of the great Maker of our frame! And again the human head—that dome of the house of life—is built upon the most perfect principles of that kind of structure; with its thicker bones in the base of the skull, like the solid masonry of a Roman arch; with its interior and supporting ridges of bone, like the flying buttresses of a Gothic cathedral. The dome of St. Sophia, in Constantinople, built in the time of the Emperor Justinian, fell three times during its erection; the dome of the Cathedral of Florence stood unfinished 120 years, for the want of an architect; and yet it has been justly said, that every man employed about them, had the model in his own head.

All nature is not only, I repeat, a world of mechanism, but it is the work of infinite art; and the artisan, the toiler, is but a student, an apprentice in that school. And when he has done all, what can he do to equal the skill of the great original he copies; to equal the wisdom of Him who has "stretched out the heavens like a curtain, who laid the beams of his chambers on the waters!" What engines can he form like those which raise up through the dark labyrinths of the mountains, the streams that gush forth in fountains from their summits? What pillars and what architecture can he lift up on high, like the mighty forest trunks and their architrave and frieze of glorious foliage? What dyes can he invent, like those which spread their ever-changing and many-coloured robes over the earth? What pictures can he cause to glow, like those which are painted on the dome of heaven?

It is the glory of art that it penetrates, and developes the wonders and bounties of nature. It draws their richness from the valleys, and their secret stores from the mountains. It leads forth every year fairer flocks and herds upon the hills; it yokes the ox to the plough, and trains the fiery steed to its car. It plants the unsightly germ, and rears it into vegetable beauty; it takes the dull ore and transfuses it into splendour, or gives it the edge of the tool or the lancet; it gathers the filaments which nature has curiously made, and weaves them into soft and compact fabrics. It sends out its ships to discover unknown seas and shores; or it plunges into its work-shops at home, to detect the secret that is locked up in mineral, or is flowing in liquid matter. It scans the spheres and systems of heaven with its far sight; or turns with microscopic eye, and finds in the drops that sparkle in the sun, other worlds crowded with life. Yet more; mechanic art is the handmaid of society. It has made man its special favourite. It clothes him with fine linen and soft raiment. It builds him houses, it kindles the cheerful fire, it lights the evening lamp, it spreads before him the manifold pages of wisdom: it delights his eye with gracefulness, it charms his ear with music: it multiplies the facilities of communication and the ties of brotherhood; it is the softener of all domestic charities, it is the bond of nations.

Gentlemen of the American Institute! you need no commendation of mine; your works speak for you; and I have only to wish, that they may advance in improvement and extend in utility; an honour to yourselves, and a blessing to our common country!

XVI.

THE IDENTITY OF ALL ART.*

GENTLEMEN OF THE APOLLO ASSOCIATION:

THE ground on which I shall place myself, in addressing to you a few observations this evening, is *the identity of all art;* identity in object, in the principles of criticism and culture, and in the reasons for promoting it. This is, at once, my subject, and my apology; my apology, I mean, for this seeming departure from my own walk. Your invitation, indeed, will acquit me of presumption with you; but this is the apology which I have offered to myself. For I do not feel that I am departing from my own walk, so far as I may at first seem to do. Letters and the arts of design, belong to the same great school. I consider *myself* as an artist, however humble, as much as any one who has placed a painting on your walls. I regard the principles of all intellectual production, as being essentially the same.

It is a common idea that painting, as an art, and pictures, as objects of criticism, stand entirely by themselves; that they do not come within the range of men's ordinary judgment and feelings; that common men have no business to say anything about them. Of an oration they think they can judge, but not of a

* An Introductory Lecture before the Apollo Association in New York, in 1840. This Institution has since taken the title of the American Art-Union.

painting; of a book, but not of a picture; of a fine landscape, but not of its representation on the canvass. But as I do not admit the propriety of this distinction, I do not feel the need of any pretension or pride of connoisseurship, to warrant me in offering some thoughts to you on the present occasion: introductory as they appropriately are for me with my limited knowledge, and as I doubt not they will be, to deeper views by others on the whole subject of art.

Let us then consider the identity of all art. If I am not mistaken, the topic will yield some reflections, not inappropriate to the purposes of this meeting and to the design of this course of Lectures.

I say the identity of all art; but I *might* say the identity of all action. As the universe is the expression of a Mind; as everything in heaven and on earth, is significant of something beyond itself; as every movement has a meaning—not a rolling world nor a falling leaf excepted—and the whole creation thus bodies forth an idea; so, within the limited range of man's action, all is expression. There is nothing of final import in the whole world of man's industry or agency but this—but expression: and he who has not seen this, has seen nothing. He has neither the artist's, nor the poet's, nor the Christian's eye. He who sees nothing around him but a hard, dull, intractable, lifeless world, nothing but machinery, brick and mortar, hewn stone and wood work—that man understands nothing, can interpret nothing, can describe, can paint nothing. He cannot paint *still*-life, without this insight. Without this, he will be but a sort of Chinese painter. The very flowers and birds which the Chinese paint so beautifully, look like wax-work; and the portraits which they copy, seem, but for some coloring, to be pictures of the dead. But the mere wooden-bowl or axe-helve that a true artist paints, has life in it. The one looks as if it had been washed a thousand times, and the other as if it had felled a thousand trees.

There is, I repeat, this identity in everything that man has wrought—that it bears the stamp of his mind. Whether it be a plough or a picture, a statue of Canova or a log-hut beyond the mountains, an airy strain of music or a massive pile of architecture, a cotton manufactory or a gallery of art—all is expression. The living thought of man not only wrestles in the heaving crowd, but it stands revealed in the stately wall; it looks out through the windows of every house-front; it breathes from the rifted arches of every mouldering ruin; it sighs through the green leaves and the tall grass where bloody battle has been done; it comes down as a presence upon every great field of momentous history like Italy, and weighs and presses upon the heart more than as if a living multitude were there. The face of the cultivated and trodden world bears the impress of human thought as its grand expression. The tissues of human hearts, have woven all round this mighty globe—over mountain and over valley, over empire and throne, and bare cottage and barren sand—a robe of life.

Now it is the peculiar province of the fine arts to unfold this life. All human action exhibits it; but art proposes this exhibition as its very purpose and end. And in this definition of art are embraced not only architecture, sculpture, painting, and music, but also oratory, and writing, whether of prose or poetry.

Let me be permitted, in passing, to claim this place for prose writing. It is as truly an art as poetry. I question, in fact, whether it is not a higher art. Poetry, indeed, is more artificial, but I doubt whether it is the higher art. It is said to be the elder-born--born of ruder ages; and I can well believe it. That is to say, I can believe that less mental culture is required to put words in that shape than in the shape of perfect prose; just as in the body, less culture would be required to walk easily in trammels, than to walk gracefully without. If Hesiod and Homer had written in prose, I doubt whether it would have been as good prose as their poetry was. And, to take a modern instance, I think no poetry of Mr. Southey shows so much real art, as his Espriella's Letters. It is sometimes said to a prose writer of genius, "Why do you not write poetry? I am certain it is in you." I am not sure—the poets and critics must pardon my extravagance—I am not sure but he might answer, "Because I am doing a better thing." "Yes, but it is so much admired. If the thoughts you have expressed had been in poetry they would have given you a reputation." "True, but this does not prove that poetry is the higher art. Whatever is unusual, is most likely to be admired. As speech is the endowment of all, few are likely to understand what an exquisite instrument it is, and what exquisite art is implied in its perfection. A military man, with epaulettes and gay costume, marching, with measured tread, at the head of his troops, will draw more eyes than he who walks gracefully along the street; and yet the military man perhaps would never reach that graceful carriage. If he be an accomplished man, he will, indeed; and so the best poets are among the best writers of prose; as, for instance, Milton and Wordsworth, and our own Bryant and Dana. This fact, I think, is in my favour; especially when taken in connection with another, viz., that when you descend from the highest walk of the art of writing, you will find more in proportion of unexceptionable and harmonious poetry, than you will of good sound prose. In other words, more men of ordinary talent, proportionably, write good poetry than good prose. You will observe that I am not speaking at all of the essence of thought; that may exist alike in both. And that I suppose is what is mostly meant by those critics who wrap up all the world's genius in poetry. But I am speaking strictly of the *form* of writing. And what I assert at the least is, that prose-writing is as high a form of art, as rhyme or rhythm. The latter is more admired, I repeat, because it is unusual; because it is a wonder; because it is more out of the common reach. But this no more proves that it is a higher art, than the same feeling would prove that court etiquette is a higher thing than true gentlemanly tact and good-breeding in a private drawing-room. 'Verse,' says Mr. Bulwer,—I beg you will bear with this digression a moment longer,—'verse cannot contain the refining, subtile thoughts, which a great prose writer embodies: the rhyme eternally cripples it; it properly deals with the common problems of human nature, which are now hackneyed; and not with the nice and philosophizing corollaries which may be drawn from them. Though it would seem at first a paradox, commonplace is the element of poetry rather than of prose. And sensible of this, even Schiller wrote the deepest of his tragedies, Fiesco, in prose.'" The wonder is, that anybody could have written a great tragedy in anything else. The formality of rhythm is not natural to it; it stands in accordance only with the buskins, the stage, the lights, the scene-shifting—in short with the artificial character of the whole thing. What would be thought, if a man should write a speech or a sermon in blank verse? Or to take a stronger instance: what would be thought if a man, in a great rage in the street, or a man in deep grief by the fire-side, should pour out his grief or anger in blank verse? Or suppose a man were to make love in blank verse. In all these cases, I think the verse would be very blank indeed, and the faces of the persons addressed, yet more so. But to tragedy especially belong these bursts of feeling—of rage, grief, terror, pity, love. And therefore we should be apt to say, that tragedy—the language of passion—should be the simplest and most natural form of human speech. If any man has got a tragedy *in* him—though he be not a verse-maker—I wish he would try it.*

If I must ask you to pardon this digression, gentlemen, I hope you will admit that it is not altogether inappropriate to my subject, or to the present occasion. I bring a new claimant, asking for a place in the goodly brotherhood of the arts. And far be it from me, in doing this, to depreciate true poetry. Whatever well embodies the loftiest forms of thought is well and worthy. But the poets have so long been considered as enjoying a kind of monopoly in the art of writing; they are so constantly spoken of by their critics as holding in their charmed vase all the finer essence of genius, that they can well afford to bear some question of this pre-eminent claim.

But to return to my general theme—what I was about to assert is the identity which exists, as I conceive, among all the fine arts.

In the first place, the object of them all is the same; to exhibit some thought, some passion, or to set forth

* Doubtless certain passages—declamations, descriptions, speeches—might be best given in blank verse; but whether this is, in general, the natural and appropriate form of dramatic writing, is the question.

simply the truth of things, to make a just representation of a thing as it is. Whether the ideal or the matter of fact be the thing in hand, all the arts—architecture, sculpture, painting, music, writing, oratory,—propose to do the same thing. Portrait painting is only telling—better indeed than words can—but still it is only telling how a man looks. Landscape painting answers to descriptive writing. Historical painting but embodies what history has recorded. And fancy pieces are but as the poet's or essayist's pictures. They are often taken directly from the poet's or the essayist's page. And that is the best painting, we are accustomed to say, "which tells its own story."

In the next place, the means used in the various arts, though dissimilar, are subject to the same laws. The procedure of thought in all is essentially the same. When a man makes an historical picture, he chooses a subject, he lays out a plan, he divides it into heads, he determines what parts he will bring out into prominence, and what he will sink into shade, and he keeps in mind, in finishing every part, the general effect he intends to produce. Precisely so is it with every well devised, well executed, artist-like speech, oration, discourse, or essay. When I look upon a painter as he proceeds with his work, I am constantly reminded of the art of writing. When I see him lay out his plan, I think of the plan of a discourse. When I see him blot a certain part, to work it out again, I think of the *sæpe verte stylum*. When I see him put his finger upon a certain point of colouring, to soften it, I am reminded of the exchange of a stronger epithet for a milder one: for all must have a keeping, a harmony; if a thing is said too strongly in one place, it will not agree with another thing said in another place. The painter's lights and shades, too, remind me of the lights and shades of a discourse. And if he seeks after too much light, strives to make all striking and glaring, I call to mind more than one novice that I have known who did the same thing in his discourse—wanted to make every paragraph brilliant, every point prominent, and so made nothing prominent, had no effective brilliancy anywhere.

II. If there be this identity in all art, then it follows that the principles of culture and the principles of criticism in all, are essentially the same; and I submit to you, as the second point in this discourse, whether it *be* not so.

Let us look, first, at the principles of criticism, and let us resume for this purpose the comparison of a picture with a discourse or essay. We demand of each that it shall say something, that it shall say it distinctly, and say it effectively; distinctly that we may understand it, and effectively that we may feel it. In order to meet these conditions there must be a reigning idea in a painting, and there must be sharpness of outline combined with softness of colouring. The first being given (*i. e.*, the reigning idea)—the trial point with a painter, if one of the unlearned may speak, is to combine the two last, (*i. e.*, the distinctness with the softness). In Murillo's paintings, and in some of Allston's, there is a softness amounting to haziness. There is a want of distinct outline. In Michael Angelo's *parcæ*, the fates, we have sharpness of outline even to harshness and severity, though perhaps his style in this respect may well suit the subject. It does not, however, as I must think, in his painting of the Last Judgment, in the Sistine Chapel. In the pictures of Leonardo da Vinci, Raphael, Guido, and

Domenichino, we have the true combination—the clearest outline with the softest colouring.

Again; it is a principle of criticism in letters, that a writing shall not pass beyond the modesty of nature into extravagance, nor fall short of the life of nature into dullness: and this, I presume, is just as true of painting. The Venetian School is an example of the former—the extravagance; the school of the Caracci of the latter—the want of vigour and spirit. In Vandyke's portraits, too, it seems to me that there is always a certain extravagance, not of colouring, but of expression; while in Holbein's there is, as far as I have seen them, a want of vividness.

True criticism, especially if it proceed upon the broad views which I now advocate, will indeed always be liberal. It will not think to bring everything to the same standard. There *are subjects* which are dream-like; where the features should look, as through a veil of mist. Such are some of Allston's; though I confess that for a general style I no more like haze in a picture than haze in a speech. It may be an obtuseness in me, but I must acknowledge that whether I read, or hear, or see, I have a great desire to know something. I do not like to be left in the dark as to what an author or a painter means. I have thought that it was his very business to tell me, that that was the very thing he professed to do; and if I am to be left in the shadows of imagination, I had rather they should be my own, than his. There is but too much of this style in our modern philosophy, poetry, and fine writing, as we call it; and I will not deny that I have intended to apply the same observation to the style of Allston. Mr. Allston is truly a poet and a man of genius; but I cannot fall in with that national spirit of self-praise, which maintains that he has already taken his place by the side of Guido, and Raphael, and Leonardo da Vinci. To see that proved, I must wait—I will say it though I die for it—I must wait for the Belshazzar.*

True criticism, I have said, is liberal. It will distinguish among the different works of the same hand. Allston's Jeremiah is not hazy, and the Baruch in that piece is admirable—soft and distinct too. So Rubens often paints—as I think it has been said, at least I have often thought it, in a "raw-head and bloody-bones" style. But when I came to see the Crucifixion of St. Peter in the church of Cologne, and especially the twelve apostles in the Rospigliosi Palace at Rome, I perceived that his genius was capable of almost any style, of the utmost delicacy, finish and beauty.

But it is time, after all this boldness, that I should say a word in *defence* of this liberty of criticism. And my defence lies in the principle I am contending for, that the great laws of all criticism on art, are essentially the same. Any one of you that is a painter will not hesitate to give your judgment on books. Why shall I not give my judgment on pictures? I contend that the art of writing is as profound and as difficult to be criticised as the art of painting; nay, and I think, more so. Painting more directly appeals to the eye—to the general observing eye—to the general and natural sense of propriety and beauty. Writing is a more recondite art; more out of reach of the common judgment. Good writing is really, though men may not know it, a greater mystery than good painting. Do I say, then, that no culture, no taste, no habit of observation is necessary to judge of painting? Far enough from it. I assert the right to

* I *have* waited, and am convinced that the finished parts of this great work have more of the stamp of the great masters upon them than anything else that Allston has produced.

judge, subject precisely to these limitations. But the same limitations apply equally to writing. I may be wrong in my judgment of one or the other. I may be quite wrong in the opinions I have ventured to offer concerning painters and paintings. But I hope I have vindicated the common right to judge, and that I shall not be charged with a want of modesty in having ventured, certainly with diffidence, to use it.

Let me add one further observation upon criticism and the arts. I have said that true criticism is liberal; and the observation I have to make is, that in all the fine arts great injustice is generally done to all but the first rate excellence. In literature and in painting a few names bear away the palm of merit. They fill the magazines, the newspapers, the mouths of the people. There is no just discrimination of the many artists and writers, who are approaching more or less nearly, and some of them very nearly, to the same excellence. This is extremely discouraging as well as unjust to modest and patient labour. It does not ask to be first, if it is not first; but it does, and does rightfully, ask to be appreciated. And the wrong done is an argument, as far as it goes, for what you are doing, Gentlemen: for spreading a truer and more discriminating taste among the people. For this it is precisely that is wanted to correct the superficial and wholesale judgments of the public. Listen to the conversation of cultivated men, and you will find that they go down from great works that rise a little above the rest—from the great and ever-quoted names, and find a thousand beauties in the regions that lie beneath. Or place a company of artists or of real connoisseurs in this gallery, and you will find that they are not altogether occupied with two or three pieces, but that they note a thing—a part of a picture for instance—beautifully done here; or a hand or an eye exquisitely painted there; and they do justice to all. Just as a hasty traveller, who has spent two or three weeks in Switzerland, comes home, talking of nothing but Mt. Blanc and Jungfrau, while one who has spent a season in travelling over it, will talk of a hundred pinnacles and of many a lovely nook and glassy lake spread all over that land of beauty; a land of which a friend of mine, once travelling with me there, said, as we stood gazing upon its wonders, "Oh! it is a glorious picture, set in the frame of the world." But the public, in the great field of literature and art, is like the hasty traveller. It does no justice to minor beauties and humbler merits. For in this respect a gallery of pictures—and I think Sir Joshua Reynolds has made the same remark in his lectures—is like a library. There is many a book in which there is an admirable chapter, though it be not admirable as a whole; and there is many a book of great merit which stands untouched upon the shelf, gathering the dust of years upon it, because Shakspeare, or Bacon, or Milton is near it. You may say that the world cannot read or study everything, and that it is best it should read the best authors—study the best artists. I wish it really and thoroughly did either; for then would it be more liberal and more discerning towards all merit. For now it talks the more about great names, the less it knows about them; and thus upholds a law of distinction—a dynasty in the world of mind, which, at least in my opinion, does cruel injustice to hundreds of meritorious authors and artists. This error, as I think it, ought to be corrected, and I believe it will be. I perceive already that this injustice is beginning to give way before a more diffusive and generous culture. The series of biographical portraits lately appearing in the English reviews, and the devotion of one entire publication—

the Retrospective Review—to the recovery of buried treasures, is some proof of this. So too it is felt, that, in the moral world, a certain notable philanthropy, is not to carry off all the honours of goodness. And it will yet come to be seen that all the world's treasures of goodness, beauty, enthusiasm, genius, greatness through ages, are not concentrated in a hundred wonderful individuals. Ay, and the hundred too will be more fully, more truly appreciated then. The vulgar stare at distinction will give place to a finer discernment of all talent and merit.

Let us now proceed from the principles of criticism to the principles of culture. What I assert is, that the principles of culture in all arts are essentially the same; and those upon which I shall briefly insist are, good sense, moral feeling, and the general cultivation of the whole man.

First, good sense. In statue, picture, poem, essay or oration, this must be a pervading characteristic. Art is never to spread its wings beyond this strict boundary. The moment that the poet or painter, the orator or sculptor, thinks that good sense is a mean quality, and to be disregarded, he is virtually ruined. In all the greatest works of the human hand, in the poems of Homer, in the orations of Demosthenes, in the Grecian sculpture, and in the best paintings of the Italian school, is ever found the clear impress of this quality. If it is not the very stuff with which genius works, yet it is the very stamp upon the true coin. Many a forgotten poet had as much imagination as the highest, but he had not good sense. Cowley's conceits were as quaint, and curious, and brilliant as Shakspeare's; but nobody reads Cowley, the poet, though his prose is admirable. The extravagant and fantastic Harvey had as much fancy as Jeremy Taylor, but he had not the good sense which is necessary to chasten, control and guide it.

I shall be asked, perhaps, what is good sense? I do not know that I can better tell than every one already knows. But it excludes everything that is unnatural, unreasonable, extravagant, improbable, unlike truth and life, unlike the genuine attitudes and expressions of real, sincere, human passion. Perhaps the most distinctive mark of it is, that the reader, the seer, must feel that *he* might have acted, looked, in the circumstances supposed, just as the picture, the essay before him represents. If not, then the matter before him wants good sense. To *him*, at least, it wants good sense. And if I be asked again, who is to be the judge of this quality? I answer, the common and universal mind of the world. Let any woman, who looks at the Judith and Holophernes of Christopher Allori, ask herself whether she or any other woman could look as the Judith is painted, in the circumstances—a woman who has just cut off the head of the sleeping satrap, and brings it in clutched by the hair and dripping with blood, and yet looks as calm and unconcerned as if she carried a milk-pail. Or, to make a more daring observation, look at the Madonna della Seggiola of Raphael. It is the mother of the long-expected Messiah. So much was this honour desired, that marriage among the Hebrews was held in special favour, and celibacy was a peculiar disgrace on this very account. And now the desire that swelled in the bosom of ages, is accomplished in the breast of this humble female, hailed with angelic congratulations, favoured and blessed among women. What a rapt expression of gratitude will there be in her countenance! What depth of thought in her eye! What visions will seem to float before her of wonders and glories to be unveiled in the future. Can it be, then—I ask with modesty—but can it be that the Madonna is fitly represented as the beau ideal of mere physical beauty—as a beautiful woman, seated of a summer's afternoon, in a luxurious bower? "Beautiful exceedingly" it is; but the question is, is it the kind of beauty that is touched with the expression that belongs to the occasion? Or, for another example—look at Allston's Jeremiah. It is a prophet in the moment of inspiration, communing with God—receiving a message from the Infinite One: and yet, but for the upward cast of the eye, it appears to me more as a warrior than as a prophet. I suppose it is the *furor divinus* that is intended to be represented; but I cannot admit that that *furor* should so entirely partake of physical and earthly qualities. I will not ask you to pardon the adventurousness of these criticisms. I am not pretending to judge of minor points in the artist's skill, but of the great and leading expression; and of this, I hold I am as much entitled to have an opinion, as I am of the leading impression of a poem or a discourse. I may be quite wrong in the opinion I have ventured to express concerning these pictures: but nevertheless a man is but a man, and I know no idols, no divine models among men; I cannot yield to the common inference that because a man is a great man, therefore *everything* which he does is great. And I will only ask you to suppose that in a poem or tale, the Judith, the Madonna, or the Jeremiah, were represented—the leading expression of their character, office or situation given, as it in those pictures, and then say, whether it satisfies you.

The second principle of culture which I have mentioned is moral feeling. Without this, without glowing conceptions, and a real love of moral beauty, there can be no successful culture. What Cicero said of the orator is equally true of the painter; he must be a good man. A bad man, a man essentially bad, devoid of all moral and spiritual emotion, cannot be a good artist. And for this plain reason: that the highest traits in everything he has to paint, are moral. It is so even in nature; it is emphatically so in the human countenance. Suppose the artist attempts to paint the countenance of the martyr; of him who in the last dread hour, amidst the blows and taunts of hardened and malignant executioners, is giving up his soul to his Maker. How is the artist to do this, if he have no conception of the feeling of the martyr, no experience in himself of faith, or prayer, or forgiveness! How otherwise is he to portray that most touching vision of all mortal loveliness and immortal triumph united; that resplendent divinity and softened humanity which blend in the dying martyr's countenance; that strength, fortitude, might, as of an angel to endure; that meekness as of a child to submit: that pity as it were of a seraph, clothed with all mortal sensibility; that forgiveness that speaks through every trembling feature, "lay not this sin to their charge"—that trust in God of the lifted eye and the parted lips—that trust swallowing up, embosoming the poor suffering nature—beaming through the last departing shadows of mortal struggle and infirmity, buoying up the sinking spirit, and bearing it away, disburthened of every earthly weight and pain and sorrow, to the bosom of God!—how, I say, is a man to do this, unless he has it in him, to feel that he too could be a martyr to truth and duty!

Hence it is that an age more skeptical than believing, more inquisitive than confiding, is not likely to be an age of any great achievements in art. This, more than anything else perhaps, explains the present decline in the world, of poetry and painting. I can conceive of no worse omens for literature and art than that their cultivators should be found separating themselves from the great bonds of religious feeling and observance—should be found bending over their desks or their easels on Sunday, rather than at church—should be found putting off one form of religion, and not putting on another. Nothing perhaps so well accounts for that extraordinary outburst of Italian poetry and painting between the thirteenth and fifteenth centuries, as the prevalence then of a religious spirit. Dante, Petrarch and Tasso, Michael Angĕlo, Leonardo da Vinci and Raphael, were filled with religious devoutness, such as it was. Christianity had then a season to sink undisturbed and unquestioned into the hearts of men. The dark ages of struggle had passed by; and the doubting age had not come. Will not the same thing be found true of every literature, Grecian, Roman or English; that it has filled just such intervals; after the moral elements of society have settled into quiet faith, and before they have been clouded by the exhalations of prosperity or choked by the steams of luxury—an interval between the rugged mountain and the low, rich valley; in other words, that the brightest constellations of genius have shone forth after the storm and before the earth-born mists and damps had risen to obscure them. I know that these comparisons may point to other than moral influences; but believing that moral influences are the most potent of all, and not only believing, but knowing, *seeing*, that every great age of literature and art has been informed, penetrated, quickened, kindled all over, with moral fervour, I am persuaded that the comparisons I have made point especially to these. Inward, confiding, believing, spiritual energy, is the soul of art and literature; it is the intellectual might of the world.

One further principle of culture I proposed to consider, and that is the cultivation of the whole man. Every work of art is the work of the whole man, and therefore will bear the stamp of his general improvement. If it were a work of the mere fingers, then extraordinary execution without a soul might make a great musician, or exquisite finish without a just plan and design might make a great painter. But it does not. If the fingers only work, without the head and the heart, the result may be pretty, finical, wonderful in its way; but it will not be a soul-moving work of art. How much of our music bears this character; mere digital dexterity, mere trilling and quavering of the voice! How rarely is a young lady told that when she seats herself at the piano-forte or harp, she should do so with the same view as a man rises up to make a speech; to say something, and so to say it that others shall understand and feel it! This is true, too, of instrumental music: it is nothing, if it does not express a sentiment; and the mere instrument in the hands of a great performer, seems to have more soul in it, than the entire man or woman who is a mere execution-machine. If this high and spiritual view of music were taken, the time now so wearily devoted to it by many, would not be felt to be lost upon the acquisition of a mere fashionable accomplishment; but it would be consecrated to the culture of the highest nature. For what would it then be, if the music were well selected, but a constant endeavour to conceive, to feel, to be embued with, the purest and noblest sentiments? It is said that the songs are almost all silly love-songs, filled with sickly sentiment. I must take leave to object to this as a general definition even of love-songs. Many of them express the noblest sentiments. I will take the first that I lay my hand on:

" And ye shall walk in silk attire,
    And siller have to spare,
Gin ye 'll consent to be his bride,
    Nor think on Donald mair.

Oh! who would buy a silken gown,
    With a poor broken heart!
And what to me 's a siller crown,
    If from my love I part?

I would na walk in silk attire,
    Nor braid with gems my hair,
Gin he whose faith is pledged wi' mine,
    Were wranged and grieving sair."

That, I aver, is no sickly sentiment; and well were it, if it sunk more deeply into the heart of every luxurious and worldly age. Save us above all, from making woman mercenary—from making the love of woman mercenary! It is like taking the richest diamond, and grinding it down to MacAdamise the streets, that the chariots of luxury may roll more smoothly over them!

But to draw the general topic on which I am descanting more directly to the present occasion; the arts of design can never flourish without a wide and generous culture of the whole man. When in my early youth I studied Cicero de Oratore, I thought I was to put myself under the teaching of a mere rhetorician; that he would tell me how to stretch out my hand and how to tone my voice, and things of that sort. But I soon found that the noble old Roman was demanding that the orator should learn everything—know everything—*be* everything; that, according to his idea, the whole rounded circuit of human perfection, came within the orator's walk. Now, I think, that this equally applies to the artist; and indeed in the greatest artists, this idea has been realized. To advert for a moment to their positive acquisitions; Michael Angelo was a great architect, sculptor, and poet, as well as painter. Raphael was studious in history, versed in art of poetry, and so distinguished for his knowledge of architecture, that he gave designs for many palaces in Rome and through Italy, and was entrusted for a while with carrying on the building of St. Peter's. Leonardo da Vinci was one of the most accomplished men of his time; conversant not only with all the fine arts, but with science, literature, the arts of mechanism, and with all manly exercises.

But positive acquisitions alone do not satisfy our idea of the fully cultivated and accomplished man. They may still leave the man quite angular, ill-shapen, defective. As all the accomplishments, which can be heaped upon a young woman, all the finishings of the schools, all the languages and all the rules got by heart, may still leave her far from being a graceful and agreeable person, so all the mere learning in the world, may fail to make a graceful and accomplished artist. The true culture, which means something very different from mere acquisition, is the culture of the heart, of the affections, of the imagination, of the taste, of beau ideal in everything. As in the human body, it takes a hundred organs, sinews, nerves, to make one graceful step, gesture, attitude; so in the mind, it requires the combination of many qualities to reach the grace of art. There is a certain fine, almost indescribable perception of the true, the fit, natural, well proportioned and harmonious, that can come from nothing but general culture. Taste in art is like good breeding in manners; it cannot be learned from rules, nor diagrams, nor schools any way; but it is the breathing out of the inward life. What but this is it, that spreads over some landscape-paintings, such an air of truth and reality, nay, and of sentiment too, as if they were touched all over with a feeling—warm without being garish, and quiet without being cold. Nothing but a loving communion with nature can produce such paintings, and that communion can never be enjoyed but by a pure, gentle and loving spirit. Claude Lorraine's pictures tell you at once that they were breathed upon by an inward life. What is it, again, that produces such different results in that favorite subject with painters—*The Descent from the Cross.* In some paintings of that scene, all is literal, cold, and desolate; death weighs upon the picture, and weighs upon your heart. But others, as that of Guerin in the Baltimore cathedral, are so composed, so coloured, so filled with triumphant expression, that you feel as you gaze, that "death is swallowed up of victory." What can account for this difference but the different feeling of the artists? In the one, death has conquered; in the other, it is swallowed up in the glory that is to come. And I will venture, indeed, to express the belief, that the highest art will never produce a result that is entirely disgusting or revolting. In a well-proportioned, well-balanced mind, this is never the view of anything; but over all, on the contrary, it spreads the relief of its own beautiful nature. Even in viewing the group of the Laocoon—scene of horror as it is—the mind is filled with a strange and thrilling pleasure. And never in nature nor in man, is there anything so dark and distressful but there is something to relieve it. But that something will not be perceived unless it is by a mind that is large and comprehensive; schooled in religion, schooled in philosophy and faith, and touched with the beautifulness of a nature divine and hopeful and triumphant.

III. Let me detain you, Gentlemen, a few moments longer, with one or two remarks, appropriate, I think, not merely to this occasion, but the particular object of your Association. And let me add that these remarks, will still fall in with the general tenor of this lecture.

For, if I have rightly set forth the essential identity of all the fine arts, it will follow that the arts of design demand to be fostered for as good reason as literature poetry, or music. They have their place in the same great work of cultivating the public mind, refining its taste, elevating its moral feeling, and promoting its highest happiness. Painting is the poetry of visible form, colour, and expression. The graver can set forth a high moral lesson as well as the pen; I need only point you for proof to the wonderful creations of Retsch That leering Devil in the Game of Life: that poor youth, so beautiful, so anxious, so sad, so irresolute, so fated—ah! many a youth might have sat for that picture; and many a wily and treacherous demon has been near, and played the game, and won it!

This Association, too, is formed to foster native art; I hope you do not say patronize it, for I must confess that *I* do not like to be patronized, and I do not believe that anybody else does. But the design is to benefit ourselves, by spreading among us the works of our own artists. Well do they deserve it: and I hope the time will come when our church walls will be opened to them. So well do they deserve it, that I will not dishonour them by comparing their claims with those of the refuse stuff that comes over in ship loads from Europe; though there be, as we are told in the advertisements, *real original* Raphaels, Titians, Guidos, and Salvator Rosas, in every one of these wonderful collections.

But grant, it may be said, that painting should be fostered as well as literature, as well as poetry and song—why not let it take its chance with the rest? Why form an association to further its objects? This objection overlooks one material difference. The *book*, when it is written, is printed. That work of art is multiplied into thousands of copies, which easily come within the reach of all who choose to read. It is not so with the painting. It is too expensive for the most of us to buy. What then so proper as a joint stock company like this, to trade for pictures, something better than furs from the North-west coast, or pearls from Ceylon: a lottery, the only good one that I ever heard of, where for five dollars one may draw a prize worth five hundred,—worth far more in the pleasure it will give. Five hundred are often spent for a dinner, a supper, an entertainment, whose pleasure passes and perishes in a night; while a picture may, in a far higher way, please us and our children after us, hundreds of years. Nor in any other way can pictures be distributed among the mass of the people. But for this they must be locked up from the public in the dwellings of the opulent. A similar institution in Edinburgh is spreading fine paintings all over Scotland. One such painting in a country village is a blessing to all its inhabitants. It is more a curiosity there: it is more looked at and studied. A few such teachers in a village would spread an influence all around them. They would speak from the silent walls to passing generations. It may be thought extravagant to say it, but I certainly should look for a higher taste and refinement in such a place.

And of what especially would paintings be teachers? I answer, of what in this country we most especially need. They would be teachers of the beau ideal, the beautiful, the sublime. This is the special province of the arts of design. Although they labour under some difficulties and defects compared with writing, yet they certainly *can* portray a beauty, a sublimity, which the pen cannot; or at any rate, they appeal more directly, and by means more appropriate, to the sense of beauty and grandeur. Now, this appeal, I repeat, is precisely what our country wants, both as a new and as a republican country. In the one character, it has no time-honoured structures, no old ruins, and fewer venerable associations, to address the eye and the heart. In the other, it has parted with many titles to respect and reverence, be they right or wrong—monarchy, a court, a nobility. By all means are enthusiasm and veneration to be cultivated here. We want them to meet the all-surrounding, everywhere-penetrating tendencies to the practical and the palpable, which, like our railroads, are binding the country in chains of iron; we want such aid to lighten the pains-taking of gain, and to assuage the anxieties of ambition.

I do not set myself against the practical spirit of the country, nor its gainful industry; it is all very well in its place; I only say that it needs to be modified by the infusion of other principles, and that it is by such united influences only that we can expect to lay the foundation and build the superstructure of a deep and solid, a fair and beautiful national character. Let religion, let preaching, let literature come with its help to this work; and let art, too, come, with its wonder-working and wonder-inspiring hand Let the sense of beauty be enshrined in the heart of the people. I would rather that one silent, calm picture of martyr-like heroism or of saintly beauty, sunk into the public heart here, than to know of some great and agitating speculation, which had put a million of gold into the public coffer.

The artist has in this country—which so much needs him—I believe, a glorious field. He has not princes indeed for his patrons; but he has a public of educated, intelligent, and increasing millions. Let him not distrust it; let *him* not be wanting, and I promise him, that *we* will not be wanting. The human heart is for ever the same; the same now that it was in the days of Vinci and Raphael. Let him not think that it is turned to stone. Or, if he thinks so, let him try it once; let him strike it with the rod of genius, and if it is not dead—and it *is not* dead—the waters will flow; and they will fertilize and beautify the land in which he lives and in which he shall die; die, and yet die not: for no noble deed shall be planted in the quickened and springing life of this youthful country, but green bays and bright flowers shall rise from it, and flourish around it, in perpetual and everlasting memorial.

XVII.

ON THE MORAL CHARACTER OF GOVERNMENT.

FOR IT IS THE MINISTER OF GOD TO THEE FOR GOOD.—Romans xiii. 4.

THIS is said of political Government. And I wish to invite your meditations this evening, my brethren, to the moral character of this great function of Government. I have long thought that this subject demands the attention of the pulpit, and especially of the American pulpit.

Of the pulpit, I say, in the first place, and of the pulpit everywhere; for what is the office of the preacher, if it is not to speak of everything that touches the national conscience, the national morality; to speak, among other things, of that regard to the common weal which should come as the sanctity and bond of religion to a people? I do not advocate a partisan pulpit. I think that the line should be distinctly drawn between party questions and the general moral questions; and that with the former the pulpit has nothing to do. The preacher indeed has a right to his opinion upon these questions, and he has a right to express it in proper places and at proper times. But the season of public worship is not the time, and the pulpit is not the place; for this plain reason, that all political parties meet here on ground that is understood to be common, and all have built up the pulpit for their common edification, and not as a post for attack upon any; and I must think that he very ill understands his place who employs it to drive away either portion of his hearers, indignant and angry from the sanctuary. But with regard to the moral function of Government, with regard to its fidelity to the people and its duty to God, the case is different. And if religious instruction—so to define the province of the pulpit—if religion, in other words, has anything to do with right and wrong, the case is plain. For what power in the world can do right or can do wrong, upon a scale so vast and stupendous as the Government? Where is there such an accumulation of moral actions and responsibilities as in the Government? What hand upon earth so holds in its grasp the weal or woe of millions living and of millions unborn, as the Government?

And to consider all this, I say, in the next place, is especially the duty of the American pulpit. Because the whole people here to whom the pulpit speaks, acts, morally or immorally, through the Government. I do not loosely say that the people *is* the Government, or that "the people *makes* the Government." We are born under a certain political Constitution. We are born members of a State; that was not for us to choose or to make; and we are bound to be in subjection to the powers that be, I conceive, by considerations far superior to our mere will. Our form of Government is a fabric of power, framed by the wisdom, and cemented in the blood of our fathers; it spreads its protecting shadow over millions of people; and unless some flagrant cause is shown for its subversion, unless some "right of revolution" can be made out, obedience to it, I hold, to be a religious duty, a duty to the God of nations, to the Governor of the world. But this state of things being established, we have ye something to do with it. To the administration of this power, we, the people, the whole people, do directly contribute: to the right or wrong then, which the Government does, to the good or the evil which it brings upon us and will bring upon our posterity, we contribute. We hold this great trust and must discharge it. The burden is upon us, and we cannot escape it. We do and must put forth this tremendous power. Rightly or wrongly, faithfully or unfaithfully, carelessly or solemnly, we do this thing. And it is the bounden duty of the pulpit to bring down this awful responsibility upon the conscience of the whole people. I cannot sufficiently express my amazement or my regret, that the pulpit should have been so long, so completely, so almost universally, wanting to this duty.

The subject of political morality is not only one which it belongs to us, but one which it deeply behoves us to consider; and to consider, I am afraid we must say, with some anxiety. The question about the national morality in every branch of it, is one, in every view, of profound concern. An immense interest for ourselves, an immense interest for the world, is embarked upon the experiment we are making at self-government. But *self*-government? The very word directs us to morality, to moral restraint, to conscience as the basis, without which every thing must sink to ruins. We may point to what material results in this country we will, to what rising cities, to what increasing commerce, to what improving and extending manufactures, and vast tillage and stupendous growth of the national wealth; but, if we are declining in morals; if we are becoming less virtuous and religious people; if corruption is silently stealing into the midst of our prosperity, we know that a canker is at the root which must ere long bring down all our flourishing honours to the dust. Nay, our very flourishing, could it continue without moral culture, were but a misery and a shame. Nations must be nurseries of *men;* national growth must produce noble men, and ever nobler men, or the grand purpose of national existence is frustrated. Now I do not look with discouragement upon our people in this view. I see evils and dangers, but I do not see a general tendency downward. A deep sense of these evils and dangers, a habit common to all ages of disparaging the present in comparison with the past, and a certain zeal in some for rapid and sweeping reforms, are uniting with foreign criticism and censure, to decry this country; but I cannot agree with the one or the other. I stand up firmly for my country, because I can do it conscientiously. I have personally compared it with other countries, and I am satisfied that in general virtue it is, to say the least, inferior to none. I sincerely believe too that the moral sentiment of this country is improving. It is manifest that several prominent vices—intemperance, gaming, profaneness—are not gaining ground but are decreasing among us, and have been for a number of years. We must not look, in this matter, at certain masses of foreign pauper population in our cities, nor in general at the cities alone, but at the whole country. And yet, after all, I must say, there is a doubt, and more than a doubt in my mind, on *one point;* and that is about our *political* morality. Not, however, that I believe even on this point the body of the people to be less pure. Certainly their party animosities are not so bitter as they were twenty and thirty years ago: they do not divide families and neighbourhoods as they did then. And this is some advance in reflection, in liberality, in good temper: some elevation of the public mind. It is into *the action of the Government*, I conceive, that corruption has entered. And it has entered, in no doubtful or equivocal form. *This* is the terrible principle that has come to be recognised in the results of every election; that *the successful party is to take all the offices;* that "to the victors" —thus grossly to state, by a common phrase, the most corrupting, the most fatal, the most detestable principle that ever entered into politics—that "to the victors belong the spoils!" Spoils! The high function of public duty; the solemn responsibility of administering the Law; the sacred investiture with the powers and attributes of sovereignty—consecrated by pledges to men, and oaths to heaven—these are denominated "spoils!" To whom belongs the "bad eminence" of introducing this principle, is not material; for it seems to have become the practice of the Government. But standing as I do in the pulpit, in what ought to be one of the moral heights of the world, I cannot do otherwise than proclaim the hatefulness, and turpitude, and terrible effects of the principle. It strikes at the moral independence of the people. It turns our elections into mere scrambles for office. Our representative system, so far as this principle acts, ceases to be the representation either of minds or even of material interests; personal ambition, personal needs, desperate fortunes only are represented. It mingles in the necessary and otherwise wholesome division of parties, the basest elements of interest. It creates an obligation, a bondage to party support and to party dictation unknown before. "I have laboured in the election; I have the reward; it is a bargain; and I am bound hand and foot"—this is the appropriate language of the principle. It tends to make the whole political action of the country "mesmeric," as I lately heard it characterized by a distinguished statesman: for it divests individual minds of their proper, personal freedom, and subjects them to the mesmerizer—the caucus, the party. He might have added, that the caucus is the galvanic battery, and nominations are the wires that convey the influence, which is to strike the successful candidates with palsy or to animate them to an irresponsible, galvanic action. I would speak with no indecorum of men in office. I know that this tendency may be controlled by individual honour and virtue, and is so; but I say, that this is the tendency.

I repeat, that I would use no indecorum, no improper lightness of speech with regard to men in office; for this, I conceive, is one of the immoral, the demoralizing and desecrating liberties of our Republican politics. Under monarchical systems, the people are accustomed to look up with respect, with loyal reverence to the Government. The sentiment may have gone too far; but it is a right sentiment, when rightly directed. And the just ground for it, is not taken away by our Republican forms. On the contrary, no Government can be so much entitled to respectful treatment, as that which has been raised up by free, popular suffrage. To brow-beat, to smite upon the face, the image of power which they have erected, is suicidal madness. This plainly is the true theory; and woe be to the people who find the fair theory overthrown by fact; who believe that no affection, no consideration, no reverence is due to the power that rules among them! Even then I would treat public office, and those who hold it, with a certain respect.

This levity, in fact, helps not a little to blind the na

tional conscience to the moral character of the great function of Government. Its proper moral agency, few men fairly recognize; and therefore the control of a just moral criticism is seldom applied to it. It is a sort of blind force, or a conjuror's wand, or an impersonal function, or a curiously devised, or recklessly working mechanism; and the actors in it are scarcely regarded as men. It is some *primum mobile* in the terrestrial system; and as certain visionary thinkers have imagined the heavenly bodies to be moved by supernal agency, angelic or demoniac, so it is that many seem to think of the earthly system. They scarcely recognize a human intervention in it; the proper agency of human minds and hearts and consciences. It is far off from them, far above them; and they see at work, demi-gods or demons; and would be surprised if they came nearer, to see instead, a company of toiling, hard-working, often perplexed, troubled, and anxious men. And in so far as the real human agency is seen, yet party spirit distorts the vision and the object. Flattery raises the favourite administration above the level of moral discrimination; reviling sinks the detested administration below it. Talk of *conscience* in the *Government;* say that a reverence for God ought to preside over the Cabinet and the Congress; demand that the administration shall feel and act as a Christian administration—men smile at the very idea of it. They have ceased to demand any such thing. Government, in fact, has ceased in their view to be a moral organism. What a tremendous default of the just and right view! What a terrible omen for the future!

Under all these influences, it is not strange that political morality should go down; that it should sink below all other morality in the country. It is separat ed from all other morality. The morals of politics, like the morals of war, are cut off from the great code of right and wrong. Political honour is severed from private worth. Honour, reputation, character, are taken into partizan keeping. The party favourite, perhaps, is a bad man. Well, many men, many presses say so. What of that? It is the talk of the hostile party; nothing else can be expected of it; it *does* really vilify *good* men. Meanwhile his own friends praise him; and that is enough. They gather around him and shield him—as they do no other man, no clergyman, lawyer, or merchant—shield him, if possible, from his own reproach. And this separation of the morals of party from general morality, leads even good men to do that in politics which they would do in no other relation. It is a state of social war; and the ordinary maxims of rectitude do not apply to it. Fraud must be circumvented by cunning. The political point must be gained at whatever strain upon the moral point. Not only, "the country right or wrong," but "the party right or wrong"—this is the law. The latter, in fact, is ordinarily what the former means. For no great *country* can be honoured by successful injustice; the country wrong, is a country dishonoured. But the party is such a thing, that it may, in its own view, often gain honour simply by winning; since, as things are ordinarily construed, its whole aim, end, life, and very being is *success*. Into such a system, bribery, corruption, selfishness easily enter to build up the Government; and that which should stand as the great and majestic image of *Right*, before the people, becomes too often instead, like one of those idols of savage worship which is honoured and caressed indeed if it is favourable, but if not, is beaten with insane fury, and trampled into dishonour and ignominy.

I tremble when I use such language as this. I hasten to say that this is no just idea of a Government. If I could strip off this distorting mask from the great image of power; if I could show that Government is a moral being; if I could make it appear, that whether acting rightly or wrongly, it is an intensely moral function, I should feel that I had not spoken in vain.

What, then, is the Government? What ought it to think of its function, and of the place it holds in human affairs? What does it *do?*

In answering these questions, let me plainly detach myself from that great bond and chain of conventional usage which is forever binding us down to base acquiescence in existing evils, and which prevents us from seeing the nobler and better way. I dismiss from my mind then, all respects of custom, all suggestions of low and temporary expediency, all pleadings of party interest; and I ask what, in the light of reason and conscience, what, as before the just God and before all wise men, is a Government, and what should it be? Say, if you please, that I am visionary; say that it is idle to lift up any high ideal of this dread attribute of sovereignty,—I do not think it is idle—but at any rate let me pursue out my own thought; and it shall be for those who hear me, to say, whether it engages their assent.

Government, then, is a *trust.* Let me endeavour to accumulate upon that word, its whole meaning. Government is a trust. Whether by hereditary descent as from God—for I leave out of the question the case of the military usurper—whether by election as from the people, Government is a trust. It is this especially, emphatically, supremely; above all things else, that it is, it is this. All its public domain and property, its finances, its army and navy, its legislative, judicial, and executive functions—all its power in every form, is a trust, and nothing but a trust. No man can say, "it is a property, it is a prerogative of *mine*, derived from nature or from my own will, to govern millions of people." Whether he be king or president, whether it be Congress or Parliament, it is the consent of the people that places them in their seats and holds them there.

Nor is it any less a trust, because it springs from the very nature and necessity of things—springs, I may say, from the will of God. When God ordained that a country, or tract of country, should be occupied by a multitude of people, he as certainly ordained as a thing necessary to its safety and well being, that the regulation and care of its interests should be committed to a few. That is to say, Government of some kind is as much an ordinance as nationality. For all the people of a country cannot come together to make laws, arrange public measures and confer with foreign nations; and they must, therefore, have a head. All the people of a district cannot exercise such public functions; they must, therefore, choose a representative. The head, the representative, has committed to him the general interest simply *in trust.*

But what is a trust? What does it imply? What does it mean? What is the essence of it? In its very essence, it is moral. It implies a duty; it appeals to a conscience; it must answer to a God above! It is holden of God and man, for the public weal. If a trust-company is responsible for the faithful discharge of its duties, so is a trust-Government responsible. It is a trustee, as much as if the taking and accounting for money were its sole office. And for what is it a trustee? For the welfare of millions; for all that which touches, in its action, their joys or their sorrows, their business or pleasure, their wealth or poverty, their weal or woe. What private interest, or party dictation can break this bond of duty to the whole people! Though a party succeed in seating itself in the place of power, yet from that moment it should cease to be a party, and should act for the whole nation. The representative system recognizes parties, indeed, but it does not recognize a party Government. No sane people, in its political compact, ever meant that such a monstrous thing should exist. If any measure presents itself, of which the acting Government is obliged to say, "this would help the party that placed us in power but would be bad for the country," it is bound by its position, as entrusted with the common welfare, to reject that measure. If this is not the *actual* political morality, it is nevertheless the *true* political morality.

But a trust, a moral trust, I still say, what is it? And I answer more emphatically, it is a bond upon the conscience. It is a bond to fidelity stronger than any other. I may not do what I will with my own unrestrained by conscience; but surely, and doubly true is it, that I may not do what I will with another's. I may refuse to take such trust; but if I accept, I must discharge it. From the moment I take it, I am bound to those from whom I receive it, and I am bound to heaven. The Government of a nation, the greatest trustee-ship in the world, is bound by solemnities of office and of oath, to the God of nations. And he who, invested with such a function, has not arrived at this view of it, has yet to learn what are the first principles of the doctrine of Government.

My Brethren, this is not a small matter, nor a matter improper for our consideration in the house of God, nor a matter impertinent to us. We elect men to office. We influence them by our very idea of what they should be. A high ideal must always go before high action. Every man and woman may thus make a lofty contribution to lofty ends. Let me create in this whole people a high and sacred sentiment and sense of what a Government ought to be, and I will lift up a power which no Government can resist. The world, I trust, is beginning to look into this matter as it never did before. And it is high time; for it has precious interests at stake, and the duty has been too long neglected. This idea of Government, which history itself has too much countenanced—that it is a high game of ambition to be played out for the pleasure or interest of a few—that its seat is a lofty stage for men to play such tricks upon before high heaven, as make the angels weep, and men beneath to groan in bitterness and sorrow—and that this is all that can be expected of a Government; could there be anything more monstrous to the eye of truth and reason, more offensive to heaven, more demoralizing to the world than this? Demoralizing, I say; for the highest visible power in the world, like a lofty tower, is seen and marked of all men and is surrounded with splendour. And an evil example from that height, will fall with tenfold crushing weight upon the people. In sovereignty there is a kind of sanctitude; there is a divinity that doth hedge about even a bad king; and when the throne of power, or the highest seat of magistracy is regarded but as a place for the intrigues of ambition or interest, it is a desecration such as if the pulpit were turned into a huckster's booth, or the sacred ermine of justice were dragged in the mire like a beggar's rags.

No, my brethren, we must not be silent. We must take up this matter. We must think of it. We have all an interest in holding up high the idea of Govern ment, in demanding of it fidelity to its trust, in demanding of it justice; and should I not say, the nobleness, the grandest embodiment of justice. It is not a mere mercantile justice that is high enough for a state. It is not to be just as a trader, who will not repudiate his debts if he can pay them; though this is a kind of justice that is to be urged, and thank God, *has* been successfully urged, upon more than one of our own States; but the sovereignty of a great people should be noble, magnanimous, beneficent; it should be temperate, dispassionate, grave; it should be too great for resentment, too high for selfishness, too majestic to do wrong; it should respect the rights and interests, not of its own subjects only, but also of other nations, and especially of weaker nations. A single man may find it hard to be just to rivals and enemies; but the collective power of a great people should not find it hard. It should take the noble part among the nations. The petty passions of men have no place in it. The brow of majesty should be calm: and its hands should be stretched out to the widest comprehension of the great interests of humanity. And as the mighty heart of the system, it should beat to the noblest emotions that the collective justice, honour and conscience of humanity and of all mankind, can pour into it.

But all this which I have been saying is enforced by another and, if possible, still stronger reason. For what does a Government *do?* Is it to the people a negative and indifferent function? Is it a piece of mechanism away up in the sky, with which people have nothing to do but to gaze at it? No; it is not. It is here; it is among us. It is a power that is felt in our daily life. It gives us business; it gives us bread, or withholds them; it is a mechanism that touches the fortunes of every family, of every individual. Every turn of every wheel in it, is as a wheel of the rack inflicting pain, or as the revolving orbs of heaven, shedding light and blessing upon the world.

What is a tariff? If a hand were every day put forth to take something from the granary and the cellar, from the kneeding-trough and the daily board, that would be what a tariff is. Even with the most careful and gradual adjustment, it affects the comfort of ten thousands of families. With violent changes, it builds up or plucks down, it settles or scatters unnumbered households. It is justice or injustice, to the capitalist and the labourer, to the buyer and seller, to the producer and consumer. It is justice or injustice to everybody.

What is legislation? What is a statute but the very law under which the whole people must walk? The law professes to enact that which is just and right, and to punish that which is unjust and wrong. It professes to be the definite exposition of that rectitude, which the law of God demands. The statute-book is the very Bible of civil life, and in many respects of moral life. The Government stands before us, and says, "thou shalt do thus and thus; or if thou wilt not, thou shalt be visited with pains and penalties." Is obedience to it an indifferent thing?

But the Government does more. It makes treaties. And all who sail upon the sea or walk upon the land, are bound by those conventions. Yet more; it makes peace or war. Are these things indifferent? Are they morally indifferent? I know not what on earth is more awful, than is sometimes the incipient step, that leads to a long and bloody war. The Government gives a direction; it is, as it were, but to lift a finger and point: it is but three lines perhaps, written in a moment, by a mortal hand: and what follows? Oh! who can sum up the horrors and woes that are accumulated in a single war! Let us not cover them over with blinding military phrases. War comes with its bloody hand into our very dwellings. It takes from thousands and ten thousands of homes, those who were abiding there in peace and comfort; around whom were thrown the tender ties of family and kindred. It carries them away to die of exposure and fever untended, in infectious climes, or to stand up in the fierce fight,—to be hacked and mangled and torn in pieces; to sink on the gory field from which they shall rise no more, or to be borne away, writhing with agony, to noisome and infectious hospitals. Nor is this all. The groans of the battle-field are echoed in sighs of bereavement from thousands of desolated hearths. Or if the soldier returns, perhaps he brings worse sorrow to his home by the infection, which he has caught, of camp vices. The country is demoralized. The whole national mind perhaps is brought down from the noble interchange of kind offices with another people, to wrath and revenge, and base pride, and the habit of measuring brute strength with brute strength—for that is mainly what a battle is. The language of the victorious country is—"we have beat them; we have whipped them"—the very language of a bully. The wasted treasure, as well as wasted morals, is not indifferent. Enough is often expended in a war, to build ten thousand churches, hospitals, universities, or to construct rail-roads across a continent: or to dry up the tears of a nation's sorrow like Ireland's. If this treasure were only sunk in the sea, it were a great calamity; but it is expended in cutting into the veins and arteries of human life, till they deluge the earth with a sea of blood.

And all this, I repeat, is done by Governments; by the pointed finger of that awful power; by three lines written with its hand. Should not all those who take such a tremendous responsibility, and all those who vote supplies, fall upon their knees before God and ask for light and guidance? Should not the conscience of the whole people and the cries of suffering humanity and the tears of widows and orphans, rise up and call upon all rulers and legislators to cast away all passion and pride, and to address themselves to the most solemn and religious thought of their duties and responsibilities? May not a suffering and sorrowing world point them to the great audit—the answer to God? And ought not this dread ministry of Government to stand before us in a new and more solemn light? Ought it not to weigh upon the heart with the burthen of an empire's welfare, and bow down the head with awe before the God of nations? When the death of Louis XV. was announced in the Court of France, the young dauphin and his wife, Louis XVI. and Marie Antoinette, amidst all-surrounding agitation, and while congratulations were ready to be poured out upon them, burst into tears, fell upon their knees and exclaimed, "O God, aid us, protect us; we reign too soon!" Fit investiture with the awfulness of sovereignty! Fit modesty! Yes, they reigned too soon. The awful days that came, and to which they were unequal, their own mournful end, proclaimed that they reigned too soon. Why shall men grasp after power? Why, as in pure and pristine ages, shall they not shrink from it with awe, or enter upon it with modesty and prayer? It is, I fear, because sanctity has gone out from power, and it is regarded as a mere worldly instrument for worldly ends. It is, I fear, because it has lost its moral venerableness. I dread lest it be found true that the people have taken it in hand only to handle it too familiarly, too rudely; only to divest its lofty seats of their sacredness, and its solemn halls of debate, of their dignity. If it be so, or if there be any tendency of this kind amidst the freedom and the swaying to and fro of public opinion, then must all the conscience that is left in the world come to the rescue; then must the pulpit come to the rescue; and well may the priests, the ministers of the Lord, weep between the porch and the altar, and say, "Spare thy people, O Lord, and give not thine heritage to reproach." We have swept away the throne and the sceptre and the crown: those prescriptive titles to the homage of mankind are gone from among us. Then must we set up the throne of justice here, and the sceptre of our power must be righteousness, and the crown of our Republican majesty must be the lowly fear of God!

It is a stupendous, it is an awful movement in human affairs—this tendency of the age to popular forms of government. This tide in the affairs of men—it is evident that the civilized world is embarked upon it; and it is rolling on to the dark and unknown future. What is to be the end of these things we know not; though for myself I am one of those who hope well of the result. But one thing is certain. As surely as there is a just God who governs the world, as surely as all history gives true augury, so sure it is that injustice and corruption shall not, shall never thrive in human affairs. If popular governments cannot be made pure; if the majestic dominion of the people that is now rising in the world, is only to spread itself over disorder and licentiousness like that before the flood, then shall another flood come, and with other tokens; then shall the great deep of society be broken up, and the windows of heaven's displeasure shall be opened; and a base and irreverent and corrupt world shall be swept away, to prepare for some new creation.

My Brethren, bear with me one moment longer. We *must think* of these things! The whole people must think of them! We, the people, contribute to make the Government what it is. We are not the Government; we do not wield that power; but we give it its moral character; we impart to it its wisdom or folly, its violence or moderation, its spirit of justice and patriotism, or of injustice and party animosity. We elect the men who shall administer the Government; and the spirit in which we choose them is the spirit in which they will govern. And I do earnestly say again and again, we must think, we the people, must think of all this. We must reform our careless ways of thinking on this subject. We must take up a new idea of the solemn and majestic function of Government. We must take up a new idea of our duties. Grave and thoughtful must be the steps that lead us to the ballot. We must remember that we are putting forth a hand there, that is to touch the weal or woe of millions of people, and of the future generations. If we choose for office bad men, be their politics what they may; if we choose reckless, headstrong, violent, unprincipled men; if we choose for a nation's guidance, men whom we would not trust with our private affairs—men to hold the reins of the supreme rule, whom we would not trust to hold the strings of our private purse; what can we expect but the displeasure of the just God, and the reproach of all just men? Who shall care for our fate, if we thus sport with it? Who will pity us in the day of our calamity? Nobody. We shall be the world's wonder and the world's scorn for our folly and guilt.

No, PEOPLE of America! the burden is upon you. The burden of the future is upon you. If you fail, heaven and earth will make inquisition for your negligence and recklessness—for never was people so favoured. Favoured and fortunate thus far; but if ever the dark days shall come—which heaven forbid!—if ever disunion and anarchy shall overspread this land; if ever its fair borders shall "shine o'er with civil swords," and be covered with blood and carnage, then shall its desolated dwellings make inquisition of you, of your pulpits, of your people. Then will God demand of you, and say, "Ah! sinful nation! a seed of evil doers! children that are corrupters! ye have forsaken the Lord; ye have provoked the holy One to anger; your country is desolate; your cities are burned with fire; your land, strangers devour it in your presence; and it is desolate as overthrown by strangers!"

XVIII.

THE SLAVERY QUESTION.

REMEMBER THEM THAT ARE IN BONDS.—Hebrews, xiii. 3.

I PROPOSE to offer some remarks, this evening, on the Slavery question. It is a question of humanity, and by that claim, they that are in bonds, are always to be remembered. It is one of the great moral questions of the day, and proper at all times to be discussed. But I think it must have been pressed upon our attention in an especial manner during the past winter, by the debates upon it that have agitated the national Legislature. It has really been, next to the Mexican war, the great question of the Session; and in point of actual interest, greater than that. It is a matter of great moral interest to us, and to every one of us; because we have, or shall have, duties to discharge in regard to it, of the highest possible moment.

For it has become apparent, I think, that the whole North will take a stand in regard to the extension of slavery, that must give to the question, a new and very solemn importance. The slavery question is fast becoming the great trial question in this country; the question on which its politics, its peace, perhaps its union depends. For myself, I cannot look without apprehension to the discussion and the legislative action, to which I see that this question is to be subjected. I cannot altogether sympathize with the tone of nonchalance with which some of our Northern and Western men say to the South, "You cannot, and you dare not, break off from us." When I have listened to the men of the South on this subject; when I have heard them on the floor of Congress, pledge conscience, honour, and life to withstand the evidently and equally fixed purpose of the North, I have seen passion, indeed, but it seemed to me a passion of the deepest sincerity and determination. It is said, I know, that interest, palpable and pressing interest, must keep us together. I answer that the bonds of interest have been a thousand times broken by the force of passion; that it is intemperate passion which we have to fear; and that there seems to be enough of this, in the case, to awaken the serious concern of all thoughtful men. I would do no injustice to the men of the South. It is not passion alone, I know, that animates them; but it is apparently the deepest sense of wrong meditated against them, as they conceive, in the fixed determination of the North to forbid all further extension of their system.

During the last winter I have entered a little within the borders of the Slave-system; I have conversed with some of the ablest and wisest men of the South on the subject; and I have come to entertain the conviction that we of the North ought to know them and their system better than we do, to render full justice to either. When Mr. Quinet, the celebrated Parisian professor, proposed to write a book on Ultra-Montanism,—i. e. the highest Roman Catholic pretensions—he determined as he tells us, though living in a Catholic country, to go to Spain, where that system exists in its fullest vigour, and to study it there. And so do I conceive that he who would write upon the Slave-system, should go to the very field, on which its character is fully displayed. He cannot know either the good or the evil of it—either the qualified good or the positive evil, without seeing it. I do not say that it is necessary to take a journey to South Carolina or Louisiana to decide that slavery is abstractly wrong; that it was wrong originally to bring men into that condition. Few question this, whether at the North or South. But to determine what can be done, what ought to be done, what is best to be done—this requires a careful, eye-witnessing study of the system, in its actual condition and complicated relations. The Southern men complain that we of the North are dealing with abstractions; that we do not understand the case; that we are mistaking names for things, and pictures of the imagination for realities. I admit that something of this is likely enough to be true. I have long since come to be convinced that we thoroughly know nothing but what we experience and see. I admit the force of all this; but I might remind our brethren of the South that it has a double application. For, I must say, neither do they seem to understand *us*. They seem to think it is all passion and fanaticism with us at the North. I have thought it very remarkable that they do not appear to know, to recognize the moral difficulties which we have with the subject; the difficulties not of fanatics, not of men who are bestirring themselves in this matter because they can't keep still about anything; but of sober and thoughtful men, who sit apart and meditate the question by themselves. For what other, I ask, than a *moral* interest *can* we have in the question? We have no immediate concern with it. What is it, in the name of reason? what can it be, but a feeling for the right and for humanity that is leading the whole North and the whole world, in fact, to take the attitude which it is assuming on this subject?

It is true, then, that neither party is likely very well

to understand the other; and in the little that I have now to say upon the subject, I will speak with all the care and candour of which I am capable. I will first state the case as I have received it from the lips of Southern men; and next, I will offer what seems to me proper to be said by way of reply. In setting forth their plea, it shall be *they* who speak. It shall be their fairest, most honourable and conscientious plea. I know that base interest has its voice there. But there are thoughtful and Christian men in the Southern States, and many such; and, although I think they are mistaken, I am willing, fairly and calmly, to hear what they say.

Thus, then, they argue:—"We do not defend the original taking of these people from Africa. The horrors of the slave-trade we give up to universal execration. The sin does not lie at our door. But here these people are among us. We found them here when we came into life. We were born into the possession and care of them. What is our duty to them? "We are willing," say the Christian and conscientious men among our brethren there, "to take the highest sense of duty for our guidance. What ought we to do? We are willing to listen to calm reasoning upon this point. We ask for light. We would not offend against God, nor against the Christian law. What ought we to do? What does justice demand? If anything can be pointed out in our relation to these people or our treatment of them, that is intrinsically wrong, we will not defend it. Wrongs will be *committed* in all human relations. Are there no *parents* among *yourselves*, who are harsh and cruel to their children? Do you not sometimes hear as you pass by a dwelling, the cries of a child that is cruelly whipped? The same thing may be witnessed as you pass by our plan-tations, though we deny that it is *common.* But we do not defend it. You ought not to speak of exceptions, springing from human infirmity and passion, but of the essential relation. And we say in the very outset that you mistake the relation. You call it cruel bondage. *We* say it is a relation of dependence, of subjection; necessary in the circumstances to the good of both parties. You say, it is the buying and selling of men; the bartering of immortal souls; the bidding off at auction and under the hammer, of that which is a spark of the Divinity, the image of God. But we say, that there is in this language much that is figurative. Thoughts, affections, the immortal spark, cannot be bought nor sold. We buy the services of these men for life. That is all we can buy; the use of bone and sinew. Do you not buy the same, when you hire a man for a year or a month? It is true there is a difference. The party with us does not consent. He does not sell his services. His will is bowed down to our will. It is true, too, that we buy the service of these men and of their *children.* And there is compulsion in the case. Abstractly, it seems a hard measure; inconsistent with the natural rights of a man. We admit it. It is a trying view of the case, we admit. Humane men among us do not sell their slaves if they can help it. It is an evil incident to the system; we grant it is an evil; it is an unwelcome and painful resort: Sell my slaves!" I have heard a Southern man exclaim: "I should almost as soon think of selling my children."

"Still, however, in any view, here is compulsion; and now we say,"—thus proceeds the argument—"this compulsion is necessary; necessary for the welfare of both parties. It is not only true that our fields, in many quarters, cannot be cultivated by any labour but that of the African man; that no other constitutions can bear it; but is it not equally true that it is best for the African man that he should labour? Is not industry better for *him* than idleness? Yet it is perfectly certain that he will not labour but under compulsion. We do not say—but under the whip. That is seldom used; it is seldom necessary. But we say that he must feel himself laid under necessity to work or he will not work."

Give your patience to this plea, my Brethren; it is meet that we should hear what our Southern people say.

"We say"—is their language—"that the African man is naturally indolent, reckless, without foresight, incorrigibly disposed to idling and amusement; unconscious of those stimulants of ambition and care for the future that animate the white race. If left free to follow their bent, they will not work. They are not fit, in this respect, to take care of themselves. We say that the condition, for ages, of the Africans at home, proves it; that the experiment in Haiti proves it; and we believe that the same thing is beginning to appear, among the emancipated slaves in the West Indies. These people want masters, guides, protectors, providers. They need them as much as little children need them. If they were left to themselves, to act their pleasure, our whole Southern country would be overspread with idleness, disorder, vice, and ruin. It would be absolutely uninhabitable.

"Then as to the results of the relation, we say they are happy; happier for them than for us. Of the affection subsisting between us and them you seem to have no idea whatever. You seem to suppose that all is severity on one side and suffering on the other. It is a total mistake. We are attached to our people and they are attached to us. We take care of them in sickness. We care for their children, and the aged and helpless of their females. Provided with food and clothing, and feeling no anxiety for the future, they enjoy life; their spirits are elastic and free; the song and the dance are more frequent with them than with any other people; they are happier and better off than multitudes of the labourers of England or the peasants of France.

"In short," say they, whose plea I am setting forth, "we hold that this is a good relation; the best, at any rate, that the case admits. We hold," say *some* among them, "that it is especially good and desirable in a Republic, where universal competition is elsewhere breeding universal discontent, vexation and pain; that it is a relation between races essentially distinct, and of which the one is essentially inferior, and will be so forever; and therefore we look upon the relation as one that ought to be permanent; that is destined, if undisturbed by fanatical interference, to last as long as the country lasts."

Now, in reply, it seems to me—I may be thought to use strong language—but it does seem to me that in all this, one element is left out of the account that is enough to split this argument into a thousand helpless fragments; and that is the great element of *human nature*. I cannot help looking upon those who make these pleas, as I should upon children unconsciously playing with toys filled with gunpowder, which is certain yet to explode, and to spread havoc and destruction all around.

Are these people MEN? That is the question. If they are *men*, it will not do to make them instruments for mere convenience; for the mere tillage of the soil. If they are *men*, it is not enough to say that they have a sort of animal freedom from care and joyance of spirits. If they are *men*, they are to be cultivated; their faculties are to be regarded as precious; they are to be improved. But all this would be fatal to the argument; fatal to their happiness in bondage; fatal to the security of their masters. It is felt, I believe, universally at the South, that it will not do to educate them beyond a certain, and that, a very low point; that it will not do to give them refinement, elevation of soul, generous and high impulses. They smile, I suppose, at the very idea of it. Refined, elevated, high-minded *slaves!* It is a solecism, a contradiction in terms. But, I ask, is this ground to be tolerated? Suppose that a child—any child—were put into my care; there he is on the ground before me, engaged in happy and merry sports! I know that he is capable of growing up towards my own intellectual stature. Well, I sustain him; I keep him; I care for his wants; I tend him in sickness; I am attached to him, suppose, and he to me; but for certain purposes connected with my convenience and safety, I deprive him of the means of intellectual development; I make laws for all my household, forbidding them to educate him; and he comes up into life, an ignorant, brutish, half-idiotic, overgrown abortion of a man! Would not all the world cry out against me as a monster? And grant that the African man of the present generation cannot be raised to our stature. Yet if in the course of ages he may be, and if it is our policy systematically to arrest or to retard his growth, does the case materially differ from what I have supposed? And, I repeat, is it a thing to be tolerated? Why, if I could raise trees in my grove, or flowers in my garden, or cattle in my pasture, ten times fairer and better than I have, I should be thought to have forfeited all claims to good *taste* and good *husbandry*, if I would not do it. But a *man!* a being capable of indefinite expansion and immortal progress! is he to want the benefit of an equal consideration—ay, and a far higher? The tree, the flower, the ox or the horse, feels no claim. But an intelligent creature, a fellow-being, a brother-man: *dare* we keep him ignorant, dwarfed, degraded for our convenience? But once more; if he is a *man*, then he is not only improveable and ought to be improved, but he *will improve*, in spite of all that we can do. The African man *has* improved in this country under all his disadvantages. And he *is* to improve yet more and yet faster. Light is breaking in upon him; sympathy is visiting him, from far and near, from this country, and from the whole civilised world beyond the sea. And he knows it. He has heard of Abolition people! And I do not know but ultra-Abolitionism, amidst all its violence and rancour, and all the evil it has done in other ways, has done good in this—that it has lifted up a glaring standard, a flaming banner before the eyes of the slave. And I plainly say, I am glad he knows that there are men in the world, who wish and pray for his elevation to the rights and dignities of manhood. I say this in no unkindness to our brethren of the South. Nor yet do I ask them to pardon me. I can ask pardon of nobody for espousing the cause of humanity, instead of that which would dwarf it and keep it down. Pardon us rather thou, poor, crushed and suffering human nature, wherever thou art, that we feel for thee so little! But we do, nevertheless, feel for it, and must express that feeling. Wherever *power* and *right* come into conflict, our part is already chosen. Has that golden sentence of old, to which once a Roman theatre rose up to do honour—"I am a man, and nothing belonging to man is foreign to me"—has it in these modern days, lost all its beauty and grandeur? God forbid!

But if this feeling is rising in the world and not dying out; if it is to penetrate into the mind and mass of slavery, with its influence—can any one doubt what the effect will be? *The slave-man will improve.* He will become more and more conscious that he is a man; and that as a man he has rights, which God and nature accord to him. And how is all this to consist with the plan of perpetual bondage! with the plan of indefinite and permanent extension! If the African man be indeed a man, it never can succeed. No; you cannot hold down the tremendous element which you propose to chain and bind for ever. Though the powers and pledges of an empire were engaged to make all fast and sure; though this broad land, stretching from sea to sea, were the bond, and the Alleghanies and the Rocky Mountains were the seals upon the bond, to hold all fast, there is an expansive force in human nature, that to be free, will rend a continent in pieces, and shake the mountains in its might. Freedom is one of the elemental forces of the moral universe. It is the undying aspiration which no mortal power can keep down.

All this, I say, follows, if the African is a man. But now I hear it said, in reply, "he is *not* a man in the sense which you suppose." It is maintained that "he is inferior; of an inferior race; and one destined for ever to remain so." What is meant, I pray, by this constantly reiterated charge of inferiority? If only that he is uncivilized, uncultivated, undeveloped, that is all very intelligible and very true. If it be only alleged that there are some peculiar marks of mental deficiency upon this people; that the higher faculties in them seem to be singularly, almost strangely slow to come forth under any circumstances; that philosophy, poetry, habits of mental abstraction have appeared but rarely among them, and in but a low degree; all this may be admitted. Their chance, certainly has been poor enough. Yet that not one Zeno or Epictetus should have arisen among them, nor anything like it, is doubtless something strange. But surely it is not meant to be denied that their faculties are human faculties. That is to say, reason and imagination and affection and conscience in them, are essentially the same as in us. Now what is the nature and tendency of these faculties? If there is any one thing about them which I know,—of which I am perfectly sure—it is this; that their nature is to improve, to expand, to grow larger and larger forever. These intellectual and moral powers are not like the instincts of animals, destined to come to a certain point, and there to find an impassable barrier. Does not the stoutest asserter of their inferiority, the strongest advocate of their perpetual depression on earth, believe that they are to rise to heaven, and there to expand in immortal vigour? Why else does he preach Christianity to them? Is it all a farce? Surely not. But if this very soul is to rise to heaven; nay, if the loftiest, the Christian means of development are applied to it; does any one believe it is the will of God that through ages, the clog and the weight and the chain should rest upon it here? It is absurd. Those who believe in the doomed and perpetual degradation of the African, should build for him no churches. Churches are not guard-houses to keep people in check, but schools of education. The ministers of God are not jailors, but teachers. And if teaching does not mean improvement; if Christian teaching does not mean indefinite expansion, it means nothing.

No, this nature, like all human nature, is destined to grow on earth. The world exists but for this. The ages are the courses of human improvement. They are lengthened out but to lead the tribes of men farther and farther, higher and higher on the scale of progress. And this African nature, if it is not an exception, if it is not to stand as a strange and terrible solecism amidst the rational works of God, is to grow. And if it is to grow, it is with equal certainty destined sooner or later to burst the chains of servitude.

I have thus attempted, though very briefly, to set forth the plea for slavery, and the answer to it: that is, the *moral* answer, for I confine myself to that. That the North and the South should understand one another on this subject; that we should end our recriminations; that we should cease to accuse one another of fanaticism and bad passion, and of mutual hatred, which the best men among us do not feel; that we should really come to understand the ground which honest and conscientious men are taking on either side; this seems to me of such importance that I can see no other chance of any but a fearful and fatal solution of this terrible question. Mutual recrimination will not settle it: calm reason, candour, mutual respect and brotherly kindness must come into this controversy, or it bodes a woful issue.

At this moment the Northern States of this Union are taking a decided stand against the further extension of the slave system. We say that we cannot consent to spread the shield of our general Government over any new slave territory. The Texas annexation sticks in our throats, and we can swallow no more. This obstinate determination is very provoking to the people of the South. They say, it is an enormous injustice to them to forbid the carrying of the slave system into California. We say, in reply, then let California alone; we do not want it; but if you will have it; if you will raise the question; then in conscience we can make but one decision. We cannot, as morally honest men, true to their convictions, sanction the spread of this system. We cannot consent to legalize it anew. Our fathers compromised with yours to let it stand within a certain domain. We will not violate that compromise. We will hold to the very letter of it; but surely not one letter of it looked to the indefinite and perpetual extension of slavery over new domains. We cannot agree to that. It may be right for you with your views; but for us with our views, it cannot be right. If you *alone* could do this, it would be morally nothing to us. But if you ask us to be parties with you in this transaction, if our hands must be put to the bond, then we must draw back. We would speak in no loftier manner to you than the occasion demands. We beseech you rather as brethren, fairly to consider our scruple. It is not chiefly political; it is not economical; it is *moral;* and thus insurmountable. Suppose that South Carolina should legalize polygamy or abolish marriage. We could not help it, that I see. Suppose that the whole South should do this; or that it had originally come into the Union on compromise, without any law of marriage. Well, we are bound by the compromise, let it be supposed. But are we bound by it to unite with our neighbours in extending their system? Can we agree to join them in conquering or buying new territories on which the system of polygamy, or of no marriage should be established; established by our laws, supported by our arms, and sanctioned by our countenance? But in the view of the people of the North, I suppose that slavery is, in principle, a clearer moral wrong, than polygamy or no marriage would be. What then, I would seriously ask the people of the South, are we to do with these convictions? Would they have us tread them under foot? It is as if they asked us to falsify our conscience or our word. We cannot do it. *No* people can be so false to itself. A Government may belie the sentiment of the people; but no *people* can be so false to itself.

In fine, if I could speak to the people of the South, I would say to them; I have faithfully endeavoured to understand your view of this great question; for thirty years I have availed myself of all proper opportunities for conversing with those of you with whom I have been acquainted; I have listened to them with all possible consideration, and may I say, candour; and I entertain now none of that rancour against you, for which you are accustomed to look at the North. I have no doubt that the body of you sincerely believe that for the present, and indeed for the future, while the African man continues to be what he is now, the relation of servitude is the best both for you and him. You believe, whether rightly or wrongly, that he is better off and is happier as he is, than he would be if he were immediately set free. You profess kindness for him. You say, that among you cruelty to him is held in the worst repute. You say that the condition of things among you generally is *not* that of grinding tyranny on the one hand and of reluctant and weeping submission on the other. You say that the African is a weak and childish being, unfit to take care of himself and that you must hold him, and ought to hold him in your care and keeping.

Then I say, in the first place—for heaven's sake and for humanity's sake, treat him as a child. Pity his degradation; *that* noble sentiment can do you no harm. Raise him from his degradation as you would any poor and ignorant creature; do not, that is to say, crush and keep him down, or neglect him and leave him prostrate, because he is a slave. How can any one live, how can he pass his whole life in the presence of one or two hundred beings, capable of the noblest elevation, capable at least of something far better than they ever reach, and yet leave them in perpetual ignorance, and almost brutish stupidity! If the very dog at our feet, could be raised to the bliss of humanity, what noble mind would not be filled with enthusiasm to achieve it! Is it said, *that* would not be safe; then, I reply, *there must be something wrong* in the relation. It *cannot possibly be right* so to hold down and bind to the earth the faculties of an immortal creature! *

In the next place, I would earnestly ask those who sustain this relation, if they have well and duly considered what a tremendous element they hold in their charge. The awfulness of this human nature!—the whole world has yet to wake up to it. But is there not a sentiment of contempt towards the slave man, that fearfully overlooks what he is. Amidst all the pro-

* It was about twenty years ago, that an aged gentleman was living in the city of London, in wealth and luxury derived from the produce of his estates in the Island of Barbadoes. Some facts came to his knowledge that led him to suspect that his slaves were cruelly treated. At the age of eighty, he left his luxurious home, and crossed the ocean to examine for himself. He dwelt among his people for ten years. He took a fatherly care of them; he improved their condition and character; he prepared them for freedom, and dying at the age of ninety, he left them with a copy-hold of his estates. Well might the Edinburgh Review say, we take shame to ourselves, that while we have been occupied with the deeds of kings and conquerors, we have never heard till now the name of Joshua Steele.

fessions of kindness and protection towards him, I think I see that in a very marked degree. The great human claim which we assert for him, is met with a smile of incredulity and indifference, if not of contempt.

This, it seems to me, is the dividing point in the whole controversy. In the Southern mind, as far as I have studied it, there appears to be no proper recognition of the *common humanity* in the African man. That the slave man is a *man*, with a man's feelings, with a man's rights, with a man's capabilities—this is precisely what is not felt. I would solicit the attention of my Southern brethren to this point. It seems to me that the long habit of using these beings as mere cattle, and disposing of them as mere chattels, has worn off from them, in the eyes of their masters, the venerable and solemn impress of humanity itself. I once put the question in conversation—"Suppose that this were a race of apes or ourang-outangs which you held in bondage, but that you believed, according to some modern theories, that they were capable of being cultivated up to humanity; would you not feel a greater moral interest in such a race, than you now do in the slave-race? Would you not be inspired with the most enthusiastic desire to bring about such a consummation? And is it not some strange habit of mind that prevents an equal interest about the improvements of human beings?

The comparison may be repelled; but is not the allegation mainly true? *Is* the *human* claim of this unhappy race felt? They say, at the South, that we do not understand the case—how *inferior* these people are: we reply, "Do you understand the case? how *human* they are. You say that you feel kindly towards them. So you do towards your dog or your horse. Is that enough? Does that satisfy the sacred relation of man with man? *Is*, we repeat, the awfulness of the human claim regarded? And will the God who has made man in his own image, permit that sacred claim to be so disregarded?

Far be it from me to invoke his displeasure; but I say in the third place that there is peril in that dread element which we have taken into our charge. The times of ignorance God winked at: but these later Christian ages cannot pass over a race oppressed, dwarfed, kept down and chained to the earth, without making terrible inquisition for it. Heaven demands, "where is thy brother?"—and earth echoes, "where is he?" It is in vain to resist that universal sentiment that is rising all over the world in behalf of this oppressed race. That universal sentiment will educate the slave; and it will educate him to wrath and resistance, if we do not educate him to intelligence, love and freedom.

If *I* were to propose a plan to meet the duties and perils of this tremendous emergency that presses upon us, I would engage the whole power of this nation, the willing co-operation of the North and the South, if it were possible, to prepare this people for freedom; and then I would give them a country beyond the mountains—say the Californias where they might be a nation by themselves. Ah! if the millions upon millions spent upon a Mexican war could be devoted to this purpose; if all the energies of this country could be employed for such an end; what a noble spectacle were it for all the world to behold, of help and redemption to an enslaved people! What a purifying and ennobling ministration for ourselves!

XIX.

PUBLIC CALAMITIES.*

I KNOW, O LORD, THAT THY JUDGMENTS ARE RIGHT, AND THAT THOU IN FAITHFULNESS HAST AFFLICTED ME.—Psalm cxix. 75.

An event has occurred in our waters within the last week, that has so occupied my mind, that I could not well have prepared to speak to you this morning on any other subject. I feel, too, that I shall probably best consult the state of *your* minds, by making it the subject of your reflections; in a place too, where such reflections most naturally come for guidance and relief—the house of God. The house of God also mourns with many private dwellings of the land; the groan that arises by their desolate hearths, is echoed from the altar. The Church of God mourns the loss of one of its holiest, dearest and most devoted servants. Dr. Follen—alas! that I must say it, and dismiss all further hope—is among the victims of that dreadful catastrophe. That name, whose utterance now fills us with grief—I know not how it was—strangely almost it seemed, stranger as he was—had mingled itself with the *home* sympathies of many hearts, and of many of the best minds among us. Yet why should I say that I know not how it was—when the beauty and purity of his life, the unfeigned sincerity and affectionateness of his disposition, the enlarged

* A Discourse delivered on the occasion of the loss of the steamer Lexington, in Long Island Sound, January 13, 1840.

and liberal views of his mind, and his martyr-like devotion to truth and duty, had naturally made him a home in that love which knows no boundaries of country or clime. God pity that nearer home, where that name is no longer the familiar utterance and bond of affection; where it is only a broken echo, from a living grave! God knows that our sympathy and prayers have hovered over it in agony; to bring, if it were possible to bring, relief and comfort.

But I must not dwell upon this; it is too painful Many other names, dear in their circles of home and friendship, are placed, in God's dread Providence, upon this mournful record. The groan that rises from this catastrophe, will spread itself over the world—to kindred in England and Germany, and to friends in France and Italy. I have spoken of the only one I knew in that fated company, and of him you will feel that it was proper that I should speak; though this is not the time to speak calmly and at length of the eminent traits of his ever to be valued and venerated character.

I could have wished, indeed, that I might have been excused from speaking of this event at all. I feel that it does itself utter a stronger language than any I can use; that your own impressions are likely to be too vivid to need any excitement from public discourse; and that the event of itself, perhaps, teacheth more wisdom than any I shall take occasion to teach from it. Besides, it seems to me as if it were a kind of sacrilege toward such an awful calamity, to take possession of it at once, ere the immediate horror is well over, as a ground even for spiritual improvement. But my original reflection recurs to me; that this event does occupy the public mind to that degree that it can scarcely be excluded even from the sanctuary ; and, therefore, I have thought it best to let it be the theme of our meditation, even though I should only express thoughts which are better conceived in your own minds.

Perhaps I may, without impropriety, enlarge the ground of this meditation. This event is but the consummation of a series of calamities, which has made the present winter the most disastrous, perhaps, that we have ever known. Never, within my memory, certainly, have so many lives been lost by shipwreck on our coast. In our cities, too, the pressure of commercial difficulties, the frequent instances of infidelity to mercantile and public trusts, the torch of the incendiary, lighting flames by day and by night, throughout the whole line of our sea-board, have united to spread distress and distrust far and wide in the public mind. We are apt to feel as if never men fell upon such evil times as we have fallen. We are tempted to ask, Where is the good Providence? Where is the security of life, and of its possessions? and, taking political considerations into view, Where is the security of nations?

In this season of public calamity, when "men's hearts are failing them for fear," I deem it the duty of the pulpit to offer what it can, of guidance, comfort, and admonition. This in my place, I shall humbly attempt.

I.—In the first place, let us not be driven by these calamities, from the conviction that GOD REIGNS. I am not about to offer any argument to prove this truth. If there be a God, we may say, indeed, that it is an obvious inference that he must reign. If there be a God, he made all things; he made this world; he made all its elements and established all its laws; and this implies his dominion over it. But not to *argue* for this truth, I say that calamity is the last thing that should be permitted to drive us from it. For in calamity it is, especially, that we cannot do without it. The fact being so, is, indeed, no weak argument for the truth. If man is so made that to consider himself the victim of chance, is to be whelmed in utter and hopeless misery; if the atmosphere of chance is one in which his mind cannot live; then, as true as there is a God who made him, is there a Providence for him to rely on. And the fact in his mind *is* so. He has no resource but trust in God. Suppose that demons had wrought that awful catastrophe in yonder waters—had maliciously plunged helpless men and women into the cold waves, to die; or suppose that human error, uncontrolled and uncared for, had involved us in the calamities on land which we are enduring; what could men do but gnash their teeth in unavailing rage and despair?

But no: there is a Providence over all things. There is wisdom in events, though we cannot fathom it. Divine Goodness does not forsake the scene of uttermost calamity. I doubt not there were hearts there, where our thoughts are now most turned, which felt that it was so—felt that God was near them in that scene of awful confusion—hearts that in their religious calmness and confidence, would rebuke our despondency and murmuring. We are apt to do injustice to the feelings of good men in such circumstances. Our imagination overspreads all with the apparent disorder. But I doubt not there were Christian hearts in that dread hour when death became inevitable, that said, "It is come!—it is come!—Father, thy will be done! Father, receive us!" And in that feeling there was a divine serenity, and the uplifted eye of triumphant faith that looked beyond the surrounding darkness and struggle, to the calm heaven—to the presence of God above.

"Why," do you say, "did not Almighty Goodness interpose for them?" Had it been best, truly best in the whole view of things, can we doubt that it would have interposed? Then it was not best. Then all was well; though in some order of things which we cannot scan. But you say, perhaps, "This was not the work of Providence, but the fruit of error." Let us consider it. Error is every year exacting of the human race thousands of lives. Error, perhaps, has exacted these. But error is not a wild and ungoverned power, that has broken into the domain of Providence. It is a part of our nature, a part of our discipline, a part of our progress and improvement. We are not made perfect. We are not trained to exacti tude in our medical systems, in our mechanic inventions, in our influence upon one another, in our processes, mental or moral, in anything that appertains to us. We take our part with weakness and imperfection; we struggle with them; we are their victims. Of almost every human being that dies, we may say that he would have lived longer had he been wiser, or had others been wiser. The agonies that surround every death-bed might make the same complaint that rises over the most awful catastrophe brought about by human imperfection. So is our lot bound up with others, and bound up with infirmity and error. If the soul perished in this alliance, there were no comfort; but the soul it is that is trained up by it to virtue, to fortitude, to sanctity, to heaven!

When we look at the martyr's soul, and see how by persecution, by sorrow, and by the last dire extremity, it is borne up to the noblest heroism and triumph; how by the flame which consumes the body, the soul is borne to heaven; there is something in this contemplation which supports us. And yet the martyr is sacrificed to the most enormous error of which the world can be guilty. But he dies, we say, for a principle; he dies for human progress. But so does every man, who falls a victim to human imperfection, mechanical, medical or political, die for human progress. Thousands of lives are annually sacrificed on the altar of human improvement; a fact which shows that life itself in this world, is not an end but a means. The Providence that is carrying every thing forward, as it marches in the greatness of its might, crushes millions with its step, mows down generations with the scythe of war, dashes in pieces the time-founded structures and empires of the world, and sweeps all earthly weal and woe from its awful path.

The dispensation, indeed, is awful; but it is so in part, let me further observe, because we look at it too much as a general picture. It is, after all, but the picture of individual life—of your life and mine. It is, more or less, the lot of us all; and it is not hurled upon us as a mountain to crush us, but it flows in separate sands through the glass of time, to measure out to us the hours of discipline, the hours of improvement. I must repeat it—that every thing is individualized in human experience. It is this in part which enables us to look, with a feeling that supports us, at the sufferings of the martyr. He stands alone. He is a single object of contemplation. We can see the workings of his mind; they are not whelmed in a mass of horrors. We do not feel as if a hundred deaths were involved and concentrated in his death. But this is what we are apt to feel when we contemplate an event which has involved a hundred lives. And yet this generalizing does not present to us the true view. Every man, in such a scene, dies for himself alone, as truly as have the hundreds, in different parts of the world, who have gone hence while I have now been speaking to you. Every man, it may be emphatically said, *is* alone when he comes to die. He is alone with his thoughts, with his prayers, with his affections to those dearest to him: he is alone with his God. Some time he must die; and his time is then; and to him it is *his* time, and not another's. If he had escaped that danger, he might have died the next month from the ignorance of his physician, or he might have fallen the solitary victim of some violent death. Hundreds die thus every year, and they are no more truly alone than he who perishes with a thousand. And this annual aggregate of ills, save to the imagination, is as truly solemn, as any life-destroying catastrophe. Both present the same case under the reign of Providence.

Did I, at present, address any one of those to whom this affliction has come near, I would pray them to consider this: to see that their case is not to be taken from beneath the general law of Providence. It is only as if their friend had died singly by an accident, or had fallen dead in the street, struck with apoplexy or paralysis—or, may I not say, as if he had died in his bed: for how often is the privilege and comfort of ministering love, purchased by the agonies of the sufferer! I know that it is common to deprecate sudden death—to pray against it: but for myself, I cannot join in that prayer. To me it appears that it would be a privilege—life's work done, the hour come—to drop suddenly from the course; no agonized partings—as full of agony perhaps as to feel that the tie is broken. Nay, how often does the survivor say, when the long and bitter struggle is ended. "Thank

God! it is over!" I do not wonder at that desire of the celebrated James Otis, so signally fulfilled, "that he might die by lightning." I have stood on the very threshold where the bolt, from the black retiring storm, descended upon him; and I confess, it seemed to me, as I stood there and thought of it, that that lightning flash was not the bolt of wrath, but the bright angel of release. The lingering pains that are usually appointed to man as the termination of his life, I believe, are less for his own sake than for what he may do for the good of others: it is *his* trial-hour, *their* hour of improvement. But, for the same reason, death is occasionally sudden, and seems disastrous. That very character of disaster arouses men's minds, and puts them upon devising guards and defences against danger. This very event, the most dreadful that ever brought horror and heart-ache into our bosoms, may be commissioned eventually to save more lives than are lost by it. Let me not seem, in saying all this, to be a cold philosopher; God is my witness how far I am from it. I know that in many a family this event is the sudden and awful wrenching of a thousand quivering ties twined all in one. But agonized sympathy seeks some relief. And I can find none but in the great Providence of God—but in seeing that this event is not a chance blow, a random accident, set apart from its beneficent dominion. I know no other comfort for the mourner; and, hard as it may be for him to turn there—hard as it may be to turn away from seeing this event as a frightful catastrophe, and to look at it as a sacred and solemn dispensation of heaven; this I would pray each one to do—to lean upon the bosom of the all-wise Providence—and to say, even as the Great Sufferer said in the dread hour, when all earthly evils and sorrows were leagued against him, "Father! thy will be done!"

Shall this event shake our faith in that Providence? The principle that would allow it to do so, would drive all faith in Providence from the world. Can we give up that faith? It is our only refuge from the overwhelming ills of life. We must cling to it. Suffering, struggling, bereaved, broken-hearted, we must cling to it, for it is our only refuge. And for my own part, as clearly do I see it, and as truly do I believe in that wise Providence reigning over life, as I see and believe that I live at all. And could one of those who have passed through that dread dispensation which we deplore, to a better life, speak to us, I doubt not he would say to his agonized friends: "Be comforted—as far as mortal trial can be comforted. All is well. I *see* that, in which you struggle to *believe.* For me it was better to depart: for you it is sorrow; but that sorrow shall be yet turned into joy. The breath of a momentary life passed away, and we shall meet again. I have died for the world's improvement—for your virtue; and beneath the great and loving Providence of God I see that all is well. Oh! then be comforted! The serene heaven which spreads over you, is but an image of the all-enfolding love of God, in which we shall yet rejoice for ever!"

But you say, "It is such a sad thing; it is such a horrible thing!" and I feel what you say. "That they should have gone forth, so thoughtless of what that very day was to bring forth!" is your reflection —"gone from the social board—perhaps from the table of feasting—gone with a smile, perhaps, saying, 'such a day I shall return,'—or gone after a long voyage at sea, feeling as if they were already at home! and then that four or five hours after they set foot on that deck, they should have been dead !—that it should all have been so sudden—in a moment—one moment sitting and conversing with a friend, and the next moment meeting death face to face—and above all, to think, if we must think, that a little calmness, a little deliberation, might have saved them: that such valuable, such precious lives should have been sacrificed, if there were any possibility of their being saved : is it not dreadful?" I know it—I feel all this; but still I cannot rest here. I must reflect upon it. I must meet the darkest mystery in Providence, the problem of human error. I must see that error is inevitable, and that it is one of the elements of human improvement. If Providence interposed to save us from the results of every mistake, the human race would be held in perpetual childhood. In the way of life, the foot slips, and plunges us into distress, into calamity, into the jaws of untimely death. Was the foot to blame? or its construction? Its very power to move, its very flexibility, the very formation that fitted it for its purpose, made it liable to slip. Mis-steps are its teachers; pain is its teacher. And thus all evils are the mind's teachers. Death, which cannot on earth benefit the individual subject, is yet the world's teacher. Untimely death teaches it prudence; and all death teaches it virtue. This is the great doctrine of a Providence; and all experience; the world's experience vindicates it.

This great doctrine, my friends, must be our repose. But I offer it to your contemplation not merely as such —not merely as necessary to be believed in—not merely as urged upon your piety, but as commended to your reflection. I pray you to see that it is true: to see that all things—great or small, common or strange —the most indifferent and the most awful alike—come under the same great, wise and benevolent order of things. Let us submit to God's wisdom. Let the hand that is involuntarily stretched out to snatch our friend from peril—let that hand, when it is too late, be lifted up to Heaven, with the prayer, "Thy will be done!" And may every one who is striken and smitten to the dust by this heavy visitation, find strength and support in that humble trust!

II. I have dwelt longer than I intended upon this consideration of the Divine Providence. I have been led on almost without regard to any order of thought —which I find it, indeed, difficult to preserve amid the agitations of a time like this. Let me now lead you to a different point of view, from which we may take a wider survey of the general calamities that press upon us: for I would willingly take refuge, for a few moments, even in the contemplation of wide-spread evils, from the immediate disaster that fills us with distress and horror.

I have said that the present is altogether a season of unprecedented calamity. But I must pray you not to yield to a view of these evils which shall overrate their magnitude or overlook their uses. We have lived so long in this country, in a state of peace and plenty, that we have almost forgotten through what sorrows and conflicts the human race has passed, to reach its present condition. We have been raised to a high level, like some of those which are found upon the mountains of this new world, till we have lost sight of the great plain of the world where the fortunes of men are wrought out with bitter toil and sorrow, where their rivers have run blood, and their fields have been fattened with slaughter. The exiles who flock to us, from many a country and clime, might well be tempted to say, "The ways of Providence are not equal." They have come from lands where liberty has been crushed down in the blood of their children, or where the dungeon has been exchanged only for exile; where famine has stalked through the dwellings of thousands, and the faces of men have grown pale, and their limbs have tottered beneath the awful scourge. Within the period of our existence as a nation, what wars have desolated the fields of Europe; what bloody battles have been the epochs of her history; what groaning hospitals have tracked the step of her armies; what shrieks of widowhood and orphanage have risen upon the air, laden with the accumulation of her calamities! Compared with this, let us not forget that our condition, with all its trials, is one of high prosperity. I would not speak lightly of these trials. I know that they are great. I know that they eat deeply into the heart of domestic happiness; that there is more suffering among us, and that, not alone in the hovels of indigence, than most men are aware of. But, one week of famine in the land, one wide sweep of the wings of pestilence over us, one cannonade from a single ship in yonder harbor, pouring its storm of hail-shot and fire upon the city, would make us feel, that to step from *that*, into the midst of all our present trials, were a blessed exchange.

I say that our condition has been, and is, comparatively a favoured one. But I cannot yield to the common readiness and easiness of inference, by which this sense of our happy fortunes is made to extend to our national character. We are in our condition, I believe, the most favoured people on earth—i. e. *as* a people—as a mass; but I am far from saying that we are the wisest and most virtuous people in the world. We have heard but too much of this boasting. We have talked about the slaves of despotism, till we have apparently forgotten that there may be a worse bondage—to private ambition, to wearing anxiety, to envy and self-will. And therefore that *distrust* which has entered in among us—distrust about the securities of property—distrust about the tendencies of the national character—though it be one of the most painful trials of the time, is not, I think, without its uses. It may do us good. It may impart a sobriety to our thoughts of the public welfare. It may turn our thoughts from our private interests to the common weal—a direction of mind greatly needed among us. It may put a salutary fear in the place of our rash confidence. It may put us upon thinking more deeply upon those deepest foundations of our welfare—virtue, simplicity, soberness of mind and a reverent and humble piety.

No blessings are to be kept, and least of all those that are enjoyed in the midst of freedom and abundance, but by a jealous fear and vigilance. Was not this truth in a measure forgotten in our prosperity? Did it not seem as if life, in this New World, was to take on quite a new character? For myself, I confess that I was deceived by the aspect of things around me. When I had looked upon the humble traders, and the hard and unrequited toilers of the Old World, and then saw many of the same classes here rising rapidly to wealth and splendour, I felt as if a new age had come; as if a new world here, were indeed opening its portals to crowding and happier generations. And I hope now that it is not altogether untrue. But I confess that I have been brought to soberer thoughts of our condition, and of the very condition of humanity. I see that life is not to be, to any people—that it must not be, a dispensation of ease and independence. I see a sublimer law revealed than that of prosperity —the law of wisdom; a higher end proposed by the

Providence of heaven than success—even virtue. I see that the old, the eternal, the Christian law, still presses upon us; that through much tribulation we must enter the kingdom of heaven; that we must learn and not forget, that we are pilgrims and strangers on earth, having here no continuing city nor abiding place.

Public calamities, then, amidst all their severity, are yet teachers of wisdom. I speak not of individual instances. I say not, it is best that those calamities should have fallen here or there. I am not obliged to say that it is best that it should have fallen any where. But since they *have* come, they may be turned to some wise account. He who can 'cause the wrath of man to praise him,' can cause even these things to praise him, in our growing wisdom. May he cause us to praise him, and be thankful. You speak, my friend, of the disasters that have befallen you. *You did not set your foot on that fated deck!* Who of you now, would not have given millions, if he had them, rather than have been there? How many survivors would give all that is left them, if they could buy back that irrevocable step. You did not take it. You were not there. Your husband, your brother, was not there. He might have been. Some of you thought of it—intended it, and were saved from it, as by a miracle. Life is still yours; the warm fireside, the happy home, is still yours. What then can you feel, amidst your blessings—what can you be, but thankful? No murmurer, methinks, is here to-day. But if there be, I say to him—*You did not set your foot on that fated deck!* And as your shuddering thought draws back from that fearful idea, let it retreat for ever into the sanctuary of thanksgiving.

III. Again, my brethren, am I brought back to this mournful theme. Let me say a word or two more to you, and I shall have discharged the sad duty which I thought it called for at my hands.

Life is dear, and it is justly of great account with us; but can it be of that supreme account which we make it? When we see it the sport of every event, of every inadvertence; when we see it extinguished by a mote in the air, or a ray of the sun; when we see that it depends upon a step, more or less; when multitudes sink to an untimely death; when the life of a whole breathing generation is swept away before us like a cloud from the earth; can such a life be the thing on which it was intended that man should set his whole heart? Can it be anything in the divine economy, but a means to something beyond? The animal dies for the advantage of a superior being; or for his own advantage, by the decay that has ended the enjoyment of his life, or by the violence from his kind that saves him from that decay, neglected, untended. Does man die for nothing—neither for his own, nor for others' advantage? But if he does die for some ulterior purpose, then his life is instrumental; and whether he continues for a term longer or shorter, is not the ultimate, the main thing. We say this of animal life; is it not just as true of human life? But the ulterior end for man—what and where can it be, but in a future life. Yet if man's essential life be thus continuous, can it be so material as we make it, when the life of this form changes? Is it not like passing from infancy to youth, or from youth to manhood? Is it not being unclothed of one form, to be clothed upon with another? The form changes; the being lives.

"What shadows we are, and what shadows we

pursue," I feel, as in imagination I stand and behold, beneath the veil of night, a hundred fellow beings perish before my eyes and pass away like a dream. I cannot help saying, when I see so many valued lives cast away like an evening vapor upon the waters—how litttle can it matter, after all, in the great account, when we die; this year or next year; to-day or to-morrow. I cannot help saying, as I look around me, "My companions, my friends, are but shadows; we all are but shadows; like shadows we alight upon the shore of time, and the breath of that shore, will soon sweep us away into the habitations of eternity." Truly is it written, "Thou carriest them away, as with a flood; they are as asleep."

One word more I must say, lest I fail to interpret the most solemn language of this solemn event; and that is upon the duty of being ever prepared for death. There are characteristics of that event which show that this is no mere matter of professional admonition, proper for the preacher to insist upon, but for no one to take home as a living admonition to his own heart. The event took place near us—on the great highway of our constant travel—and in a mode of conveyance to which we are continually resorting. And the frenzy that seizes men's minds at such a moment, must show the most thoughtless and irreligious among us, that whatever we may think now of being prepared for death, we shall feel no indifference when the hour comes. We know that the same fate may, in any month, overtake us; and we see, as in a glass, what we shall then feel.

Pardon me, my friends but I cannot pursue the theme. I cannot utter common-place warnings, in the presence of that awful Admonisher. Alas! that all that I can do is to speak—when others have died!

Alas! that I can only meditate here—when the hearts of many are rent with agony! Oh! poor and unavailing it seems, only to take part, in weak sympathy, with their bitter sorrow. But human help cannot avail, and we can only say in our impotence and grief—May God comfort them!

www.ingramcontent.com/pod-product-compliance
Lightning Source LLC
LaVergne TN
LVHW020126110826
845151LV00001B/284

* 9 7 8 1 4 2 5 5 4 1 9 1 0 *